Integrated COMPLIANCE — and — *Total Risk* MANAGEMENT

MARK G. ARTHUS

Creating a Bankwide
Compliance Program that Works

A BANKLINE PUBLICATION
PROBUS PUBLISHING COMPANY
Chicago, Illinois
Cambridge, England

ISBN 1-55738-397-9

Printed in the United States of America

BB

1 2 3 4 5 6 7 8 9 0

I dedicate this work
to the memory of my dad,
Napoleon Arthus.

Contents

Preface

My dad was a man of few words who had little need or desire for pomp or flashy displays. The most elaborate thing about him was his first name—Napoleon—but then again, he used to go simply by "Nap." What he did have was a very strong focus and high regard for practical application, especially in terms of time and resource utility. My father as well as my mother taught me much about life and actually prepared me quite well, much better than I had initially thought. Mostly what they taught was the importance of honesty, values, and principles and how these things fit into the big scheme of everyday life. In relation to organizational skill, one of the strongest lessons was on the real value of time and the efficient use of limited resources.

Many things happen in one's life on a continuous, always-moving-forward basis. The trick is to manage these things while having the most amount of fun doing it. I can still hear my mother saying to me when I was caught getting into trouble, "If you have nothing more constructive to do then I'll give you something to do," and her "something to do" was usually a house chore that was never very enjoyable. That constant reprimand eventually motivated me to always look ahead and consciously think about utilizing my limited time and resources to accomplish as much as possible with the least amount of effort and waste. Whether it was figuring out how many kick ball games we could play before it got dark or how I could juggle three part-time jobs and still finish my senior year of high school, the goal was to squeeze every bit of utility possible out of every minute available. Over time this started to become a common way of doing things for me to the point where it has become almost automatic.

This leads into one of the biggest management lessons my dad ever taught me. It is a lesson that I have carried with me from that point on and applied in so many ways that I never dreamed I would (or could, for that matter). It is a lesson that is firmly embedded in everything that is discussed in this book and a lesson which, if not learned, would have made this work virtually impossible.

It's a lesson I learned the hard way a long time ago as a stubborn young teenager of 15. I had just bought my first car, a 1965 Mustang coupe, and was very excited over the prospect of having my own "set of wheels." There was only one minor hitch to my elaborate plans—the car didn't start. Well, at the time I thought of myself as a good scholar and so the week preceding the day I was going to repair my car I did all my research. I read several repair manuals, spoke with some mechanics on possible repair scenarios, and I even created a troubleshooting checklist of possible solutions.

The big day came and I was up bright and early that Saturday morning to begin the work on my car. I had charged the battery overnight, and when the morning began I changed the points, plugs, and wires. With all the important parts new and the battery charged, I was ready to roll. After several hours passed with my futile attempts to start my Mustang, Dad came by to ask what I was doing. I proudly explained my problem and my approach of how I would find, *unassisted*, the problem using my research and checklist. My dad didn't comment, he just looked under the hood, shook some wires including the battery terminals, smiled, and walked away. I simply thought that he was proud of me and so impressed that he had nothing to add or any suggestions to make. The rest of the day came and went, as did my dad occasionally with his smile and nothing more, but my car was still unrepaired. All I had to show for my day's work was a pair of greasy hands.

Although I was a bit frustrated I vowed to continue the next day, and without asking Dad for any help. This I did the following day, with the entire morning passing and still no Mustang that would start. It was now late afternoon and my frustration was quickly mounting. My dad apparently sensed this because when he came by once more he did more than smile. Without saying more than excuse me, he proceeded to reach under the car hood, and remove and clean the battery terminals. After replacing the terminals he simply went to the ignition, turned the key, and started the car right up.

I was livid and very embarrassed and let my dad know this. After my verbal demonstration was complete and I was calm enough to talk, I asked my dad why he let me waste a day and one-half trying to start a car when he already knew the problem and the solution. In his usual parental fashion he said "I wanted to teach you a lesson." I replied rather curtly, "What lesson, that I should ask you first before I try to start my car?" He laughed and said "No," but that "it was a lesson in time management and problem solving," and then he explained.

The simplicity of my dad's lesson is still for me today such a striking contrast to its strong impact and broad utility. The lesson I learned that day is, whenever you are looking for the solution to any problem, car repair or otherwise, start from the beginning and always look to the simplest solutions first. This is important for two big reasons: first, the complicated solutions are always difficult and time consuming to test for and even if they work, they are always difficult, time consuming, and costly to implement. In the end you may find that you can't apply them precisely because of their complexity. Or you may realize that you simply don't have the time or the money to implement them. This being the case, then why even test for them? The second part is that you may find that the simple solution works, in which case you have just saved a ton of effort, time, and money. In my case with the Mustang it would have saved almost an entire weekend and the total embarrassment of it all.

Quite often, we overlook the obvious because the simple solution seems too simple to work. As my dad had shown me during my Mustang endeavor and many times thereafter, the simpler the solution the better and more desirable the results. "Keep it simple," he used to say. My response to that lesson has been a simple one: Thanks, "Old Man." Thank you for that wisdom and much more; I never got the chance to say goodbye and that I loved you. Your spirit is still alive and strong in our memory and especially in our son. Brian, in some ways, is a three-and-one-half-foot version of you. Funny how the good things always seem to find a way to continue.

Acknowledgements

First and foremost I must thank Mr. Locklin Nelson for ultimately making this book possible. Although he directly contributed very little to the actual work, he was the "key man" who opened the first doors. He is a very intelligent, exceptionally talented, and very forward-thinking man who is well on his way to doing big things one day. Lock, I can't stop thanking you for the many times you listened to your "gut," and to me, and stuck your neck out for me. You are always looking for new and better talent and ideas; and that involves risk, but also, as you well know, provides wonderful rewards and exciting opportunities. Keep looking and taking those risks and never become one of those comfortable "suits" who sit behind their desks and always bet on the "sure thing." Keep listening to your "gut"; it knows well what it's doing.

I thank Mr. John Grozier, who has been another "key man" but more importantly an inspiration for his honesty and integrity. John has been in several difficult situations over his almost thirty-year corporate career and could have, many times, taken the easy way out by employing unethical or inappropriate means. Instead, he chose to take the lumps and has shown time and again and very clearly that you can work in less-than-perfect conditions and still succeed while keeping your principles intact. Even while the people around you, the very same people who control much of the power, unfairly take advantage and continually break the rules. John's ultimate and continuous triumph is one of the greatest measures of success.

I also wish to thank all of the numerous people who have listened to me talk over the past few years and questioned, challenged, and greatly added to my knowledge and understanding. This is probably as much your work as it is mine.

Finally, thanks, Mom, for all of your wonderful, level-headed insight over the years; my hope is to one day be as good as you. And thanks to my wife Karen for being there; and my three fantastic, best-in-the-world children, Brian, Lisa and little Jillian Rose—*I love you all, in and out of the coconut tree!*

Introduction

One of the biggest problems with compliance and risk management is that they both mean many different things to many different people. This holds even more true when individuals in different departments or disciplines are questioned. Probably the biggest reason for this is that both compliance and risk management are not thought of on a regular basis by most organization members; they always seem to be someone else's concern. The only time they are really looked at closely is when a serious problem has arisen and something must be done to lessen the damage. The most common definitions of the two are that compliance is abiding by legal regulation and risk management is having the proper insurance coverage. Both of these definitions are correct, but they are only a small portion of the much bigger picture. The real definitions of both are much broader and actually involve all aspects of the organization.

This book will discuss compliance and risk management in great detail. We will show that they are and should be concerns of *every* organization member. They are two separate but heavily interdependent disciplines, and are not the responsibility of only a few individuals or one department but every organization member and every department. We will start off by defining what compliance really is and then do the same for risk management. We will see how they are both much broader in scope than most people believe and not as great a mystery as many people fear. We will look at all of the aspects of compliance and risk management, such as daily tasks and consistency of practice. We will show how these aspects must be integrated into the process and not performed as a separate function.

This book will detail the benefits of integrated compliance and total risk management, and demonstrate how it does not have to be implemented "verbatim" but can be mixed and matched to custom fit to your needs while still being exceptionally effective. We give lots of case studies which demonstrate the successes and failures of other organizations and provide examples of what to expect if you incorporate all, or only parts, of the program. We offer examples of sample documents, manuals, and other useful tools along with defining the steps and the various modules of the program. We discuss everyone's role, from the Board of Directors' down to the department clerks', along with the importance of their contribution and how a compliance and risk management team can be established in any organization without causing major upheaval or suffering great cost.

It is true that this approach is new, but it is also true that several organizations are already using it very successfully. It is also a fact that if fully employed, this program should give greater success than *any* other program currently known, and it will use fewer resources while creating higher efficiency, productivity, and quality. And best of all, it does not require any special tools, talent, or outside help. This is not a program where an outside consultant is brought in to "fix your problems." Those "fix-it" jobs rarely work, and those that do rarely have any permanence. This program allows an organization to do what we believe to be the only successful and long lasting approach—implement or "fix-it" from the inside of the organization. Doing the work from the inside out—as opposed to the outside in, as most consultants would do—allows for a tailored program that is created by the organization members. This gives the program great strength because it has the backing of the organization members, selectivity because the members choose how and what is done, flexibility because it is custom made and can be easily modified by the people who created it, and permanence because it is home grown and owned by the members and changes with the needs of the organization.

Everything said in this book probably sounds great, but you may think, "I don't have the expertise, the time, or the understanding to do it." We will show you how you already have the expertise and will get the time through the tremendous savings the program brings. Finally, this book will give you the necessary understanding through a detailed "how-to" of the step-by-step development of an Integrated Compliance and Total Risk Management Program. It may seem too good to be true, but this program is not complex: it is based on simplicity; it is not difficult to implement due to its flexibility; and it actually saves money due to its integration concept. You will probably even find that you are already doing parts of this program now. So it may be even easier than you thought.

Part I

Total Integrated Compliance

Integrated Risk-Based Compliance— A Better Solution

Compliance and risk management typically have been viewed as two distinct, legal necessities that only demand attention when a problem surfaces or special attention is paid (such as when an audit is scheduled). Like ignoring warning signs along a dangerous road, traveling into the areas of compliance and risk management without identifying and managing the risk and remaining constantly attentive can be potentially destructive and perhaps even fatal to an organization through legal penalties, public humiliation, and large financial loss.

If an organization is to be successful in its compliance and risk management, it must build a complete program that is integrated from the very top of the organization down through its most basic levels. A risk-based, Total Integrated Compliance and Risk Management program is a program whereby compliance and risk management are integrated or "built in" to *every* aspect of the organization and are *everyone's* responsibility. In this integrated program, risk management and compliance are considered in *every* process, function, task, and action performed in the organization. No matter how small the process, function, task or action, everything must be reviewed for compliance and risk management.

Compliance and risk management, although they cover many issues, must first focus on "the big picture" and attempt to address all of the essential areas of the compliance and risk management concern. Concentrating on legal regulation or proper insurance coverage is only part of their function. What is needed for this new approach to compliance and risk management is to greatly expand the current definition of compliance and risk management. Historically, compliance in the financial industry has been looked upon as the legal requirement to follow specific regulatory laws. Therefore, if the organization took a specific action in line with the legal requirement, it was in compliance. Since compliance was the responsibility of the compliance department, management, on the whole, would not concern itself with compliance issues unless the compliance officer or the auditors identified a problem. Since we can now see that compliance must be the responsibility of the line manager, this definition is no longer complete.

A line manager is simply any manager who has direct responsibility for a department or process. They either perform the functions or tasks themselves or directly supervise the people who do. Line managers may have different titles in various organizations, such as department manager, unit manager, area supervisor, team leader, unit head, and so on. For the sake of consistency we call them all line managers in this book.

Today, total integrated compliance is largely defined as complying with:

- **Legal regulation:** All federal, state, and local regulations and laws.
- **Corporate policy:** Every corporate policy, no matter how small it may seem. If it is important enough to state as a policy, it is important enough to be complied with.
- **Sound productivity practices:** Every process, which includes all corporate policy and procedures, must be reviewed for productivity considerations. All unproductive situations bear unacceptable risk and must be considered a compliance violation.
- **Sound efficiency practices:** Every process, which includes all corporate policy and procedures, must be reviewed for efficiency considerations. All inefficient situations must be considered a compliance violation.
- **Quality control:** Poor quality is at the root of virtually all risk situations. Quality control is a very large part of sound compliance and risk management; with strong quality control, risk is reduced and managed more effectively. Quality control makes an organization more productive, more efficient, and more profitable.
- **Training and education:** A critical part of compliance and risk management, it must not be limited to compliance and risk issues. Training of new employees along with cross-training and retraining of existing employees must be a requirement. A well-trained staff will always manage risk better and provide a higher quality product.
- **Sound human resource management:** Knowing your people is just as important as knowing your customer—and for the same reasons. Risk and profitability will always be better managed and more predictable when competent and knowledgeable people are involved. The right

people in the right places will ensure effective compliance and risk management.

- **The corporate mission statement:** An organization must have a comprehensive and long-term plan that is clearly communicated to all members. This statement of direction is critical for growth and survival. It also must be properly communicated to all organization members and continually compared to the actual direction of the organization for reassessment or redirection of corporate efforts.

- **The strategic plan:** Great strategy always lays the groundwork for great results. Sound strategy that is effectively communicated and carefully followed must be continually validated to ensure compliance and risk management.

- **The business plan:** Each business and department must have a realistic and clearly defined plan that they are required to follow. Compliance with the business plan must be a requirement of management that is frequently validated.

- **The budget:** Once a realistic budget is developed, management should be required to adhere to it. Just as the budget must allow management to meet the business and strategic plans as well as the corporate mission statement, management must provide detailed explanations for all variances on a monthly basis. The sound management of risk that this provides, along with the prevention of surprises, will reduce inefficiency and losses and increase profitability.

- **Contingency planning:** One has only to take a brief look at the multitude of disasters—both natural and man-made—to clearly appreciate the necessity of a emergency contingency plan for sound compliance and risk management. No critical department, system, or function should be without an emergency contingency plan.

- **Strong ethical and moral social behavior:** The stronger the ethical and moral fiber of an organization, the greater the risk management. It is a very simple formula.

- **Profitability requirements:** Profitable organizations are rarely desperate ones. Desperate organizations make foolish mistakes and take high-risk chances. It seems obvious that profitability must be a goal, but this is not always the case on the individual level. Sometimes personal motivations get in the way. Compliance with profitability goals must be continually validated to identify any necessary adjustments in business direction and/or personnel changes.

Using this definition it becomes clear that compliance is not just government regulations any more. It encompasses virtually everything an organization does—remember, if it is important enough to do in the first place, it is important enough do to right, no matter how small the task. Compliance is all about doing things right. When compliance and risk management are defined in this manner, an organization will become strong, well-run, and profitable. It will minimize its risk and manage it effectively. And it will be poised to become (or remain) the dominant leader in its market. Almost by default, the organization will be in compliance with governmental laws and regulations.

Compliance Validation, and Not Testing, As a Risk Management Tool

There are distinct differences between testing for compliance, validating compliance, and identifying risk. To test is to judge the end result. To validate and identify is to study the effectiveness of or inconsistencies in a system. Inconsistencies are the events which produce unexpected or undesirable results or operate differently than policy and procedure may require. Even though in the end it may be better to leave the process alone and instead change expectations, an inconsistency must always be addressed.

Testing has, over time, been the most popular way to identify inconsistencies or potential problems. Yet, its application often creates more problems for an organization because it is an incomplete process. A test is basically a one-time snapshot or a still photograph of an event. It allows the study of a specific transaction that has already taken place sometime in the past. For example, in testing for an organization's compliance with the procedure that client accounts be properly reviewed for investment objectives, one would sample a population of files and "test" to see if the appropriate transactions are present. Depending upon the organizational procedure, one might look for current objective setting forms or documents that define the client's objectives. These would then be compared with evidence of the actual investment strategy. Perhaps other required evidence would be proof of conversations with the client, or written acknowledgment by the portfolio manager that the objectives have been reviewed and understood. Regardless of the specifics, *testing, as it has been applied, always looks at the end result of the process.* Since the end result already occurred and cannot be changed or prevented, any action taken on problems discovered this way will always be reactionary. Since you will only know of a problem if an error occurs and is found, you are, in effect, waiting for risk, liability, or loss to happen **before you react.** That is like saying that you should wait for your car to run out of gas in order to determine that fuel is required. This approach failed miserably for American manufacturing where they put their quality control people at the end of the assembly line to "test" the finished products. As we all know, this is always a more costly approach and, at best, marginally effective. If similar problems are to be prevented in the future, the *process* must be reviewed and corrected **while in progress.**

If testing can be compared to a still photograph, then validation can be compared to a motion picture. Validation views the process that causes the transaction from start to finish. The process is followed on a step-by-step basis looking for inconsistencies, flaws, inefficiencies, or poor design. The actual process flow is compared to what is expected, which includes organizational expectations and written documentation detailing how it should function. In our previous example, a population of client files would have been tested for the appropriate investment reviews performed by the portfolio manager. In validation, the actual reviews might be witnessed taking place. Committee reviews can be witnessed from beginning to end, or the individual portfolio manager's client reviews can be followed. There are several ways to accomplish this validation. The point is that validation follows the entire process with the full knowledge and understanding of how it is supposed to be executed, while testing settles for a cursory study of the end result. It is the difference between asking "What?", which lets you understand the consequence, and asking "Why?", which lets you understand the cause. If the process itself is sound, one can be confident that the desired results will be achieved. If there is a fault in the process, then it should be detected through validation.

We all know that a faulty process can still, at times, give the correct end result, which can be quite misleading. By merely studying the end result, one can miss an unidentified risk, and never be fully confident of avoiding future problems.

Validation, a Break with Tradition

Let's take a look at an experience of a manager at a large institution. His area was under review for regulatory and corporate compliance. The compliance officer in charge was performing a methodical compliance test using his compliance checklist. When he reached the item which required that "all files must have the client contract, objective setting form, and client form," he discovered that several files were missing the client form. Accordingly, the compliance officer wrote a report which stated that "account files were found to be out of compliance with corporate policy, as the client form was missing from several files." When the manager was notified of the finding, he did what most line managers would do: since the document was easily reproduced, he placed a copy of the client form into all of the deficient files.

It is true that the manager was forced to bring those specific files into compliance, but a lot of effort was spent to resolve the consequence without addressing its cause. As a result of the compliance approach to this problem and the line manager's subsequent reaction, he will very likely find himself with the same issue the next time the compliance officer comes to visit. Perhaps the manager will remember the finding and ensure that the client form is present in all files prior to the compliance officer's visit. Regardless, the real issue and any resulting risk were not addressed.

Rather than search *for* the necessary documents, the compliance review should have focused on whether or not those documents *needed to be there in the first place.* Assuming they were necessary, the review should then have answered the question: what caused the failure in the process? Only when the process questions have been resolved, will the manager be able to ensure that subsequent transactions are completed satisfactorily and that all risk is adequately managed.

Focusing on the transaction rather than the process is analogous to the farmer who keeps his prize horse in a barn with a faulty latch on the door. Every time the horse runs away, the farmer hires a helper to run out and catch it. The actual solution is to focus on the process—in this case the faulty latch—and stop the problem at its source.

Assessment of Common Problems and Resulting Risk to an Organization

Every organization faces problems in its daily operations that are simply a part of doing business. Sometimes the problems are internally created while others are created by external factors that may be a part of the political, social, economic, or competitive environment. The most successful organizations are the ones that handle these problems effectively and often turn them to an advantage.

There are generally two types of problems: those that exist now and those that will exist in the future. The existence of problems is a given; whether they will be addressed effectively is up to an organization's ability to anticipate, identify, and manage them. As we discussed earlier, the pro-active planned approach is the best way to address problems. This is done through an integrated compliance and risk management approach, assigning responsibility where it belongs, along with the proper training and validation testing for pro-active assessment.

No matter how good management or the compliance and risk management program is, problems will exist. The effectiveness of management and its compliance and risk management program will dictate the amount and degree of the problems and how quickly they are resolved. There are several problems that are typical of uninformed management and an ineffective compliance and risk management program. These are real problems that have existed and still exist in many organizations. Below is a listing of seven of these most common and serious problems organizations continually face. They are good lessons to learn from and as we will see later in this book, all can be remedied with an integrated compliance and risk management program.

I. There Is No Consistent, Formal, Organization-Wide Approach to Compliance and Risk Management

Many organizations will say that they do have a formal approach to compliance and risk management that is consistent. Their response is usually something like, "we practice good compliance and risk management; we do everything the auditors and regulators tell us to do."

The problems with this statement are several: (1) all actions are reactive to the findings of the auditors and regulators; (2) there is no consistent ownership or individual responsibility for compliance and risk management through all levels of the organization; (3) the only real formality is the actual audit or examination report. This situation is a result when ownership and responsibility is passed to the auditors and compliance people. Management waits to be directed on what compliance actions to take.

When management will not acknowledge the potential for improvement in their compliance processes or even accept responsibility for the task, no one in the organization will. Lacking a formal approach to compliance and risk management makes it even more difficult to comply successfully with all necessary regulations.

When there is no consistent, formal, and organization-wide approach to compliance and risk management, an organization has a tendency to wait for problems to arise before addressing them. Dilemmas and issues are left untouched as long as they do not get "too large." The common cry with this approach is "why worry about getting the safe fixed, we haven't had any money missing in over two years."

Many organizations also fail to "own" the success (or failure) of the process by making compliance and risk management everyone's responsibility. In various parts of the organization similar and sometimes identical tasks are performed differently and with varied degrees and levels of control and effort. Identical situations are treated as if they actually require these custom-made approaches. The not-made-here mentality prevails where "we know the better way to do it." At times, it may even be hard to identify the fact that identical businesses, jobs, functions, or tasks are the same because they are performed and treated so differently. The problems that grow from this approach can be large and many:

- The various parts of an organization do not learn from each other's mistakes. Errors are made in isolation and are often hidden from the full group. This prevents other areas from being aware of and looking out for the same mistakes. The same error or problem can be repeated throughout an organization without any connection.

- This "reinventing of the wheel" causes inefficiency and low productivity throughout an organization. Poor communication and interaction of ideas and solutions cause the various parts of an organization to approach similar situations separately, and in many cases, differently.
- Client issues and sales problems result. For example, a client may have several accounts with the same organization but at several locations. The result can be that each account is handled differently, usually causing frustration and confusion for the client—"how come I get two different answers from your organization for the same question, don't you guys talk to each other?"
- There is confusion over training issues and inefficiency when management or staff move to another area. A manager or staff member may move from one branch to another and find that the same applications are handled quite differently. This creates a larger learning curve and inevitably, mistakes and errors and even hurt feelings due to the "my way is better" attitude. All of this eventually drops to the bottom line via higher costs and duplicate effort and resources.

In this type of environment, senior management does not oversee or get involved in the compliance and risk management of the organization. Senior management only gets involved during changes or serious problems. Outside of this, their usual involvement is the perfunctory quarterly or annual review. Under this scenario virtually all problems (and opportunities) do not reach senior management until they have been completely washed through the bureaucracy, at which time the problems are glossed over even though they may be enormous, and the opportunities are usually sterile. There are volumes of case history to support this condition: simply look at many of the failed banks, General Motors, IBM, Bank of America several years back, and Citibank. Senior management in many of these cases seemed to be the last to know there were any serious problems with the organization.

II. Outdated, Incomplete, and Inconsistently Applied Policies and Procedures

Having policies and procedures that are out-of-date, not accurate or comprehensive, and not fully or properly adhered to can sometimes be as bad as not having any at all. What happens is that the organization members interpret the poorly defined policies and procedures their own way, which is usually not as originally intended. Because everyone understands them differently, several versions of the policy or procedure exist in actuality. The application of these different versions, in turn, causes varied results. Also, because documentation is poor, the word-of-mouth system is used to convey the policy or procedure and this almost always includes the "favorite short cuts" of the individual communicating that policy or procedure. Since short cuts are usually nothing more than leaving some parts out and changing others, and word-of-mouth does leave parts out and changes, others, the incompleteness and accuracy of the policy or procedure's application will undoubtedly occur along with an incomplete and inaccurate result.

This happens quite often and is usually unknown to upper management. In the process it exposes the organization to a great deal of unidentified, undefined, and unmanaged risk. Sometimes the risk is minor, such as lost productivity in a task that takes a little longer to perform than necessary. While other times the risk is great where a task is performed incorrectly that leads to direct loss of funds or liability exposure through a civil lawsuit.

With outdated, incomplete, and inconsistently applied policies and procedures the following is usually evident:

- *Key operating policy and procedure manuals are outdated in several areas and are not comprehensive across all functions.* There is no current documentation on what the policy is or how the procedures should be performed. As a result, consulting these documents could lead to error and/or misunderstanding. Since many policies and procedures are not documented at all, information is passed on by word-of-mouth which invariably leads to omission, distortion, and error. The defense made by some organization members is "if I don't write it down I can't be audited on it or held responsible" and "we already know how it works so we do not need some document to tell us" and "it's such a waste of time, I have better things to do." If everyone in the department does not have the same basis to begin with—a well documented policy and procedure—reliable and accurate results cannot be obtained.

- *Policies are not well communicated or understood by staff and management and they are not consistently followed throughout the organization.* No real effort is made by management to properly communicate the actual policies and procedures. This is not always a conscious effort by management where they intentionally say, "we are not going to let everyone know the policy or procedure," it is rather, a simple oversight or omission. It appears that the job is getting done so attention is not paid to communication; this of course results in incomplete understanding and inconsistent application.

    Also, when policy or procedure is changed or amended, updates are not well communicated to all interested parties. Because of the poor communication and lack of complete understanding, shortcuts that compromise the effectiveness and integrity of the policy or procedure are often taken. When new or existing staff needs to be educated or informed of a particular policy or procedure, they are instructed to sit with the most knowledgeable member of the department to learn the facts. Or what is even worse, the new individual is not given the most knowledgeable member, but the first available one. This is done instead of giving the individual a current and comprehensive document to review before being instructed by a competent individual.

Note: This is not to say that it is better to learn from a document rather than from a knowledgeable staff member or manager. It is simply stating that a firm foundation must exist that is consistent and can be referenced when necessary. The only way information can be communicated in a thorough and consistent fashion is if the lesson starts from a written document. Schools do not use textbooks so the students have something to carry into class. The textbooks are used to teach, reference, and allow the students to all learn from the same beginning and basis of understanding.

- *All procedures are not formalized or documented.* Many procedures are deemed informal and are performed in an ad hoc manner with no documentation to assess accuracy or consistency. Information is passed strictly by word-of-mouth with each member adding his or her personal stamp to the approach. This causes incomplete execution of functions and transactions, as well as an inability to monitor and establish risk controls. The attitude of "I don't do it that way, I do it this way" prevails.

  Informal policies and procedures often develop during growing stages when everything is moving faster than formal declarations of intention or effort. In many cases, these informal procedures are very "quiet" and go unnoticed by auditors and even some management for long periods of time. Many are not found until after a problem pops up caused by a defect in the procedure or the application. *No matter how small or seemingly inconsequential the procedure may be, it must be formalized into the organization and properly documented for everyone to see and understand. If it is important enough to do, it is important enough to do right.*

- *Identical functions are performed differently among businesses, areas, and/or departments.* The same functions and tasks are executed differently in similar situations which causes gross inefficiency, lower productivity, and an inability to share resources and information. What results is the same errors and risk situations are repeated throughout the organization because everyone does it their own way and no one learns from previous example.

  Although four departments perform the same process, because they have been separated by physical location (different floor, building, or state) they no longer communicate or interact closely. This has caused revisions and "evolutionary change" in the processes as time has passed and people have changed. The no-reason-to-see-how-they-do-it-because-our-way-is-better syndrome has prevailed. The outcome is identical errors repeated throughout the four departments, waste of resources creating and revising the same things, and the persistence of the "us versus them" mentality.

III. Compliance and Risk Management Education and Awareness Are Poor

Many organizations suffer from the attitude that compliance and risk management are not the concern of management and staff; they are something that is only considered during audits and regulatory examinations. They become the responsibility of the compliance and risk management departments, since they are the experts and line management does not have the time or the understanding of compliance or risk management. Since most departments and areas have never had a problem, any concern is seen as "overkill" and a waste of time.

Excuses like "the cost cannot be justified" and "there is no time and resources to structure and maintain a formal compliance and risk management training process," are often easily accepted. Any issues that may come along are viewed as rare exceptions; to discuss them with the entire group is unproductive.

These arguments seem ageless and are heard often in the face of any attempt to educate, formally or otherwise, a group of management or staff in compliance and risk management. They all are, of course, completely without merit and counter to the ultimate goal of profitability. With such poor education and awareness, the following is usually evident:

- *No formalized education or training process.* New hires, new recruits in the department, internal promotions, and the like are not given formalized training. They are instead instructed through the "sink-or-swim method": sitting with an overworked individual who has a unique set of short cuts; getting a ten-minute lecture by the boss; and given an ancient, out-of-date manual and told that "some things are still relevant." This always leads to poor communication of job expectations, requirements, policies, and procedures—which in turn causes errors, liability, and serious risk, not to mention the blow to morale of the new hire or transfer.

  Many a new hire or transfer can relate to being given a stack of documents and told to review and fully understand them only to find out later that no one uses them because they are out of date. Since there is no formal training program, no one really has the time to properly educate the new hire and the organization ends up paying several times over the cost of a formal program through errors and low productivity of the new hire.

- *The board of directors, committees, senior management, and key employees are not fully aware of important policy and procedure.* Although at one time everyone might have been knowledgeable of key policy and procedure, it is subject to change along with the environment and business of the organization. These changes are often not communicated to upper management, who occasionally believe that such knowledge is unnecessary for their jobs. The board of directors does not take the time to fully understand the policy and procedures and even the forecast and budget of the organization. They get the bulk of their information from two-hour board meetings four times a year and short two-page summaries that highlight events. Virtually everything they are told is prescreened by the organization and presented in a fashion that benefits the desires of the organization. None of this is done with malice or direct intention to mislead; it is seen by the organization as "polishing the facts" so the board can better understand them. It is often assumed that the board does not want to hear and will not understand the details of involved issues.

  Senior management is treated in a similar manner as the board, with no facts presented to them without careful scrutiny and "rewording" by lower management. Senior management does not express a desire for detail, "I don't have the time," and lower management eagerly accommodates them by pouring on the good news and candy coating the bad.

  Without accurate knowledge of what must be done, upper management cannot effectively oversee the organization, ensure that risk is properly managed, and that assets are effectively safeguarded. It also sends the wrong message to the rest of the organization regarding the importance of a strong working knowledge of the rules. "I know enough to do my job, that other stuff is unimportant."

- *No mechanism for identifying education, training and compliance needs.* There is no facility in place that can recognize the need for educating or updating organization members. Problems are addressed on a reactive basis, which is usually very costly, and often too late. The belief is that time and the resources do not exist to keep everyone informed and properly knowledgeable. On-the-job training is the rule with the need-to-know following close behind. "We've never seen any problems so why worry." Many an organization has wished belatedly that they were pro-active in identifying education and training needs. The majority of errors and risk to the company is not due to fraud or incompetence but to lack of understanding and poor training.

- *Not everyone understands that compliance and risk management is good for business.* It is the belief of many organization members that any compliance and risk management effort is costly, time consuming, and usually unnecessary. At minimum it is someone else's responsibility.

IV. Lack of or Poor Compliance and Risk Management Controls

In some organizations, the systems people print out reams of reports on a daily basis and dutifully have them distributed throughout the organization. Everyone who sees them thinks these reports are wonderful and very impressive. They are placed on the corner of desks and then sent to subordinates with important instructions to file. Out of the dozens of reports perhaps two or three are used, and even those are not used as initially intended. No one, not even the systems people who create them, seems to fully understand their purpose or possible use, and no one seems to have the time or desi.e to try.

Very often other controls such as sign-offs and verifications are either bypassed altogether or mechanically performed without any actual understanding or attention. In several areas, controls have been dropped completely and in the newer areas controls were never developed. The "controls and verifications are double work and largely unnecessary" school of thought is prevalent throughout organizations. Omissions, errors, and issues are only addressed when they get too costly or they are too large and can no longer be hidden.

In many organizations it is difficult to argue the need for adequate compliance and risk management controls. To many individuals they are non-income producing, costly burdens on productivity that are a resource luxury. The problem faced by many organizations is not only internal resistance to controls, but their inability to properly define a control or, conversely, avoid the temptation of creating too many controls. Controls will be discussed in great detail later on in this book, but briefly defined, a control verifies that an action was performed properly. A good control does this through an approach different from the verified action's approach and not by recreating or redoing the action.

Poor controls usually go unnoticed until a serious problem is discovered. The following are some characteristics of organizations with poor controls issues:

- *Ineffective and inefficient controls that are often ignored by staff and management because they are error-prone, hard to evaluate, or too complex to fully execute.* These types of controls are actually worse than none at all because they only get in the way of the process, sometimes mask the real results, and give a false sense of security. They ultimately result in risk exposure, liability, and undetected mistakes. Controls have long been touted by audit departments as necessary aspects of all functions and areas. The problem has been that historically, controls were tagged on to a process after it was created and instituted instead of built into the process.

- *Inability to identify actual and potential risk and compliance concerns until well after they have occurred.* Problems and issues and even inefficiencies are not found until long after they are large and serious. Because of weak controls, any effort to address compliance and risk issues only occurs after the problems surface. There is no successful effort to actively seek out weak spots or identify potential problems. "If only we would have known, we could have done something" becomes the common cry after an issue has blown and the risk of loss is great.

V. No Compliance Validation Program

Another problem in organizations is a lack of compliance validation or self-verification testing in the various departments and areas. The line managers rely completely on internal audit and the compliance department to tell them where their problems are and what corrections are necessary. "I know it seems like a problem and the way we do it doesn't really make sense but the auditors have never said anything about it so I guess it is O.K.; anyway the auditors will let us know if it is not. And besides, if it ain't broke don't fix it."

Without a compliance validation program there is no way to truly assess the complete soundness of the compliance and risk management of the department or area. Third parties such as auditors, compliance officers, and risk managers can do a review and assessment and probably find areas of weakness. However, due to the simple fact that they are not part of the department and not there daily "in the trenches," they can never be as thorough, understanding, and accurate. No one knows the job better than the individual doing it; so it follows that no one is better prepared to find the problems if properly trained.

Some characteristics found in an organization without a validation program are:

- *Since there is no compliance validation or self-testing, there is an inability to verify that compliance controls are working in the organization.* This prevents management from fully and pro-actively assessing the compliance and risk situation. The responsibility then falls upon audit, which has neither the time nor the full expertise to identify all or even most of the potential issues. Audit often can recognize a problem after it has occurred but usually lacks the process understanding and the time to act in a pro-active manner. Since audit does not have the in-depth expertise of the area and its process and controls, they resort to transaction testing. This after-the-fact checking is very costly in the long run and does not identify potential problems, only those that already exist.
- *There is a very low confidence level in risk assessment as well as an incapacity to consistently demonstrate whether a process is functioning properly.* There

is no way to demonstrate that there is total compliance with regulation, law, and corporate policy. It is assumed by default that they are in compliance because no serious problems have popped up and no one has told them otherwise.

A lack of a validation process promotes a reactive approach to out-of-compliance situations and changes, resulting in poor response time. Action is usually taken only after risk exposure is high, losses have occurred, or serious liability exists. "I don't think there are any problems but I certainly cannot guarantee it; that is the auditor's job."

- *There is no compliance oversight function on the individual department level or the organizational level.* The only "compliance" that occurs is worked into the annual internal audit and that only concentrates on major regulatory situations. In effect, compliance oversight is delegated to the compliance or audit department. As a result, true validation is not performed and inefficient processes and controls are often not improved. There is no individual compliance designate in each department and instead one compliance officer is assigned to multiple departments and businesses.

VI. No Business-Wide Management Review

No business-wide management review means management's involvement and review occur only in situations that are new, need to be changed, or are problematic. In organizations where management performs reviews in pockets and isolated situations, the rest of the business, which is the daily operations, is left to people not as fully qualified as the managers themselves might be. These people are the staff members, auditors, compliance and risk management officers. The staff members may be experts in their immediate jobs but they have not been instructed or educated to perform any kind of review. The auditors, and compliance and risk management people know how to perform a review but they are not experts in all areas and do not have the time to thoroughly learn and review all areas.

This is not saying that an auditor or a compliance or risk manager could not walk into an area or department and find possible problems; they obviously do this all the time. The point is that they do miss most of what is wrong through their lack of expertise of the intimate details of the department, their lack of time, their limited concern with only perceived major risk issues, and their historical, after-the-fact transaction testing approach. With the transaction testing approach they must wait and can only find a problem *after* it has occurred.

The result is a tremendous amount of lost opportunity in terms of efficiency and productivity improvements, an inability to pro-actively identify problems, and an after-the-fact problem resolution approach that is ultimately very costly.

Management simply never sits down and says, "let's review what we are doing now to see if it makes sense and if there is a better way." Because either no one has told them or they have not identified any problems themselves it is left alone. "If it is working leave it alone, we don't have the luxury to make pretty tweaks in our processes." In other words they do not have the time to do it more efficiently, productively, and profitably; they are working too hard to save time and money and to do it better. In the pay-me-now-or-pay-me-latter scenario this is definitely a pay-me-later at several times the cost. This holds true for any size business, large or small.

Too Much Business to Make a Good Profit or Too Busy to Do It Better

A small businessman owned and operated his own produce delivery business that employed a total of three people including himself. He worked six days a week; five days were spent in pickup and delivery and one soliciting orders from his existing customers along with doing the record keeping. He was making a profit and he, as well as others, regarded his business as generally successful.

His day started very early in the morning, so early in fact that it actually started at 11:30 p.m. the night before. On his five delivery days, he would get up and drive 50 miles to the produce market for purchase of his day's delivery. He would fill his order, have his truck loaded, and then return the 50 miles to begin his delivery stops. His customers at the time were approximately 35 delicatessens and two restaurants.

This businessman did appear successful; his days were completely full and to him it seemed that he could not take on any more business. He was not happy though; frustration began to grow as he felt his profit wasn't large enough and he wanted more customers. The businessman then decided to consult with his accountant to see what could be done to increase his business. It was a surprise to him when she told him nothing much could be done since his days were already full with work. The way she saw it he was an intelligent hard worker who was already working at capacity. Unless he wanted to work more hours, which would be very difficult, the only other choice, according to her, was to borrow money, buy another truck, and hire another driver. She had seen these things before, she said; she audited many companies large and small and knew what the options were. Other than that, she didn't have any valuable advice.

After thinking long and hard about his situation, the small businessman realized that his accountant knew his books well but not the intricacies of his business. It is true that the accountant was good at her trade and had seen and audited many companies, but she had never owned or operated a produce delivery service before, no less worked at his. Since the accountant was essentially a third party individual from the outside looking in, her knowledge was limited and this caused her transactional, end result judgment and conclusions.

He decided that in order to get the right answers to his problem he would have to turn to the only expert in his small business. Someone who knew his business inside out, lived it every day, and knew every small detail down to the disposal of the empty cardboard boxes. That expert was of course himself. What the small businessman then did was step back and take a fresh look at his business or, as we know it, perform a compliance review and validation.

The first thing he did before he established any conclusions was to gather the important facts. He found that 60 percent of his profit came from only two customers, who were the two restaurants. He also found that almost 95 percent of his time was spent on the 35 delis with very little time spent on the restaurants. As it turned out, the delicatessens placed very small orders on almost a daily basis and bought only enough product to get them through the next day or two. They would even call him the same day he had already delivered to return for an additional product delivery that often wouldn't even cover his gas consumption. Since they were his customers, he would deliver anyway. He realized that he was literally running in circles for the delicatessens.

The restaurants, in comparison, placed one large order weekly with an occasional second large order on busy weeks. This actually allowed him do more business in one 15-minute stop to a restaurant than he did in a full day of stops to over 15 delicatessens. The reason he had never seen any of this before was that he was too busy and didn't take the time to review his situation. Anyway, his business seemed to be working fine with nothing to review—or so he thought.

When the small businessman realized what was happening, he immediately took action. To free up some time he dropped the most unprofitable delicatessens and then used that extra time to solicit other restaurants in a twenty mile radius from his home office. He gradually, over a six-month period, took on more restaurants and dropped 15 of the delicatessens with the remaining 20 being told they could place only one order a week and at a minimum size. All of this gave him shocking results; he is now working fewer hours than before at twice the profit. He also devised a way to grow his business without any material effort or expense.

In his analysis he realized that an additional problem was that his route was too spread out over physical distance. The majority of his customers were in one 10-mile radius and five were 20 miles away. He considered dropping those five customers altogether, but one of those customers was one of his very profitable restaurants. After considerable thought in reviewing the situation he devised an excellent solution. He found someone with a small truck of his own whom he hired to deliver the produce to those five customers. The small businessman would meet this man after his morning pickup, give him his order, and then begin his own deliveries. This way the small businessman kept his customers that he was going to drop because they were too far away, and part of the profit, without all the effort and wasted time. The driver had a part-time job with good pay and the customers still got excellent product and service. He had found a way to add an additional driver with more room for growth that didn't require capital he didn't have.

In the end, our small businessman realized two things: first, taking the time for management to review the business is an excellent way to devise good solutions for tough problems and continuous review allows continuous growth. Second, simply because your day is full and you are working your bottom off does not mean you are accomplishing all that can be done. Time is key and it very often can be used more effectively.

Even though this was only a small business, the lessons learned are large ones. Although something appears to be working, it may not be working at its optimum and management review of the entire business is a necessary and a very valuable business tool to determine and correct this. The final question must be asked—Is a business successful because it is making a profit even though if managed differently, without additional money or resources, its profit would be considerably higher?

Some of the situations that exist in organizations without business-wide management review are:

- *Compliance and risk management review is not seen as an income producing event.* It is one of those things that is forced upon the organization by the regulators and the auditors; people who don't understand profit or efficient business. It is viewed as an unnecessary expense that only wastes resources and reduces the bottom line. To reduce the pain to the bottom line as much as possible it is an expense area delegated to a clerk or a lower manager. A review is only performed, and then by a third party, because of either a demand by audit or fear that the upcoming audit might not be favorable. Most reviews are checklist mechanical reviews with predictable results. You can't find what you don't look for. These reviews do not look for or think they will find anything.

- *Senior management, fiduciary examining committees, and board of directors get their information through slide presentations and bullet memos.* "These people are too important and busy to confuse or waste their time with minutia that they probably wouldn't understand anyway." All of the detail is then crunched and glossed over leaving sterile and usually trivial comments describing serious and important events. Although it is not viewed this way, feeding information to top management in this fashion is the same as lying to them because it rarely tells the whole or even the true story. Information is screened, edited, and rearranged to be represented in the most positive light. Bad information is glossed over or completely ignored and good information is exaggerated. In this type of environment top management is the last to know when something important is happening or has gone wrong.

- *There is no consistent business-wide management communication top down or bottom up.* There are no clear, simple, or well defined strategies, goals, or objects for the organization or any consistent short- or long-term planning communicated to all organization members. These things do exist in various forms on paper but they are not usefully employed in the daily operations. They are written in general terms using words such as "strategic advantage," "synergistic positioning," "cooperative alliance," "we're all on board," "team player," and other such phrases that sound impressive but say nothing.

Discussion of daily activities does not occur between management and staff at any level in the organization. All communication is done formally during special meetings and presentations and is on either major topics or special situations. When upper management communicates to the organization it is done with specially picked words to impress. "We've had difficulty over the past two years and must reassess our positioning in the marketplace. We are confident we can come through this stronger than ever by using strategic expense realignment and leveraging the inherent synergies of our business along with select key talent. This may cause us to tighten our belts a little and bite the bullet. But if we all dig down deep into our reserves and each of us gives a little extra we will come through this as better employees and a better organization. We hope that everyone will be on board with our goal and we need everyone to be a team player."

The translation by the rest of the organization is: "We are getting our pants kicked by our competitors in the marketplace and the losses over the past two years are unacceptable. There will be budget cut backs, lay-offs, and longer hours without additional pay. There will be no bonuses or holiday party and all pay increases will be frozen and we can no longer use fax cover sheets. We must accept all of this or look for a job elsewhere. And, none of this applies to upper management."

Middle management and the staff is no better at communicating with upper management. Whenever possible the information passed on to upper management is edited and spoon fed to minimize reaction and involvement. "I know those are the real numbers but you'd better make them look better than that. I don't want to have to explain to the board why we did so poorly." Too often posturing goes on in an organization where all sides try to ensure that information communicated is politically correct for each other. So much is lost in the translation, along with creating misinterpretations and even harmful rumors.

- *Senior management, fiduciary examining committees, and boards of directors do not hold regularly scheduled compliance and risk reviews and thus, are not always kept current on compliance and risk matters.* Information is often brought to their attention only after it has become a serious problem. Their expertise is rarely tapped for pro-active management of risk or even daily management of the business; at times parts of the organization actually expend much effort in keeping issues away from them! "Only tell the board exactly what we have to and no more, and then only discuss the issues that we think we've already solved. The last thing we want to do is alarm anyone." Keeping senior management, fiduciary examining committees, and board of directors in the dark as much as possible seems to be a corporate pastime in many organizations. This is not only looked upon with strong disfavor by the regulators but it is more harmful to the organization than many people realize.

VII. Weak Internal Audit Relationship and Interface

Internal audit and management appear to be staunch enemies. Someone looking in from outside the organization might not realize that both groups work for the same organization. They work more against each other than they do with each other. Information is hidden on both sides and there are regular, subtle, sometimes even blatant, attempts to mislead each other in order to gain advantage and look good or prevent themselves from looking bad.

Manager addressing his staff—"Audit is coming today, quick— lock the file rooms, hide the keys to the desks, clear off all paperwork and send John and Susan home early because they always talk too much. And remember, never offer any information and always try to give less than they ask you for. And always ask why they need the information and then take as long as possible to give it to them. If you hold off long enough they may even forget they asked."

Audit manager addressing her staff—"We are going to start the audit today so make sure you check in the file rooms, don't accept that nonsense about lost desk keys, and be sure to speak with John and Susan because they always give us good information to zap them. When you ask for information always set delivery deadlines and let me know if they are stalling again. And remember, don't reveal your motives until absolutely necessary, don't allow them to see any of your audit work, and don't trust anything they tell you until it is verified."

This scene is repeated time and again throughout the organization every time an audit is about to take place. It is completely counterproductive to all good principles of sound business management, yet it persists. Management seems to be happiest when either they show-up audit or they are not audited at all and audit is happiest when they can find problems in the areas they audit.

Here are some common occurrences in a weak management-audit relationship:

MANAGEMENT

- *There is a general lack of strong communication between management and audit in terms of teamwork, goals, and the organizational benefit.* Although it is not done openly, the different sides spend a great deal of time working against each other. Management will only tell the auditors what is absolutely necessary and then try hard to hide the rest, while audit plays the "gotcha" game. Management does things and makes changes to please audit, not necessarily to improve risk management, efficiency, productivity, or profitability. Finding problems, risk or compliance issues is the responsibility of audit and is only a management concern if something is identified. Should a department get audited and no issues found, management assumes that they are in perfect shape and nothing else needs to be reviewed. This approach causes a definite lack of pro-active management and sound management of risk and compliance.

- *Line managers have a limited understanding of audit's purpose and therefore regard them as an outside intervention into their department.* Management does not view audit's purpose as critical to the internal control factor and necessary for sound risk management. Audit is instead viewed as an expensive nuisance and rarely relied upon as a good source for risk identification. They do nothing but "waste management's time" and when performing audits they get in the way of daily operations and hinder performance and profit. "Without audit management the entire operation would probably function better." Management does not at all understand the mission of the audit department and audit has not made any effort to ease their ignorance.

- *Line managers have a limited understanding of the audit process and therefore do not utilize audit as a compliance and risk management tool and information source.* The entire audit process is not fully understood by management. There is no clear explanation by audit of how an audit is performed, what is looked for, and what is done with the results. The auditors keep their audit programs hidden from the line managers for fear of losing their independence. This leads to greater suspicion by line management of the audit process and actually makes the auditors' job more difficult.

- *The consequence of all this is too many surprises in the audit findings and very little understanding of the final outcome.* Due to the lack of communication and poor understanding, the results or findings of the audits are usually a surprise to management. Since management does not view audits as a productive exercise, little of real value results. Management only takes the post-audit actions they feel they are forced to take—and often reverses those same actions at the very first opportunity. A strong clue to this condition is the constant repeat audit findings from year-to-year with only token efforts to address them. The tug-of-war between audit and management seems to continue from one year to the next with no end in sight. When the entire affair is over very little, if any, productive results occur. In this atmosphere of conflict the organization can get deeply exposed to risk and wastes a tremendous amount of resources in both the actual audit exercise and the missed opportunities because of the poor cooperation.

AUDITORS

- *There is no complete verification of the effectiveness and efficiency of the compliance and risk management function.* It is not regarded as a formal management task and therefore not management's responsibility. Any focus in this area occurs strictly through the review of specific events and transactions. The same audit agenda is repeated from year to year with very little change. Audit has their checklists which are virtually identical to the previous year's checklists. These checklists basically become their annual fill-in-the-blanks exercise. Since there is no strong communication between management and audit and virtually no communication at all between audits; the audit approach, direction, and programs rarely change.

  Because of this lack of communication, problems may ensue. Entire processes are not audited as they were created after the audit program was written, and so they don't get covered by the audit program's checklists. Management does not tell audit about this oversight since they are glad for the reprieve.

  Although the business and the department along with it has changed, the audit programs have not. The result is an audit that often looks at the wrong things. The auditors are auditing for apple trees when the department now only grows orange trees. Department problems and issues are frequently hidden from the auditors for fear of them being put on public display. This negates any benefit that can be gained from the auditors' experience and knowledge.

  Although the problem has already been identified by management and is being properly addressed and therefore no longer holds risk, the auditors still insist on publishing the problem as a finding in their report. This serves to only punish management for attempting to address the issue. This also encourages management to try to cover up and hide future issues instead of making them known for the rest of the organization to learn from.

There is a continuous us-against-them mentality that is strongly founded in the attitudes of both sides. Management expends a great deal of time and resources to mislead the auditors and to rush through an audit as quickly as possible. The auditors feel that their job is not done *until* they find something wrong, even if it is a small meaningless issue. Many people actually look upon this type of constant exchange between management and audit as healthy because it shows a strong division and independence by the auditors. This animosity between audit and management is not only tremendously harmful to the organization, but it is actually contrary to audit's purpose and sound compliance and risk management.

- *The audits do not focus on process and controls, but rather test only historical transactions.* The audit tests do not concentrate on *how* or *why* something happened or even if it should have happened, only whether it happened correctly or not according to history or some previous understanding. This allows issues, inefficiencies, and risks to go unnoticed and at times actually encourages them to exist. It also never fosters real understanding of a department, process or task. Without complete understanding accuracy, completeness, or effectiveness cannot be fully determined.

Ours Is Not to Question Why!

This particular department was undergoing their annual audit. The audit was going fairly well and uneventfully. The department was basically well-run and was acknowledged company-wide as having a knowledgeable manager and staff. The department appeared to have kept current with everything and audit had not found any major issues in years. One area where the department was not current was their policy and procedure manual, and this created a problem.

Because of automation there was a particular form that became redundant and was no longer completed. It was a form that contained historical information which was now kept in the computer. In going down their checklist during the annual audit the auditors noticed that all of the newer files did not contain this form. Since the entire focus was on the end transaction, which was this information form, the auditors never considered the process and so never understood the use or purpose of the form and that it was now redundant. All the auditors saw was that the policy and procedures manual and their checklist required this form in the files and this was not happening.

No matter how hard the manager tried to explain that the form was not necessary, the auditors could not understand. "And besides," the auditors countered, "it states right here in your policy and procedure manual that every file must have this form." It was a big deal for the manager to now convince everyone otherwise. It required a hearing before the review board, a complete update, and a possible rewrite of the manual—not to mention all those memos back and forth to explain why his manual says it is required when he feels it isn't. In the end this manager felt it was easier to submit to the auditors and he now puts this redundant form in every file. The loser in this situation is obviously the organization in both wasted resources and possibly good managers who leave through frustration. The point is that if the auditors were process oriented they would have considered the actual value of the form. Instead, since they were transactionally oriented and only looked to the end result, real understanding was not important. The how and the why did not matter—only the what. This approach is perhaps ignoring the most important points.

- *The audit focus does not cause management to concentrate on areas that are sensitive to business risk and overall compliance.* Because the audit focus is so narrow and the checklist transactional testing so limited, it never really addresses the broader and more important issue of business risk and sound compliance. In order to pass the audits management is forced to concentrate on the limited audit scope and any resulting issues from that audit instead of addressing real risk and sound compliance. The net outcome is that management's actions are directed towards passing audits and not on sound compliance and risk management. This of course exposes the department and the organization to greater risk in all areas.

Why a New Approach Is Necessary. Why the Old Approach Won't Work

As the previous chapter's examples demonstrate, compliance and risk management typically has been viewed as a nonproductive, required cost. It has been in many cases practiced in name only, with the great majority of institutions giving it little more than lip service. In many organizations, this viewpoint has changed somewhat of late as fraud, embezzlement, insider trading, inept management, and more have caused major monetary losses along with serious regulatory liability and civil actions. Most organizations in these situations have overreacted by amassing large compliance staffs and greatly increasing their compliance budgets. This typical approach is not only costly, but ultimately ineffective.

The Compliance Army—Costly and Ineffective

Let's study the compliance department of a well-known major banking institution. This organization seemingly had a green light to do and spend what they felt was necessary to ensure total compliance. Their resulting overall effort was quite impressive from both a resource and documentation standpoint: the compliance department consisted of a senior manager, line manager, and nine compliance officers along with supporting clerical staff. The documentation they used included reference books, checklists, compliance audits, and a thorough schedule outlining the entire process. They had what appeared to be the most organized, comprehensive, and systematic compliance process anyone could envision—and most banks could only dream of. The compliance officers literally spent 12 months a year making the rounds from office to office, performing their highly detailed checklist audits. It appeared as though they scrutinized virtually every possible compliance issue and not even the smallest issue could get past them. In fact, everyone felt that the process was so good that bank management didn't even think about compliance and risk management . . . until it was too late.

This approach turned out to be a very painful experience for the organization as the compliance army failed to duplicate even the smallest successes achieved by the programs at Citibank Trust California and Barnett Trust (which we will study shortly). In the past few years, there have been several million dollars in issues apparently created through negligence and fraud along with an entire host of issues identified in the bank's recent, highly critical, and very unfavorable, federal regulatory examination. By any measure, the compliance and risk management program was an abject failure. Of course, the compliance department and the internal auditors received most of the blame for the messy outcome; after all, they were responsible for compliance and risk management. This was not fully deserved since line management should have been accountable for what occurred in their own areas.

Where did this admirable compliance effort fail? We can see the major reason by looking at a driving scenario, where the driver of a car depends on an auditor to ensure his compliance with traffic laws. When the auditor is in the car, the driver pays very close attention to the law. However, when the auditor is absent, the driver will not be as attentive and will even ignore the laws when they are particularly inconvenient. Since it is the auditor's responsibility to ensure compliance with the traffic laws, the driver is not concerned. Similarly, at the above institution, line management felt that compliance was the responsibility of the compliance department and therefore they didn't concern themselves with controls and risk management. If compliance ownership does not exist with management, compliance will never become a priority; sometimes, it won't even become a small consideration.

Why a Small Compliance Staff Is Better Than a Large One

The overall advantages of an integrated line management compliance and risk management program are considerable. As efficiency and productivity increase, better quality and a long-term cost savings can be achieved in many areas through:

- *Smaller compliance and risk management staff.* Because compliance and risk management is integrated into the process and controls and line management is directly responsible for compliance and risk management, the compliance and risk management people spend their time training and monitoring instead of "fire fighting." This approach requires considerably less staff than does the traditional program of having the compliance and risk management people perform extensive year-round audits, reviews, and tests.

- *Pro-active management.* By placing compliance in the hands of the line manager, the program becomes pro-active rather than reactive. Problems and inefficiencies are identified by the manager at their source instead of by an auditor, examiner, or the client long after their occurrence, when the risk is always much greater. There is a quicker response time to emergencies. Issues are resolved before they become costly and serious.

- *Easy identification of training needs.* Since the manager is very involved in the effectiveness of the process and controls, he or she becomes very much aware of each individual staff member's skills, knowledge, and effectiveness. Identification of any training needs becomes easy since third party information about individual staff members is less relevant and firsthand observation and involvement become the rule. This is not to suggest that the manager actually performs staff functions along with his or her subordinates, but that greater knowledge and understanding of the staff is achieved through an integrated program.

- *Cross-training.* Cross-training is critical in every organization and more so in smaller ones. It is often not fully considered until the time of need where a key organization member is out sick for an extended period of time or one has unexpectedly left. In an integrated program where monitoring, review, knowledge, and control are pushed down to the lowest levels where the events actually occur, cross-training not only becomes easier, but its benefits become immediately apparent to everyone.

- *More accurate information.* With an integrated program, the manager and his or her staff, and the organization members actually performing the functions, are responsible for compliance and risk identification. This causes the information gathered to be firsthand instead of third party which always leads to a higher opportunity for greater accuracy. The information that is gathered often does not require interpretation from a third party (compliance or risk manager) who must first understand the intricacies of the department or area and then understand the ramifications. Misinformation can result from this third-party approach when there are time restraints that disallow the third party the time necessary to fully learn the department or area. Without complete information, complete and accurate decisions cannot be made.

- *Better controls and organization.* In an integrated program, the controls are simple and more direct along with the manager and staff being better informed through more current and accurate data. This is true because they are closer to and more involved in the processes and controls at a greater level. In other words, since the organization members who are the experts in the area, the manager and his or her staff, are directly responsible for the functioning and effectiveness of the controls, firsthand monitoring and adjustments can be performed daily. This will always produce better controls and overall organization through accuracy and efficiency, while increasing overall productivity.

Effective compliance and risk management is not something that is done once a week, month, or quarter when a compliance review or audit happens. It needs to be monitored, reviewed, and sometimes updated daily. Risk management, although it is being more broadly defined of late, has historically been associated with proper insurance coverage. The principal job of a risk manager in most organizations was to ensure the proper management of risk in the organization through the appropriate insurance coverage. While we will see later on that the right insurance coverage is critical in many situations and a good way to manage risk, it is only part of overall risk management. Looking at compliance and risk management from a total comprehensive organizational standpoint, it becomes clear that it is impossible for any one individual or a group of individuals to perform daily compliance and risk management for the entire organization. There are many benefits to having an integrated compliance and risk management program; it is really the only way to ensure complete and fully effective compliance and risk management. Any approach that assigns a third party team the responsibility can only ensure occasional compliance and risk management.

This approach is already in place and providing excellent results at several institutions.

Citibank's Success

Citibank, one of the nation's largest in the trust business, has a trust operation in California: Citibank Trust California. A few years ago, its compliance program was not a top management priority and it showed. Their latest internal audit was highly critical of things such as an out-of-date policy and procedures manual, weak processes and controls, and a general lack of attention to compliance and risk management. Not surprisingly, the federal regulator, the Office of the Comptroller of the Currency (OCC), exam that followed the same year was equally critical. Something had to be drastically changed or Citibank would be in deep trouble as risk exposure was high and the auditors, examiners, and senior management were very uncomfortable.

The initial reaction by management in California was to request additional staff dedicated to a full-time compliance program in order to tackle the current issues and ensure an effective future effort. This seemed like a reasonable request, especially since it was also what the auditors had recommended. However, this solution was not to be: a major cost-cutting program was already underway business-wide and California had been slated for expense and staff reductions. What ultimately resulted was a cutback of five full-time staff in California and a temporary loan of one compliance officer from New York.

Predictably, the reaction of California management was not pleasant. The seeming impossibility of this effort was compounded by the expected return of the internal auditors and the OCC in less than one year's time, and the directive from senior management that "there will not, under any circumstances, be any more poor audit or examination results going forward." California management realized that things would not get better unless they took matters into their own hands. The biggest hurdle for them was the acceptance of the compliance officer from New York as a resource who would help them gain ownership of compliance, not as someone who was going to do compliance for them.

Utilizing the compliance officer from New York as their trainer and advisor, they proceeded to build, beyond even their own expectations, an exceptionally strong and well-focused integrated line management compliance and risk management program. California management, with guidance from the compliance officer, rewrote their trust company policy and procedures manual, developed several necessary risk controls and procedures, held compliance meetings, performed their own compliance validation to identify weaknesses, and got the business Audit and Examining Committee along with the Board of Directors to be more knowledgeable and involved in their operations. All of this was accomplished with the strength of the knowledge they had gained from the compliance officer and the understanding that they had sole ownership and responsibility for compliance.

In the end, the results were phenomenal: Citibank Trust California not only passed their internal audit with high marks, but did equally well on their following OCC exam. The parting comments of auditors and examiners alike pointed to the exceptional improvement in process, controls, and understanding of risk management all achieved in a relatively short period of time. Although the compliance officer obviously played an important role in this turnaround, he was not the key element because the changes and implementation were actually effected by the trust company's management. Compliance is now part of the daily process and routine at Citibank Trust California; they no longer "take time out to perform compliance" and no one tries to do it for them. Perhaps the most impressive statistic is that this success occurred directly after the 20 percent cut in office staff.

Barnett Banks Trust Company's Integrated Compliance and Risk Management Program

Citibank Trust California is not the only bank that has seen the wisdom of line management ownership. Another bank that practices it quite successfully is Barnett Banks Trust Company NA, with headquarters in Jacksonville, Florida, with over $6 billion in assets under management. They've developed a compliance and risk management program that gives complete ownership and accountability to line management. As a direct result, they have a strong handle on compliance, and line management has a good understanding of business risk. All of this is accomplished with a compliance staff of only four people, including the compliance director and her secretary. This effort has been successful by leveraging management expertise through the implementation of a nonconventional integrated compliance and risk management approach. One important aspect of their program is the compliance certification process. The compliance director at Barnett, a very forward-thinking individual, implemented a compliance certification program whereby line management, on a quarterly basis, certifies, via signed affidavit, the compliance soundness of their respective areas. From the affidavits, which are collected from all the areas and checked for completeness, a single certification is then made to the Board of Directors attesting to the compliance soundness of the entire operation. What this ingenious program does, in effect, is replace the need for scores of compliance staff who would ordinarily comb through the operation looking for issues and weaknesses. Instead, management performs their own compliance validation, and with design assistance and approval from compliance, assesses the results and implements any necessary changes.

The compliance director now spends her time monitoring, training, and validating the overall compliance effectiveness of the bank. Line management does not have to "take time out" to perform compliance, and they have become pro-active instead of reactive to potential client and risk issues. As Barnett Trust and others realize, this is not only the most effective use of their compliance staff, but also the most efficient use of limited bank resources. In the end, there is sound compliance, risk is managed effectively, and the resulting product is of the highest quality.

If It Isn't Broken See If It Needs Fixing

Management in many organizations takes the view that if something is working don't bother with it. In their opinion if it does not require their immediate attention then it is to be left alone. However, when the flow of internal operations is inconsistent throughout an organization—and nothing out-of-the-ordinary is occurring—the resulting inefficiency and low productivity may go unnoticed. Even worse, high risk exposure can go unchecked: "We've never had a problem; we must be well controlled." These words seem to be the favorite first line defense for justification against a serious audit, review, or validation or any resource expense for a soundness check. What often follows these words directly after an error, loss, or liability pops up is "if I only knew there was a problem, I could have done something."

When discrepancies are found it is often during: training sessions, serious audits, process reviews, the relocation and reorganization of departments and businesses, or when any event occurs that causes management to take a closer look. What then comes to light is that these inconsistencies are usually created by or go unnoticed because of poor processes and controls, poorly trained management or staff, and poor planning. What is also revealed is that almost all share the common weakness of no pro-active management or validation testing and poor communication throughout the organization.

Once these issues are identified, the overall costs and risks involved must be understood. Too often it seems that if a process or system gives the right end result, even part of the time, we fail to review it for complete process flow accuracy and consistency, or, "if it ain't broke, don't fix it." A flawed process can result in future losses when the underlying issues are not resolved. When a process is not completely reviewed, from start to finish, for accuracy and consistency because "we have never had a problem," an organization is not only missing an opportunity to improve its operations, it is risking exposure to severe liability and loss. Many organizations have wished belatedly they'd reviewed processes that didn't appear broken.

Cleaning Up the Mess

Organization ABC prides itself on its money management skills. This organization, however, has had more than its share of broken processes not fixed until after major liability and losses were exposed. It has found serious shortcomings with areas such as credit and loan review, consumer mortgage lending, and credit card management, all of which were not reviewed regularly for deficiencies until after multi-million dollar liability and losses occurred. Their most recent example occurred in this organization's employee 401(k) plan. The current plan has been in existence for over eight years with approximately 30,000 participants and over $1 billion in assets. Every quarter, participant holdings statements were sent out to all participants detailing the composite returns and the total holdings for their individual accounts. Everything seemed in order, both the internal and external audits were clean, there were no complaints, and so no specific questions, let alone the right ones, were ever asked. As a result, the total process that controlled the plan was never reviewed for accuracy and consistency from start to finish. It is true that parts were tested during audits, but the pieces were never put together to see if anything was missed or not working properly.

It took almost eight years, but someone finally stumbled upon a big hole in the process. The composite returns for the holdings were being calculated incorrectly, which caused the participants' accounts to be overstated in aggregate by approximately $63 million. Until this point, no one ever reconciled the total holdings in the plan to the individual participant statements to see if they were of an equal amount. Everything seemed in order so it did not appear necessary to management to take any action. Now, this may seem like an obvious proof and test which would have been similar to what we all do with our check books—see if our deposits and withdrawals match our bank statement; however, since it was not customary in Organization ABC to test or validate that which did not appear broken, no one ever thought to verify that the proper reconciliations were being performed—not, at least, until after the error was found. They have since regretted this and now have a big mess to resolve.

Compliance and risk management in a financial institution is often looked upon as a necessary expense/evil, and many parts, if not the whole, are often treated as a last consideration. Management under these conditions becomes reactionary to problems and never really looks to systems and processes as a risk manager, profit enhancement, or a quality control; approached the correct way, they can be all of these things. The moral is a simple one: don't wait until serious liability or loss occurs to review departments, systems, processes, controls, and functions; review and validate these regularly for accuracy and consistency—*if it isn't broken still see if it needs fixing.*

You May Know More Than You Think!

Before you ever sat in the driver's seat of a car, you were probably familiar with most traffic laws. You understood the concepts of speed limits, traffic lights, and lanes. You knew that failure to obey the law could have several consequences including tickets, revocation of your license, or even an accident, potentially fatal. You further understood that although traffic laws may occasionally slow our progress, we are better off collectively and as individuals for complying with them.

Just as you understand the benefits of traffic law compliance, you have probably begun to understand the value of sound compliance and risk management in your own organization. If you haven't read the articles or listened in on any of the multitude of discussions, then your regulators have surely made the point sufficiently clear. The challenge that confronts you now is to develop a compliance program that is not only effective, but simple in structure and easy to implement. The good news is that any institution can establish a compliance and risk management program that meets all of the above criteria. Furthermore, this can be accomplished without an army of compliance officers marching through the organization wielding clipboards and checklists. The program has many subtleties, but its basis relies on two fundamental principles: (1) keep it simple; (2) line management must be responsible.

1. Keep It Simple

Any compliance and risk management program—especially its processes and controls—must remain *simple*.

Simplicity is critical for several reasons:

- *Education and training.* Simple processes and controls by their very nature are easy to learn. They require less time and resources to communicate and generally require a less sophisticated knowledge base to understand. Things that are easily learned are quickly learned with less resources and effort and therefore can be communicated to a broader base of staff. This will greatly benefit the organization through less dependency on "specialists" and greater availability of cross-trained staff members. This not only presents advantages when emergency situations arise, such as long-term illness or unexpected departure of key personnel, but it is a good compliance and risk management tool. Since more members can be knowledgeable of the process and control, there can be more eyes to watch for errors that may occur.

- *Execution and daily application.* Because there are fewer steps in a simple process or control as compared to complex ones, performing the process or control on a daily basis takes less time and effort. This frees the staff members to spend more time on other tasks and lessens the need for short cuts, especially during crunch time which can expose an organization to unnecessary risk through mistakes and errors.

- *Maintenance and monitoring.* Simple processes and controls are easy to learn, take less effort to perform, and will therefore take less time and effort to monitor and maintain. This is very important from a compliance and risk perspective. All resources are finite, especially those used for tracking and monitoring problems and errors. This can allow a smaller amount of resources used to monitor a greater amount of processes and controls. This in turn allows for a more thorough and comprehensive control system that can cover a larger organizational base. The more comprehensive (not complex) the monitoring and control system, the better risk can be managed from a total organization standpoint.

    Additionally, since the processes and controls are easy to understand and therefore make identifying inconsistencies easier, the managers and staff directly responsible for the process can readily monitor their accurate operation. This negates the need for an army of third party, outside "experts" to perform this function. Because anyone outside of the process cannot possibly understand or monitor it as closely as the individuals performing the process, the entire system becomes more efficient and effective.

- *Identification and problem resolution.* It is always harder to see if a complex process is working properly as compared to a simple one. What often must be done to learn or repair a complex process, is to break it down into easily understandable or simple parts. Only then can it be clearly viewed and followed for flow and consistency. Once it is looked upon this way the cost reduction becomes apparent as less time is spent identifying, learning, and fixing the problems, freeing time and resources to do other, perhaps more productive and profitable actions.

- *Modification or replacement.* Even if a process or control is not broken or faulty, there are times when it is necessary to modify or replace it completely. This can be necessary due to the changing and growing demands of an organization, marketplace, or regulatory environment. A complex process or control will not only always take more time and resources to change or dismantle but often will create unforeseen ramifications. Because it is complex, it will usually touch several functions in ways not easily identifiable, and its modification or replacement can have an undesirable ripple effect on these other functions. In other words, it is like changing code in a computer program to fix a bug; in doing so, four more bugs can be created. Change is always best when it is largely "invisible" and affects the least amount of people and areas.

Simple processes and controls reduce cost through increased efficiency and productivity and in general make life considerably easier for those involved. Creating processes and controls that are simple, direct, and selective in what they are to accomplish will cause the entire system to function better. The key words for any process or control are: simplicity, flexibility, and selectivity.

Complex processes and controls should be avoided! By making a process complex, an organization gives its staff an excuse for not fully participating in the compliance and risk management effort, and dooming it to failure. This does not mean to imply that people are lazy, dishonest, or unwilling to do a complete job. In today's environment it is often a requirement to do things quickly and to do more in less time. Complex events cause people to abbreviate involved situations or find a way to go around them.

All of us at one time or another have experienced a manager, coworker, or associate who tended to write long-winded or verbose memos. If it could be said in 10 words they would use 50 or five pages instead of one. We may have read the first one or two memos, but after that we started to skim for the important points and visually cut the memo short. Although this may have caused us to miss some important detail, the time expense seemed too great to do otherwise. Besides, imagine if everyone wrote memos like this? We'd spend our whole day reading memos. Don't do in 10 steps that which can be done in one. When processes or controls are cut short by the people involved, it is their judgment that decides what is or is not important. Since they may not be fully informed, this can lead to some serious risk when the wrong things are left out.

Electricity and the Path of Least Resistance

An organization was particularly sensitive and concerned about the security and control of the cash movement and disbursements in its client accounts. They felt that the current paper process with the executive level sign-offs, was not secure enough to properly control the risk and opportunity for fraud. Documents could be altered and even forged which would allow inappropriate cash disbursements from the client accounts. Since they had recently experienced an incident such as this which caused a fairly large monetary loss, they decided to create a foolproof system that would monitor and control all cash transactions. The system they finally decided upon was felt to be ingenious because it employed the latest technology and automation. Essentially, what this organization created was a computerized system that required three separate approvals in order to release all transactions. The approvals were performed with a magnetic "swipe" card similar to a credit card, with the authorization code recorded on the magnetic strip. These three approvals amounted to a verification, double verification, and triple or super verification.

The process began when the cash clerk would input the cash transaction request into the system. After the clerk was satisfied with the accuracy of the entry, he would seek the first level of approval. This involved the designated individual being notified by the clerk, and physically being present to pass his or her authorization card through the magnetic reader. The authorization process was completed after this approval procedure was repeated twice more by the other two designated cardholders. After all appropriate approvals, the transaction was electronically released for final execution.

With no papers to forge or documents to alter, it seemed a great system since it would also simultaneously record all transaction times, approvals, and rejections. As the organization was to eventually find out, there was one major drawback with this complex and comprehensive system in that it was very time consuming to get a cash movement to occur, since every transaction required the involvement of four separate people. With virtually all tasks in this organization, as it is with almost any organization, productivity was a factor and the cash clerks were continually encouraged to improve their transaction process and approval time. They did this by employing their own common-sense approach which improved their productivity fivefold and didn't appear to hurt the overall accuracy of the process.

It was not until sometime much later into this new automated cash movement and disbursement process that the supervising manager found exactly why the clerks' processing time had improved so impressively. The clerks had negotiated and secured in their possession, all three approval cards which effectively allowed immediate authorization at all three levels simultaneously. Precisely because this process was so onerous, what evolved in due time was an agreement between clerk and approver to streamline the control and make it acceptable in their business terms. Inevitably, both clerk and approver tired of the daily back and forth required to execute each transaction so they devised this effective way to save everyone aggravation, increase efficiency and productivity, while seemingly not hurting quality. Of course, this approach by the staff rendered this wonderful control totally useless.

Looking at it from hindsight, this process requiring the automated sign-offs was far from simple. It was also very apparent that the creators of this system never considered the impact on the staff that had to employ the system. Many organization members, especially the good ones, are like electricity in several ways, but especially in the principle of always choosing the path of least resistance. The shorter the steps, the fewer people involved along with the least amount of energy expended to accomplish a task is always the desired approach. As well it should be!

Avoid the Book-in-the-Door Syndrome

A bank with strict security rules needed to regulate the flow of traffic through a doorway to a sensitive computer area. To ensure top security, they installed a combination key pad/electronic ID card reader at the door. Everyone entering or exiting had to undergo a two-step process which let them in and out while recording all IDs.

Proper security in this area was critical due to the client-sensitive information stored and processed there. On paper, the system seemed perfect. In reality, the individuals who needed access several times daily found this two-step process to be time consuming, inconvenient, and inefficient. As a result, when no compliance people were looking, they simply held the door ajar with a book which allowed quick access and kept their hands free for their work, since they didn't have to fumble for ID cards. In the end analysis, this complex control system was ineffective and failed because it took much less effort to bypass the control than it did to use it. Processes and controls must be developed that take more effort to go around than they do to cut short or avoid. Remember, you want to make your organization better controlled, not more inefficient.

We all, at times, fall into the habit of believing that the more complex and technically involved the system, the better it will work. No matter how good a system seems in performing or controlling a specific action, it will be ineffective if people work around it.

Thought of differently, if an organization is constantly prodding its employees to be more productive and time conscious, how should these same employees react to a complex and involved process? When developing a system to perform or control something, we must not only consider its desired result but also how this system will impact the jobs of the staff that must work with the system. The best system in the world will only work if it is fully and accurately employed. For this reason, a simple control that is used will always be more effective that an expensive, complex system that is cut short or bypassed altogether.

2. Line Management Must Be Responsible

The second fundamental principle of total integrated compliance and risk management is that compliance should be the responsibility of *line management*. As we discussed in Chapter 1, a line manager is simply any manager who has direct responsibility for a process or department. Although the compliance department and internal auditors play a crucial role, the ultimate responsibility for compliance must belong to the line manager and his or her staff. Although many people including line managers may offer objections to this principle, they all come down to the same three arguments, each of which is easy to defeat:

- *"Line managers can't be trusted with compliance and risk management."* Some may argue that a line manager will not uncover compliance or risk issues in his or her area, but rather hide or ignore them. This is untrue. To begin with, a good manager doesn't lie—to himself, herself, or others. If a line manager chooses to ignore a compliance issue, or claims to be in compliance while knowing that's not the case, then the problem isn't one of compliance; it's management. And if a manager is misrepresenting compliance problems, chances are other issues may be misrepresented as well.

  Fortunately, the vast majority of managers are concerned with doing a complete job, including compliance, and would rather find and fix their own issues than have them made public. With the proper education, managers can be entrusted to ensure their own complete compliance. As we will see, no one else is better.

- *"Line managers don't have the expertise to perform compliance and risk management."* This objection is confusing. After all, who knows a department better than its manager? A compliance officer or auditor must first learn the department's processes and controls before even beginning to evaluate compliance and risk issues. On the other hand, once a line manager is properly educated, no one is better qualified to review and identify problem areas. No one else is there all day, every day to identify them. No one else can be pro-active to daily issues. At best, an outside compliance officer is a part-time risk manager for each area.

  From a practical standpoint, it is considerably easier and takes much less effort to teach a manager the principles of sound compliance and risk management than it does to teach a compliance officer about every aspect of an organization. Some have even argued that the only way to teach a compliance officer everything he or she needs to know about a department would be the equivalent of making him or her as knowledgeable as the manager. This of course would be impossible, and besides, what is the point?

- *"Line managers don't have the time to practice compliance and risk management."* The argument continues that if you force line managers to perform their own compliance and risk management, then you are taking away their time for "what they do best." Many managers themselves will tell you this. However, if the correct processes and controls are in place, then compliance will become a part of managers' daily routine; they won't need to "take time out" to perform compliance functions because they would be integrated into the system. In general, a manager should never have to perform a task and then have someone perform compliance; both should be virtually simultaneous.

If you analyze these objections in the context of our automotive analogy, you can better understand why they don't really apply:

- *Trust.* Even though it may not suit us as individuals to comply with traffic laws, we obey them because we understand the ramifications of failing to do so. If line managers and their staffs understand why a compliance program is necessary, they can be entrusted to execute it.

- *Expertise.* Once you received your license, you probably never doubted your ability to drive a car. Conversely, if you lacked the expertise, you knew you wouldn't have received your license. Once an individual becomes a manager, he or she has the expertise. If compliance responsibility is expected of line management and sufficient training is made available, they will not lack for expertise.

- *Time.* When you drive, you are aware of traffic laws and you drive accordingly. When you learned to drive, obeying the law was just a part of the driving process; you did not do one without the other. By integrating compliance into the job function, it becomes second nature and requires almost no extra time or effort.

- *Conventional wisdom.* What if we approached the driving issue the way some organizations approach their compliance management issue? Let's assume that drivers lack the expertise to drive, can't be trusted to obey traffic laws, nor have the time to do so. If that were the case, then whenever no one important was looking, drivers would stop only when they wanted, would drive in whatever lane they chose, and would travel at whatever speed they found desirable. It's obvious that under these circumstances almost no one would make it to work on time; many wouldn't make it at all. The conventional solution would be to have a compliance officer ride with each driver on occasion to observe whether the driver was complying with the traffic laws. Of course, in this scenario, drivers would pay strict attention to traffic laws while being audited, but drive however they pleased when not. This solution, unfortunately, is comparable to the traditional compliance program. It is ineffective, grossly expensive, and impractical in the long term.

As we can see from the driving example, ensuring occasional compliance is easy. Maintaining constant compliance is difficult and can only be done by the individual performing the task. Police officers, compliance staff, and auditors can provide monitoring, education, and enforcement; but they can't ensure complete and constant compliance. Whether driving a car, managing a department, or running an institution, we are the only ones who can really ensure our own compliance.

4

Achieving a More Competitive Offering

Integrated risk-based compliance and risk management has many benefits, not the least of which is higher quality, lower costs, and a consistently stronger product offering to the customer. The product offering becomes stronger for several reasons as a result of the integration process which allows the entire organization to work more as a team.

A quality product resulting in a more competitive organization is to some people an unusual and unexpected benefit from achieving sound compliance and risk management. It is unusual to some because they assume that the more time spent on things like compliance and risk management the less time there is to do the real stuff, like run the business and make a profit. They could not be more wrong. The stronger the integrated compliance and risk management, the more efficient, productive, and profitable the organization will be.

We can go back to the Citibank Trust California example in Chapter 2, where employing integrated compliance and risk management got them much more than a clean internal audit and OCC examination. Their organization ran more efficiently with greatly reduced errors, and productivity in many areas was increased along with greater risk awareness by management and staff. Citibank management also felt they had better control and understanding of the organization through ownership of compliance and risk management, which they felt resulted in a better product offering to their current and prospective clients. Management for the first time knew fully what they could and could not do in terms of operation and management of their business. And the best part at Citibank was that they didn't do it with more staff or even the same amount of staff, but their tremendous success was achieved after a 20 percent reduction in staff. They did more and better with less and increased profits all at the same time. Incredible as it may seem, sound compliance and risk management goes hand-in-hand with quality and reduced costs.

When everyone in the organization is thinking about, talking about, making a commitment to, and practicing integrated compliance and risk management, daily quality will be the outcome. There is only one major catch with this entire approach and without it success will never be achieved. When we say everyone, that means everyone from the mailroom clerks all the way up to the Board of Directors. The Board of Directors and senior management especially must think about, talk about, make a commitment to, and practice integrated compliance and risk management daily. All of the memos, meetings, and directives in the world can be heaped upon the staff and it all will be meaningless if the staff sees that upper management does not take it seriously and practice it themselves.

An Education at Westinghouse Electric

Many years ago when Westinghouse Electric was still heavily into manufacturing products from light bulbs to small appliances to elevators, they were well known for their employee education programs. They took great care, paid special attention, and seemed to spare very little cost in educating their new and existing managers in many very important areas such as ethics, communication, people skills, teamwork, supervisory skills, and so on. On paper they had one of the best programs of all the large corporations; it was often used as a model for other companies. Westinghouse was well known then, and still is today, for their creative, inventive, and technological expertise. However, even with their ambitious education program, the overall corporate management expertise in many areas did not seem up to par. This may be hard to understand considering all of the time and effort they invested in their management. Looking at a brief story of the experience of a young manager in Westinghouse several years ago, we can understand why.

A young, intelligent, and very ambitious man fresh out of undergraduate school started in the Westinghouse Electric Treasury department as a treasury representative, otherwise known as a credit manager. He was not with the company three months when they began sending him to Pittsburgh, Pennsylvania, the Westinghouse headquarters, to begin a series of education programs. The very first program was a one-week-long orientation where he met and worked with several other treasury reps from around the country. He was very excited to say the least, and very anxious to begin learning the "Westinghouse way" and other skills that would help grow his young career. He took five courses that week, one each day, and met every one daily with a voracious appetite. The young man learned about Westinghouse's data control system, their credit practices, management skills, and even a course on teamwork. The course on teamwork was one of those great exercises where you are with a group of people in a plane that crashes in Alaska with no civilization around for miles. Those that cooperated and worked together survived, those groups that did not became human popsicles. The first four days were wonderful.

The fifth and last day had the best course of all. It was a course on communication, interaction, and presenting and discussing concepts, ideas, and solutions to problems with other people. The entire day was a real eye opener, especially in the area of communication. The young man learned how very few people are good listeners and how many don't even try. He realized that no one can talk, listen, or concentrate on different thoughts all at the same time. This meant that if you were talking to someone and they began a rebuttal before you were finished talking, they weren't really listening to you. They heard some of the things you said but certainly not all and perhaps not clearly. The same holds true when the other person jumps to conclusions before your explanation is done; they obviously were not completely listening.

Now at first the young man had a "so what" reaction, thinking that as long as you hear most of what is said that's good enough. He later learned how wrong this was, why so many people misunderstand each other, and why so often subordinates never fully understand what a manager really wants. Both sides are guilty of poor listening; the manager is often the guiltier party. The young man also learned that when people listen to each other the words are not the only thing they hear; the actions taken before or after those words often speak much louder than the words themselves.

At the end of the day the young man saw a video of a perfect manager who listened, interacted, and explained herself very clearly. His next thought was since all of his senior managers have already gone through this course they already know how a perfect manager should act. Westinghouse must have a great number of perfect managers and working there was going to be fantastic.

When the young man got back to his office he realized that his manager did not behave the way the "perfect manager" in the film did, but this was not going to be a problem. He would simply remind his manager of good communication and then the manager would remember his course several years ago and correct his behavior. Being young is sometimes wonderful because your expectations can be limitless and it is true that high expectations yield high rewards. Yet, being young can also mean being idealistic. This was the case for the young man who thought his manager would change.

The following day the young man was enthusiastic and ready to roar. He met his manager first thing in the morning and was promptly devastated by his manager's "I'm-the-boss-and-you're-the servant speech" and "I don't ever have to listen to anything you have to say." Although extremely upset and disappointed, the young man was not immediately deterred as he did have a lot of pride and ambition and he convinced himself that his current manager was an exception in the organization. It took him about eighteen months and several courses more to discover he was wrong. He then found employment elsewhere. In the end, the education programs the young man attended actually did more harm than good because he learned the ideal at the programs and compared that to his flawed organization's practices.

Westinghouse had one of the best education and management training programs around; how could even one manager like the young man's boss exist? The answer is a simple one. Senior management supported these fine programs by making the funds available, but that was as far as it went. They did not think about, talk about, make other commitments to, and practice many of the principles taught in their education programs on a daily basis or, in some cases, at all. The old parent cry of "do as I say and not as I do" unfortunately still holds true in many organizations. The actions of senior management demonstrate their commitment tremendously more than any education program, no matter how well devised and executed. If senior management does not buy into the integrated compliance and risk management program and demonstrate it on a daily basis, every other effort is a waste of time and money, and quality or any other benefit will remain unattainable.

The lessons learned at Westinghouse Electric and other similar situations strike one basic chord in regard to quality and success: words are not enough; they need to be supported and followed up with actions matching those words. An integrated compliance and risk management program will provide quality and success in meeting its goals and, in the process, it will more effectively utilize resources and reduce the cost of those resources, but only if faithfully practiced by everyone.

Quality

These are specific concepts that must be inherent in the upper management's vocabulary. Only then will they filter down through the organization. To achieve high quality, the following concepts must be regularly discussed and applied.

- *Consistency of operations.* Processes and controls must be consistent throughout the organization. This allows for quality results through ease of application and execution, as well as less confusion in communication and understanding.

    The example of the organization that has grown over time by acquiring other branches in a number of states across the country is a good one for showing how inconsistency can really hurt. For over several years this growth continued where the new branches were added to the family and in most cases the old management was kept with little else changed. Although many of these branches were not strongly profitable (some even had negative earnings), the business as a whole was seen by the organization as successful. Corporate headquarters positioned the branch system as successful to the shareholders when in fact profits in most cases were only marginal. The biggest problem with this operation was the lack of consistency and coordination of the branch system. The branches all essentially performed the same functions and operated the same business but the approaches and processes they employed were quite different. They often acted as if they belonged to different organizations.

Quality varied throughout the branch system and very little co-operation existed. Their approach had to be changed with all the individual branches working in concert. As Bank One and other successful organizations have shown, there is a strong quality product and great profit to be made through an organized consistent approach.

- *Reducing complexity.* One of the key requirements and goals of integrated compliance is keeping it simple. Simplicity allows for ease in understanding, application, change, validation, and assessment. It also gives a much better opportunity for the process or control to be done completely, accurately, and in a shorter time frame as compared to a complex situation. Integrated compliance does this through constantly reviewing and questioning why things are done and how they can be improved.

- *Educating management and staff.* Organization members are able to identify issues and problems pro-actively instead of waiting for them to occur. By having an excellent working knowledge and understanding of their job and the organization, they are able to better recognize what is right and wrong and what is good and bad. Their ability to act quickly and decisively also enhances the quality result. As we have said before, most errors are committed through ignorance as compared to incompetence.

- *Empowering the individuals doing the job.* It puts ownership in the hands of the managers and staff who are performing the function. Ownership and responsibility for the results and full understanding of the outcome of their actions is critical for quality and effectiveness. Empowering does not allow a third party to be responsible for doing the job right. When the members understand the organization's objectives and how to reach them, they will excel and produce a high quality product. Poor quality is not the result of ineffective workers, but ineffective training and systems and organization members who do not have ownership.

- *Allowing greater teamwork.* Since the organization members are more aware and knowledgeable of tasks outside of their direct responsibility, it is easier to act in concert and more difficult to gives excuses of "your job, my job." Cooperation in general will increase and people will work more as a team and shed the "problems are O.K. as long as they are not mine" attitude. People like to be involved in the process and feel that they have a real impact in the decision-making and results. To do something and really make a difference is one of the greatest motivations an organization can give to its members.

Responsibility and individual accountability will cause people to look beyond their immediate tasks and compare their surroundings with the rest of the organization. The integration concept teaches everyone to "think risk" on a daily basis and consider their actions and what their impact may be on other parts of the organization.

Before the integrated compliance and risk management program took effect in her organization, Sally was just doing what she was told and not considering her actions at all. Every day she would walk around to each manager and collect the client checks that were mailed to them. She would tally them, fill out a bank deposit slip and a data entry form, put them in an unsealed envelope, and place them in the out-bin for collection by the mail clerk. Then she began to learn the principles of integrated compliance and risk management through meetings and sessions held by her department manager.

Sally realized that many of her actions were filled with risk and by employing minor changes, which she devised, would greatly reduce much of the risk. She saw that leaving the "live" checks on top of her desk when she went to lunch exposed them to the possibility of someone taking them. She also saw that leaving them in the usual out-bin was bad for two reasons. The first was that everyone knew she put the daily checks there; some people would even add to them without her knowing. The second reason was that the out-bin was in an open hallway trafficked by dozens of people daily, any of whom could simply remove the envelope without detection.

Sally discussed her concerns with the managers, the mail clerk, and her associates and they all agreed with her observations and conclusions. A few simple changes were made; locking the checks in her desk when she went to lunch, any additional checks would always be brought directly to her and the check envelope was held for direct pickup by the mail clerk. All of these efforts took virtually no additional time and the risk of check loss or fraudulent behavior was greatly reduced. Teamwork was employed for the solution and client service quality was increased since a lost check would require going back to the client for replacement.

- *Changing the performance system.* Quality will not be increased and risk will not be reduced unless the individual organization members want them to be. The organization members will not care about quality and risk if they are told not to care by the way they are measured and rewarded. A manager cannot tell his or her staff that they have to process error-free client transactions and then rate them solely on the number of transactions they complete in one hour. The real message that is sent is always much more important than any verbal or written demand. The wrong rewards will actually be counterproductive to the ultimate goals.

A Chargeback Reversal

An organization was in the business of processing credit card sales slips for its clients who were retail merchants. In the credit card trade language the organization was called a credit card processor or a bank card Acquirer. The Acquirer would take the credit card sales from the merchant, exchange the slips for cash at a discount to the merchant, and process them, which involved batching, tallying, and so on. These processed batches were then sent electronically to the appropriate credit card association, VISA, Mastercard, Amex, or Discover, who would then pay the face value of the sales slip less an interchange fee to the Acquirer. The profit to the Acquirer was small, usually measured in basis points, but with high volume, efficient processes, and low chargeback write-offs, a great deal of money could be made.

In the credit card industry, the thing most feared by merchant and Acquirer alike besides fraud is the chargeback. A chargeback occurs when the cardholder, under certain rules and conditions, can request their bank, the cardholder or issuing bank, to remove the charge from their account and reverse it back to the merchant. In this case the charge or total value of the sale actually gets debited by the issuer to the Acquirer's account with the association. At this point the Acquirer has effectively funded the chargeback since the merchant has been paid for the sale and the charge has been credited or deducted from the cardholder's statement.

The Acquirer must then go to the merchant for the appropriate documentation to prove the validity of the sale to the issuer, or in trade terms, dispute the chargeback. If the merchant cannot provide the necessary documentation, in which case the chargeback is deemed valid, then the Acquirer must recover from the merchant the full value of the chargeback or face a write-off. Recovery of the chargeback amount by the Acquirer is usually easy, but only if the merchant is still a client of theirs, or is still in business or the Acquirer meets the necessary time frames for charging the merchant.

A chargeback that is effectively disputed is called a chargeback reversal. There are fairly strict rules in which a chargeback can be reversed back to the issuer and ultimately the cardholder, but the biggest overriding factor is the time restraint. The Acquirer, the one who originally got the credit card sales slip from the merchant and processed it to the association, has a 30-, 60-, or 90-day window depending on the reason for the chargeback, to dispute it and provide the appropriate evidence to reverse the chargeback to the issuer. If for any reason the Acquirer misses this window, outside of a "good faith" arrangement with the issuer, the Acquirer usually gets stuck with the chargeback and must write off the amount as a loss.

This particular organization was especially sensitive to time frames because stale chargebacks, those that are past time frames, often could not be charged to the merchants and instead had to be written off by the organization. These stale chargebacks were also growing in number along with the concern of senior management.

Due to the small profit margins, a $500 chargeback write-off would require several thousand dollars in new processed sales just to break even. This made it critical to work all chargebacks in a timely fashion and avoid any subsequent write-offs. To ensure timely chargeback handling, management responsible for chargeback processing developed a chargeback clerk performance program. This program was designed to speed the processing of chargebacks and ultimately reduce the total write-offs. The logic employed was that if chargebacks were handled within the allotted time frames, any resulting write-offs would be inconsequential. This concept may have been sound, but it ignored one very important point. No one ever asked the staff why there was a large number of stale chargebacks and write-offs. Management simply assumed that the staff was not working hard enough.

At the outset of the program all of the clerks were told they had a daily chargeback processing quota to meet and those that exceeded the quota would get immediate rewards of gifts and year-end rewards of better pay raises and bonuses. For additional incentive they even placed a large sign in the middle of the floor counting the chargebacks processed by the hour. Management also had daily morning meetings discussing the previous day's accomplishments and gave numerous words of encouragement. Many of the walls were also wonderfully decorated with several signs that read "quality is number one" and "think smart, reduce write-offs." All of the clerks responded fantastically to this new program with greatly increased volumes and many exceeded quotas. It appeared that management was brilliant and the program would make industry headlines.

It took approximately six months for management to realize that their incentive program was a disaster. In the end the program did not solve their problem of stale chargebacks and high write-offs. In actuality the cure was worse than the disease, as it made the stale chargebacks and write-offs increase. It does not really matter what is said or how many silly posters are plastered on the walls; the actual measure of performance ultimately dictates the staff's actions and what will be accomplished. The organization can scream quality all they want but the measurement, ranking, assessment, and rewards for performance send the true message. "My boss says she wants me to satisfy every caller and answer all of their questions; but during my annual review she criticized me for having one of the lowest calls-per-hour ratios. She also gave me a lousy raise and said unless I increase the number of calls handled per hour I will be in trouble; so from now on once a call is more than five seconds old I'll just disconnect." The rewards of a performance system must be in the right place. If you want volume, reward for volume; if you want quality, don't reward for volume and punish for quality.

The problem with our credit card processing organization's incentive program was that since the emphasis and performance system were based on items processed and not on the accuracy or quality of the processed chargeback, the difficult chargebacks that could not be resolved quickly were continually put to the bottom of the pile to make way for the easy ones. This of course caused several chargebacks to become stale and they eventually had to be written off even though everyone was meeting the quota daily. As write-offs continually mounted management realized that the new performance system eventually caused exactly what they were trying to avoid. Management did want quality and obviously wanted to reduce chargebacks, they continually said it in discussions, meetings and memos and even posted signs, but they unwittingly never said it where it counted—in the performance system.

When it comes to a performance system in particular, it is critical to have the rewards and measurements send the desired message. Don't tell your credit managers that the organization does not want to be exposed to marginal loans and then criticize them because they reject too many loans. This is precisely how many organizations got in trouble with bad real estate loans in the 1980s. They said one thing and rewarded for another.

Management almost never intends to ignore quality; they in fact, often demand quality in all their discussions and meetings with staff. As we have seen, this is not enough; the performance measurements must be in line with objectives and expectations. For an organization to get quality they have to create an environment for and reward for quality.

- *An integrated process.* It demands that the performance system reward for hard work, teamwork, quality work, and continuously thinking improvement.

The organization members must have a say in the decisions that affect their work. No one knows their job better than the individual doing it. To make major changes or assumptions without consulting the person performing the task, regardless of their position, is a good way to lay the groundwork for failure. Even if the change or assumption is correct, everyone likes and even needs to feel they have a say and some control over their destiny. The best way to get buy-in and ownership of a change or new program is to let the individuals who will be part of the change or new program feel that the decision was at least partly theirs. This is something that is so often overlooked by management but is so crucial to effectiveness and quality. "My boss always changes his mind and never explains anything to me; he must think I'm stupid. Well he is the one who is not too bright because anyone who does my job can see that the changes he makes don't work."

The organization must provide the appropriate education and training. We've mentioned it before, but education and training also comes up a lot in any discussion involving quality. It's a fact that the majority of errors made are a result of poor understanding and knowledge and not incompetence. Education should be organized and not the word-of-mouth system.

There must be support and commitment from top down. Culture, commitment, and quality always start at the top. Without senior management support every other effort will be a waste of time.

Communication must be strong and organization wide. The greater the communication the more efficient, effective, productive, and quality driven an organization will be. Mistakes are not repeated as often, people learn from each other, there is a greater sense of teamwork and less of the "us vs. them" attitude, more resources are shared, and there less duplication of effort. "I didn't know that my report was so important to your department and you used it for your calculations. I can make some minor changes that will speed up your process and improve the report's accuracy."

It is hard to find your way in the dark and even harder to do it with poor directions. The more clearly and simply goals and objectives are stated the less of an opportunity for multiple interpretations and the less time is spent figuring out first what they mean and then how to get there. What often happens in these situations is that people make it up as they go along.

Say It Simply and Clearly

There is little worse than statements that have no tangible meaning and send no clear message. "Our goal is to be the leader in the industry and we will get there with a cohesive strategy through leveraging the synergies inherent in our talent and our competitive advantage. We will demand quality and achieve it through Total Quality Management and a commitment to excellence." This statement is corporate gibberish; it says nothing, gives no direction, and will actually confuse anyone trying to make sense out of it; yet it is not that dissimilar from many corporate mission statements.

"Our goal is to achieve a 20 percent market share in the New Jersey mortgage business by 1998 and we can get there by having our branches concentrate on the prospective customers in their area. They will do this through local print media, working closely with local real estate agencies, and by making personal visits to potential customers. We will abide closely with our current credit standards and not deviate by concentrating only on the targeted class of customers." This statement, even though the approach may or may not be good, sends a direct message that is easily understood.

Now the individual organization members have something to follow, debate or change but at least it can be defined and measured. You cannot easily define or measure a "cohesive strategy" or a "competitive advantage" but you can measure "20 percent market share in the New Jersey mortgage business" and the effectiveness of "local print media, working closely with local real estate agencies, and making personal visits to potential customers."

The performance system must directly reward for achieving the objectives and goals. As we have discussed, the measurements and rewards will dictate the results achieved. If the performance system is fair and equitable and rewards for the right things, the results will not disappoint the drive for the expected goals.

- *Setting higher standards.* High standards must be set in order to achieve great things. The setting of the highest standards for performance, efficiency, productivity, and ethical behavior will send a clear message to everyone that the organization will accept nothing short of the best. This may sound like a cliché and one of those empty and superfluous motivational statements, but it is really a simple and basic formula for quality. No one ever achieved excellence by shooting for mediocrity.

In the 1970s and the early 1980s American manufacturers had very low standards for quality of workmanship. Some manufacturers accepted defect rates of 10 percent or less as excellent, contrasted today by manufacturers such as Motorola, which feels even 1/2 percent is too high.

These poor standards were nowhere more evident than in the electronics and automotive industries where poor quality seemed to be the rule and anything made well occurred by pure chance. New television sets were shipped with parts missing and cars were sold that fell apart while leaving the showroom. Standards were low due in large part to the belief that during those times of high inflation and soaring costs, quality and attention to detail was too costly and would kill profits.

As we all now know, nothing killed profit and companies quicker than the junk that was produced and sold by many American manufacturers. These same companies, the ones that are still in business, have finally realized and changed their ways so that they now produce some of the best quality products in the world. And they do it by setting and achieving very high, and formerly unbelievable, standards.

Go ahead and try it, take you current standards and double them and see what happens. After everyone gets done screaming and crying and they realize you're serious, they will buckle down and get to work. If the performance system is fair and has the proper rewards, you may be surprised at the results that are achieved.

Low standards effectively tell the organization members not to work too hard and that it is O.K. to waste time and resources. For some probably very unscientific reason it always seems that the more time there is the more things there are to do. We have all heard the comment that "sure we can use additional people, we can always find them something to do." This is said even though everything in the department is getting accomplished completely with the current staff. People work best when they are challenged and get bored when the task is too easy. The organization must continually challenge its people with standards that remain high. This also means that they have to be continually revised because any standard that is achieved is no longer the highest achievable. Computer technology is an excellent example of this; performance standards seem to be increased every six months with no immediate end in sight. This should be everyone's goal.

- *Strong policy, procedure and controls can improve quality of operations.*

  Achieve and maintain quality
  - If the program is effective and consistent throughout the organization, it will cause applications along with their execution to be cleaner and less error-prone.
  - Consistency of operations is realized through simply defined policies, procedures, and controls that everyone can follow and understand.
  - Higher standards become the trademark of the operation that will result in stronger and more effective controls and therefore fewer errors, compliance issues, and fraud.

Lower Costs

With an integrated program, containing and reducing costs becomes a daily function that is everyone's concern. Once all of the organization members understand the actual costs involved in their functions, they can begin to constantly identify opportunities for reducing costs. The key point is to constantly question everything that they do and ask why it must be done and then how can it be done in less time and use less resources while giving better results. This holds true with every task, not just the high profile, but the lesser everyday tasks as well. In the long run with cost reduction, it is usually these low level tasks that are more important to manage for efficiency simply because they are considerably more numerous and usually often ignored.

Overworked, Underutilized

A medium size manufacturer had just lost its manager of credit, collections, and billing. The new manager who was hired to replace him had started with formal introductions to most of the management team. The other managers not being available, he was told he'd met them sooner or later. He was then introduced to his staff and finally his desk, and told to get to work. Since there was no management training program and no other management available to instruct him of his daily tasks or even show him around the department, he had to depend on the head clerk to educate him. The head clerk was almost twice his age, hardworking, intelligent, and very used to things being done just-so.

The head clerk had everything down to a system with morning ledgers and reports, early afternoon collections, afternoon check postings, and late afternoon reports and ledgers. It took everyone in the department about 11 full hours daily to finish all of their tasks. By all accounts this new manager had a very hardworking and dedicated staff that had everything under control; they did not appear to need any guidance and he could not have possibly squeezed one more minute of work from them. His staff was even kind enough to point this fact out and also occasionally remind him lest he forget.

Since the business was growing, work in his department was growing along with it so the dilemma the manager faced was how to handle the new work without any additional staff, only employing an already worked-to-the-limit staff. He did not know his new department well enough to even begin to guess where to start. He decided that the best approach to take was to do nothing for the first three months. He only intended to observe and ask simple questions like, "What is this?" and "Why do we do it?" After three months he had learned enough to begin the necessary changes.

Starting that following Monday he began to ask slightly different questions of the department staff. They were more direct questions that challenged the staff, forced them to think, and at times forced them to defend their long held beliefs and assumptions. The questions asked were, "Why do we need to do this?" and "Why do we need to do it this way?" and "Is there a quicker or better way to do it?" and "Who else depends on this task?" No task was exempt from review and every staff member had to take a close look at what they did and why they did it. The manager made only one rule and that was: "If you cannot explain to me why you are doing this and what the benefit to the organization is then you must stop doing it. And the responses of 'because so-and-so told me or that's how we've always done it' are not acceptable."

Not surprisingly, he was met at first with skepticism, then with disbelief, and finally with resistance when everyone realized he was serious. What helped the manager's cause was when the staff understood that no changes would be made unless they fully agreed to them and even initiated them. Challenging everything in the department became one of those "impossible" goals that they all began to strive for. Over the course of the next eight months, task after task was questioned with most being changed and many being eliminated.

Because the staff never before completely understood the total purpose of their department or even their own jobs, nothing was ever questioned until now. If an individual does not understand the purpose of their task and what impact it has on the other parts of the organization, he or she cannot begin to question or challenge why it is done or how it can be done better. By questioning the staff and forcing them to understand, and sometimes defend, specific tasks, the manager caused the staff to look past their immediate jobs and at the surrounding areas to fully understand what they were doing. The ultimate rewards from this exercise were amazing. Each staff member on average reduced their hours worked from over 11 to under four hours a day. The most shocking aspect of all to the staff was that the quality of their work increased although the time spent in producing those results decreased. They realized that the simpler the process and the fewer steps employed produces fewer errors made and requires less time for review and validation.

What the staff found was that a tremendous number of unnecessary steps were performed in many processes, some tasks were totally unneeded although at one time they probably were, and many reports and ledgers were much more complicated than required. Without changing the major functions of the department, the staff, the tools, the equipment, or the surroundings, productivity was increased almost threefold and overall quality, morale, and loyalty was never higher. Not to mention that the new work coming into the department was welcomed with open arms.

The lessons learned at the medium sized manufacturer and other similar situations point out the fallacy in the "more is better" attitude. In the case of the credit, collections, and billing department, they did more work more effectively in less time and without increasing staff. As businesses expand, the steps employed to perform the growing number of functions inevitably increase, often without reason or need. It seems to be a common belief that size requires complexity. Such complexity is usually nothing more than layers of people, reports, and steps to a process. Like the government, it seems to grow every year whether necessary or not.

What is not always understood is that the resources and steps necessary to accomplish a task do not grow on a one-to-one basis as the task grows. Economies of scale allow you to do much more with relatively much less. These economies, however, are only attainable if the situation is fully efficient. Perhaps the simplest way to create these efficiencies and benefit from the economies is by employing the "straight line" principle, better known as, "the shortest distance between two points is a straight line." What you do is basic: look at where you are and where you want to be, and then cut out all of the unnecessary obstacles that block your way in getting to your goal. If in order for a transaction to get processed it requires five people to handle it, see if it can be done with two or three. It is often amazing how people don't miss unnecessary steps in a transaction.

So-What?

A good way to trash the garbage-in-the-middle is to use the "so-what" test. This is a neat little test that can be used time and again; the more it is used, the more accustomed all of the organization members get to it. After a while people even begin to anticipate the asking and eventually ask themselves before anyone else gets a chance. The *so-what* test is a series of simple questions, just like the ones in our manufacturer example, that causes one to think in terms of real utility and need for a step, task, process, control, and so on. It eventually flushes out the waste in all applications. Some of the questions in the test are:

- So what does this really do?
- So what do we really need it for?
- So what happens if we stop doing it?
- So what if we do it this way instead?
- So what if we cut out these steps?
- So what? (as in: who cares, big deal, prove to me we need that step, task, process, control, etc., convince me otherwise or we stop or change)

Other people have referred to the *so-what* test as the cutting-out-the-fat test, but that name is too long; it is simpler just to say *so-what*.

The most important point that must be stressed is that every step, task, function, process, control, etc., must be reviewed, no matter how small. It is the small ones especially that need to be scrutinized because they are so numerous and tend to be overlooked. The multitude of small steps add up to minutes, hours, days, and even months of effort. What manager wouldn't want an extra three or six hours a week of "found time" in their department to use as they choose? Every current resource expense must be fairly challenged along with every call for additional resources. It is not enough to say, "my people are working 10 hours a day now," or "I'm getting more work so I need more people"—*So-What!* Reducing expense is an attainable goal reached through teamwork and smart work; work smarter, not harder is still an excellent axiom.

Lower costs are achieved through:

- *Cooperation between organization members, areas, and businesses.* The word is cooperation and not competition. Everyone moves in the same direction and as a single group or team and there is no us-against-them mentality. Information is shared, communication is strong, and mistakes aren't repeated from area to area or year to year.
- *Efficiency in processes and applications.* Simple processes and applications where possible in similar areas, regions, and businesses, allow

ease of application, understanding, implementation and revision. This is the "cookie cutter" approach where all like steps, tasks, functions, processes, controls, etc., are cut out of the same mold. This all leads to increased efficiency and productivity in ease of application, training, and modification.

- *More knowledgeable management and staff.* Since everyone doesn't have to learn all these unique tasks, it allows for a strong general knowledge base which in turn creates a greater general understanding of the organization's operations and goals. All of this leads to lower costs. Consistency equals efficiency equals lower costs and higher profitability, and lower risk.

Lower costs will be the result in the long run

- Fewer errors, compliance issues, and fraud directly affect the bottom line by way of lower costs and fewer legal expenses.
- Efficiency in processes and applications will result in quality and consistency.
- Consistency will develop between areas and/or the businesses as they all will speak the same language. This always results is less time spent in communicating and understanding actions. Less time spent here is more time spent on money-generating endeavors.
- The simpler and more efficient an operation, the less staff is required to perform the functions and generate the desired results.
- More knowledgeable management and staff will be a by-product of a quality program.

Strong policy, procedure, processes, and controls that are fully integrated can improve quality and reduce cost!

5

Responding to the Increased Sensitivity of the Regulators

In almost every industry today the government regulators are showing a growing interest and concern in the actual management of the business. They are no longer solely concerned with just strict compliance with regulation. The fact that no compliance violations have been found is not a guarantee of a clean examination. More and more the regulators are beginning to review management's credentials, approach, knowledge, and risk awareness. If the regulators are very comfortable with their first impression of the management controls and risk awareness in the organization, they are much less likely to give as thorough a review of the detail or come back as often. This benefits both the organization and the regulators, as less time and effort is spent on both sides. This unused effort and resources can be applied to profit generation for the organization and for additional investigations elsewhere for the regulators. As we will see later in our example, some regulators, such as the Office of the Comptroller of the Currency (OCC), have adopted this approach more thoroughly than others. All of the regulators appear to be moving in this direction if for no other reason than it makes sense and works.

This approach is considerably more in-depth and subjective than the previous approach as the regulators will no longer simply verify such things as the existence of a policy manual but go much farther into the facts of how current it is, its completeness and relevance to the business, whether or not it is fully understood and communicated to management and staff, and so on. In short, they will be looking very closely at process and performance vs. corporate policy and business planning.

The following is an outline of the regulators' Risk Management Assessment Examination approach. This approach was principally developed by the OCC:

I.   Compliance and Risk Management Examination

- *New focus on Top Down vs. old focus on Bottom Up.* The Bottom Up approach is when compliance is viewed from the end result with the individual who performed the action. In other words, you would verify that the completed trade had a signed and time stamped trade ticket and that the trader noted it appropriately in his log. The Top Down approach is when compliance and risk management is viewed from the most senior manager level, usually the Board of Directors, down through the ranks to the end result. The Top Down approach looks for the entire management level, top down, to be knowledgeable, concerned, and involved in compliance and risk management. The top down approach would start with corporate trading policy and see if it is correct and well communicated. It would then assess the soundness of the process and test the knowledge of the participants before looking at the existance of the logs and the execution of the trades.

- *Fiduciary activities and responsibilities encompass more than simple compliance.* It is not good enough to just demonstrate that there are not any compliance violations. Management must show that proper due care is taken and sound compliance is practiced. This is done through compliance and risk management processes and controls, awareness, and education and training.

- *Importance of the quality of management's supervision of fiduciary activities.* Strong compliance and risk management controls are critical to ensure the effectiveness of the processes which will result in a quality product. The quality of the supervision and management of these processes and controls directly impacts the results.

II.   Risk Management Examinations

- *Directors and senior management are responsible and will be held accountable for supervising fiduciary activities.* It is not acceptable to plead innocence through ignorance of events or staff actions. Whether the directors and senior management are aware of a situation or not, they are still held accountable. Accountability and responsibility start at the top and flow downward.

- Examination Objectives:
  - Ensure that the fiduciary activities are administered in a safe and sound manner; including compliance with laws, regulations, and sound fiduciary principles.
  - Determine the quality and effectiveness of the fiduciary risk management process.
  - Assess the degree of risk present in the subject fiduciary activities and how well it is understood and managed by the organization.
  - Verify that management does maintain a formal and systematic approach to fiduciary risk management.
- Initial analysis focuses on four major components of risk management:
  - Risk Tolerance—How well the organizational structure can endure risk.
    - Policies
    - Planning
    - Underwriting standards for accounts and new products
  - Risk Identification—How well the organizational structure can recognize and support risk.
    - Management reporting systems
    - Loss reserves
    - Capital adequacy
    - Insurance
    - Litigation
  - Risk Supervision—How well the organizational structure can manage risk.
    - Management structure
    - Operating systems
    - Internal controls
  - Risk Monitoring—How well the organizational structure can check for and keep track of risk.
    - Compliance systems
    - Audit committee
    - Audit programs and coverage
- Mandatory testing by the regulator to validate preliminary findings of the interviews:
  - Test in the following areas:
    - Operations
    - Administration
    - Investments
  - How well does management know the following:
    - Systematic concerns
    - Weaknesses identified during the risk management analysis or during previous examinations

- Systems, investments, or account types requiring the greatest technical expertise
- High growth investment or account categories
- Investments or account types that test legal barriers
- Any other factors that may contribute to a higher than normal level of risk

The ramifications of failing an examination or even achieving a marginal pass can be quite costly for the organization in terms of current and future resource expense, limited ability to participate in desired markets, public relations image, and overall profitability.

As we discussed earlier, using this new approach, the regulators can find serious fault in the management and operation of an organization even if no actual compliance violations are found. Such was the case with the OCC's review of the bank in the following example. Although no actual violations of government regulations were found, the OCC came down strong on the bank and even suggested that they close one area of their business because the product was so poorly understood and run by the bank.

OCC Review of Another Bank

Senior Management Review

The first two weeks were spent by the regulators interviewing senior management in all relevant areas. They scheduled meetings with senior management to discuss their understanding of the business and related risk. The OCC did not depend on credentials, titles, written documents of the organization, memos, or meeting minutes; they instead questioned each manager individually to learn their understanding and expertise in the business. From these discussions the OCC formed the basis of their main investigations. This is different from previous approaches of performing samples, scrutinizing documents, and the like to identify compliance issues. Here, instead of starting at the bottom, they began at the top, with management, and looked for broader based issues which then funneled down to the specific issues of real concern.

Scrutinized Employee Records

The OCC in their review required the organization to supply turnover rate of employees, copies of exit interviews of employees, and listing of employees for the last three years. *Here the OCC was looking for weak management of staff, disgruntled employees, and worsening trends in the organization that could all lead to future risk to the business and clients. Often the best way to understand the quality of the existing employees is to look at those employees who are no longer there.*

Product Investigation

The OCC spent a good deal of time reviewing the various products the organization offered. They considered things such as business fit in terms of resource support, expertise, complimentary products, client commitment, and profitability. From their general review of the bank's products the OCC got specific and requested a large amount of information on corporate trusts. No compliance or regulatory violations were found in the corporate trust area. However, the OCC suggested they consider leaving the business. The OCC determined from their review that management knowledge and expertise in the business was severely lacking, controls and risk monitoring were poor, and the appropriate resource dedication from the bank was not evident. *The message here is not so much about corporate trusts, but rather the way they approached the function. Strong consideration was given to management quality, risk monitoring, and controls. As a result of the weak controls, the OCC made the strong recommendation of leaving the business. This shows how serious the OCC is about risk and management understanding.*

New Products

The OCC thoroughly scrutinized the organization's project planning on new product development and analysis. They considered product fit with the current organization structure, resource dedication, knowledge, and expertise in the product, legal consideration by the organization, and long-term commitment. The OCC found that the organization's previous new product attempts were flawed due largely to a lack of formalized review policy for new products and projects. *Most organizations do not have a new product planning process in the comprehensive approach the OCC desires; many organizations do not have one at all. The majority of organizations that do have a new product planning process employ the linear approach where the idea or concept goes to marketing first, then systems, staffing, and legal, and so on down the line. Instead of sitting everyone down at the same time to discuss major obstacles up front, they go from department to department. Sometimes, after great resource expense, it is discovered that the product is not a good fit for the organization.*

There was one organization that spent an entire year and several thousand dollars developing a new product and the systems and staff to support it and actually sold the product to some clients only to discover later that the product was illegal. Since in this case the legal department was at the end of their long linear approach the illegality was not found until great expense and even liability was suffered—not to mention the embarrassment and public relations nightmare that followed.

OCC Questionnaire

Before their actual visit the OCC sent a questionnaire that consisted of several dozen fact finding queries to the bank. They asked for things such as education, background, and experience of individual key management to training programs and risk reviews to type, size, longevity, and strategic direction of the business. They were also very interested in profitability of the business and asked for two years worth of full financial records.

This organization had a 25-page response to the questionnaire. *The OCC scrutinized these answers and developed the basis for their questioning and review of the bank's management and operations.*

Account Acceptance Procedures

The OCC criticized them because they do not centralize and standardize account acceptance procedures across the bank. *Although this makes perfect sense, many organizations do not have standardized procedures throughout the organization. This seems especially true with the larger organizations. The lack of standardization is usually not intentional; it results from the organization growing at a fast or sporadic rate.*

Where possible, the OCC wanted procedures for acceptance of risk across business lines. *This must be done centrally with policies on what type of business the organization will and will not accept.*

Overdrafts

The OCC cited the possibility that the bank was exceeding their legal lending limits due to overdrafts. Overdrafts must be reported on call reports as loans. This will tie into lending limits; 15 percent of capital is legal limit. *Most organizations never viewed overdrafts in this manner and therefore do not have the tight process and controls.*

Pledging of Collateral

Reviewed procedures for pledging against cash in excess of $100,000. The holding company can't pledge for the main bank so this practice had to be stopped.

Environmental Policy

The OCC focused on their environmental policy and the education and awareness of staff and how its actual application took place. *Many organiza-*

tions do not have a formal policy. Although this a critical risk management tool, it is often one not thought of until a serious liability results.

Risk Management

The regulators looked for the risk management process to be a formalized process in planning and exceptions to planning. They started with the strategic goals of the organization, worked down through the business plan and departmental budgets, and actually tried to tie them into the individual management and sales goals. *In other words, strategic and business plans, budgets, and individual management goals, should all relate and tie in and have risk management built into them. This makes perfect sense but it is still surprising how many organizations seem to develop their plans, budgets, and goals in isolation of one another, not even thinking of the importance of linking them together.*

Audit and Examining Committee

The OCC verified that the Audit and Examining Committee approved and was the oversight of audits and audit programs. They recommended that the committee meet quarterly and develop a way to catch aggregate exceptions (profit planning, strategic plan, account acceptance plan, etc.). *The OCC wants real substance out of this committee. They were very concerned that it was in fact an independent body and not simply a "rubber stamp" for audit findings and programs. The committee is supposed to attest to the effectiveness and independence of audit. Many organizations need to take a strong look at their committees to see that they are really meaningful and not just a paper support of a poor process.*

Conflict of Interests

The focus was on insider trading and bank policy with securities transactions. They sampled employee trades, looked for front running, etc. *The importance of these controls is even more critical in light of the new technology, products, and government attention.*

The review of this organization was not focused on the adherence to key regulation and identification of any violations. These were still important considerations of the review; however, the approach was essentially to understand management's risk processes and controls along with their knowledge of their business and outside environment. The OCC's thinking was that if the process and controls are sound and management is experienced and knowledgeable, this will be the cornerstone of the organization and ensure good risk management and profitability for the bank. If the opposite is true, even if no violations or problems currently exist, their occurrence in the future will be almost guaranteed. Most laws and regulations simply ask that a thing be done properly and honestly. If the focus is on this concept and not on the wording of the law itself, a great deal of time and money can be saved along with ensuring compliance with the laws and regulations.

Some of the above points and comments by the OCC may be familiar to you and some may not. The specifics of the points are not as important as the overall message that is conveyed. The message is *don't lose sight of the real issues by getting bogged down in the detail or limiting your attention to just doing what's necessary to comply or get by for the day.* Understand what the real goals are and always keep them in sight. Those goals may be things such as market share, profitability, and long-term growth; they may be client service and reduced expenses or they may be a combination of all these things. Regardless, these "big picture" considerations are what actually drives all the specifics and detail that consume the daily activities. It is often easy to be so busy with everyday events that you lose sight of the real goals. This all boils down to having a clear understanding and continuous sensitivity to the big picture. It always seems very easy to see where an organization lost sight after they are defunct; the trick is to see this long beforehand.

Seeing the Big Picture

As unbelievable as it sounds there are times when we know something so well that it prevents us from seeing the simple problems. All of us have been in at least one situation where we knew something so well it seemed that we could do it in our sleep. Either through many repetitions or through many years we learned a system, process, piece of equipment, job, or department better than almost anyone else around the organization. This caused us to be the expert who was looked to during important situations or unsolved problems. What happens often when someone becomes an "expert" is that they do not have to approach the situation as a less experienced individual might. When a problem arises, they feel that they can get right to the issues and find a quick resolution and not bother with all the beginning and ending steps. This method works some of the time, but after a while it usually becomes more abbreviated and ad hoc.

Especially in problem solving where we are familiar with how the event should properly occur, we can lose sight of the big picture and only see the individual parts we choose to focus on. What then happens is a haphazard approach that quite often becomes a guessing game. We may get lucky and chance upon the correct solution, but many times much effort is wasted bouncing around from place to place trying to find what may be right under our nose. In every situation we must always keep the big picture in mind when striving for any goal. This may sound like a generality, or an obvious statement, or even a cliché; nevertheless it is very important where time is limited and resources are scarce, which is the case in every organization.

The big picture does not always have to be particular to a specific event; it can be something as general as the common purpose of the organization. The importance of the big picture or common purpose has never been so painfully obvious as was the case with American banking in the 1980s. Between the bad real estate loans and the massive purchases of junk bonds, management in many organizations had to finally step back and take a fresh look at their real common purpose.

As has always been the case, the common purpose of every bank is to make a profit through good management and decision-making, growing market share, and long-term viability. One of the ways in which this is achieved is through growing the portfolio of good commercial loans that will generate a constant revenue stream throughout their life. During the 1980s, it seems that both the sales and the credit departments forgot about the common purpose of generating a profit through good management and decision-making, growing market share, and long-term viability, and focused on the short-term business of just making loans. It appeared that real estate loans were given to almost anyone who asked without prudent regard for things such as credit worthiness or ability to pay. Sales thought their purpose was to write as many loans as possible and credit thought theirs was to approve as many loans as possible. The current disaster speaks for itself in regard to lost sight of the big picture. Even though on the surface one would think that a sales and credit department might have a different purpose, in reality both must be loyal to the same common purpose—it is the means that may vary.

Whether trying to achieve successful results or trying to solve a problem, we must always remember to pick our heads up, look around, and make sure we understand our actions clearly and that they are organized, directed, purposeful, and meet the overall plan. This is true in big things as we have seen in common purpose and the lesser things as we shall see in problem solving.

The Master Learns from the Apprentice

There was a master printer who jointly carried the title of master mechanic for a certain manufacture of printing presses. The printing press was a special type that was a large sheet-fed three-color press. It was so large it could fill a small room and so complex it was made up of several hundred parts. This master prided himself in his ability to produce quality work from his press that usually far exceeded any work from that of his peers, even his more seasoned peers. In his work he always seemed to make fewer mistakes, produce more work in a shorter period of time, and often identified problems before they actually occurred. Since he was also a master mechanic, a dual designation that few other master printers had, he was continually sought out to repair, or at least identify the problems when the other presses broke down.

On one particular morning the master printer's mood was very sour. His new apprentice had just come in ready to continue learning the trade from one of the best only to find the press stopped with pieces sprawled out on the floor and the master printer black with ink and grease up to his elbows. After several queries by the apprentice, most of which were ignored by the master printer, he had learned that the press had broken down two days ago and the master printer/mechanic was at a loss as to the cause. He had seemingly tried everything and could not understand where the malfunction was or what had caused it. By this time the master printer had come to the conclusion that he was not going to find the problem without help.

The master printer, being bombarded by questions from the young apprentice, decided to put him to good use. He turned to the apprentice and said, "you're going to find what is wrong with this press." The apprentice was dumbfounded and replied, "you are a master mechanic and you could not find the problem; how can I possibly do what you could not?" The master printer then explained that he apparently was not approaching the situation correctly; the problem was probably obvious at this point, and he needed a fresh new look. The master printer further explained that although the apprentice did not know this particular printing press, he did know some smaller ones quite well and fully understood the principle of offset printing. The apprentice was still unconvinced but agreed to try.

It took approximately 45 minutes for the apprentice to find the problem, which was a small lever in the paper feed unit that was broken and out of place. The apprentice was shocked, the master printer delighted, and the press was up and running in two hours. What the apprentice unknowingly did was to use a very simple but powerful problem solving approach. Because the apprentice did not know the inner workings of the machine, he did the only thing he could—ask questions about it to understand.

For 45 minutes he asked "what's this for" and "what does that do" and "explain how this mechanism works." In doing this, the apprentice forced the master printer to answer these questions and as a result look at the press in its simplest and most basic terms. In answering the questions the master printer quickly saw the problem and also realized why he would never have found it using his old approach. Instead of asking himself questions in a progressive order, the master printer was deciding on solutions first and then looking to see if he was right. In other words, he would decide that the air pump must be broken and then look to see if it was and if not, continue with this conventional trouble-shooting approach. This method is similar to the child's game of pin-the-tail-on-the-donkey where the child tries to pin the tail in the right place while blindfolded. The child makes an assumption or guesses where the tail belongs and then attaches it with the result unknown by the child until the blindfold is removed. It is true that remembering previous failures may get the child closer the next time but it is still basically a guessing game.

With trouble-shooting the master printer was guessing at what the problem was and didn't know the result until after he looked, or "removed his blindfold." Using the apprentice he was forced to review the situation through answering the apprentice's questions, which got progressively more involved. He started with the overall big picture and got more specific. In doing this the possibilities were systematically narrowed down and focused to the actual problem.

Often the best way to solve an issue is to start from the beginning and work through it until it is understood, or in the apprentice's case start by asking where the paper and ink goes into the press. Then follow, along with the master through the apprentice's questioning, the paper and ink's journey through the press. Not being ignorant, but assuming initial ignorance in problem solving by questioning even the smallest detail, will always paint a much more lucid picture of the situation. This does not always happen when we are knowledgeable, because then we feel we can "skip the obvious" which usually starts us some place in the middle. We then follow by way of a zigzag trouble-shooting exercise and find that it is very difficult to piece or string facts together for a growing picture that can give an answer. It then becomes a hit or miss game. Our master printer finally avoided this by allowing his young apprentice to force him to start from the beginning, and review the obvious through simply answering questions. The asking of questions ultimately led to the answer to his problem. So next time when you hear someone say, "don't ask me more questions; give me answers," you will see that they are missing the point and almost certainly a fast solution to their problem.

A manager's process in a banking organization should be no different. Don't trouble-shoot or manage while blindfolded; too often this makes you go after the symptoms and not the real issue. Without keeping the big picture in mind, the solutions will be temporary and the approach short-term. By focusing on the big picture, the real goals, the decision will be broad based, effective, and long term. Cause actions to have an ultimate purpose for sound decisions and healing of issues, not the quick fix and temporary band-aids.

Part II

Total Risk Management

6

Effective Risk Management: Identify, Minimize, and Manage Risk—At All Levels

It seems that everyone today is including the word risk in almost every discussion that involves business. It is quoted regarding virtually all actions taken by an organization in terms of business, organizational, and social risk. When discussed, it seems risk is described as an evil to be avoided at all costs. Unfortunately this misconception has led to some strong misunderstandings about risk in both its definition and its unavoidable existence. If the ultimate goal is to make a profit, then risk cannot be avoided. Surely, just being in business is associated with some degree of risk. In fact, if the goal is to make a profit, then risk should not be avoided in many cases, only managed properly.

Many experts have long believed that the greater the risk, the greater the return or profit. It then follows that the organization that deals most effectively with the highest level of risk will reap the highest level of profit. The answer then is not to attempt to avoid or do away with risk, but to identify, minimize, and manage it at all levels to the optimum degree for that organization. When this is accomplished, risk is no longer an ominous specter, but rather just another aspect of business that can be dealt with effectively.

The best way to effectively handle risk is to integrate its understanding into all aspects and levels of the organization. In other words, instead of creating complex and time consuming risk matrices, scoring sheets, or "risk management departments," teach risk definition and identification to everyone so it can be both minimized and managed effectively. Since all employees are already experts in their respective areas, they can each learn how to minimize and manage risk there once they learn its definition and symptoms.

Quantitative tools, such as matrices or scoring for risk assessment for large populations—such as life insurance categories and consumer loans or credit cards—can work well. There are various reasons for this, but it is largely because the law of averages will negate the high and low extremes while keeping the average constant and somewhat predictable. Actuaries have proven this approach to be very successful where the starting assumptions and data are correct.

This, however, is not the case where populations are small or events occur infrequently and the mix of variables is high. There are many reasons why consistently predicting an outcome is difficult, but by far the most important factor is the large variable mix, where the bottom line whole is the same but the parts that make it up are different in each situation, and something we call the human element. When individual judgments are involved in small populations or infrequent events, there is not enough interplay to allow the law of averages to hold true, and although the factors may be the same, judgment can change with the individual.

When we speak of the human element, we are not necessarily talking about blatant judgment errors, which are somewhat predictable, but rather, the more subtle ones. These can occur due to variables such as experience or "instinct," overall temperament, stress for the moment, decisions based on incomplete knowledge, work load, timing, and so on. All of these subtle factors are often overlooked or ignored, mostly because they are largely unquantifiable and very unpredictable on an individual basis. Precisely because these factors are so difficult to predict is why they often can have a major impact on total risk exposure.

If, however, these factors are dealt with on the "big picture" plane, they are much more manageable and even somewhat predictable from a gross total sense. In other words, if the organization as a whole moved towards identifying and managing risk, these individual and subtle variables will have less impact as other parts of the organization will counter to minimize and sometimes offset them. In this way the risk is not totally avoided, but at least it is managed effectively.

With current quantitative tools, especially those used by actuaries, the prediction of future occurrences is based on past events or historical data. For example, using this approach an insurance company may say that 10 out of every 1,000 men will live to the age of 90. This is stated with a fair amount of confidence because over time this has been the average. Now, they may try and refine this prediction more by isolating specific height, weight, smokers, and so on; however, the more finite they make the prediction, the less accurate it is precisely because the populations they are working with are shrinking.

In the service industry where something occurs in only one account, or once a month, or even once a year, the population of events is too small to predict future results simply because there isn't enough experience or historical data to determine a trend. Likewise, if a situation often repeats itself, it can still be largely unpredictable because the variables that make up the situation are different for each occurrence, causing the end results to vary.

Therefore, the goal is not to isolate and confront risk in specific individual events, but to define the entire *situation* in terms of risk from a manageable, organizational standpoint. This is not accomplished through scoring or risk-ranking specific circumstances and then instructing the individual organization member to handle accordingly. Instead, work it the other way around. Create ways to educate and train each individual on risk identification and minimization and have them manage the risk, at all levels.

What then follows is the greater the risk, the higher the level of organizational involvement. In this manner, risk can be more efficiently managed at optimum levels. Don't tell your organization members what is and is not a specific risk event; let them tell you. If properly educated, no one will do it better. Teach everyone that it is not only okay, but essential to "think risk." (Of course the next hurdle is how to properly educate and train these individuals. This will be addressed later on in this book.)

To better understand these concepts, we can take the example of the client trust account. A large organization may have several hundred trust accounts, so the logic of quantitative risk assessment would follow that some consistent conclusions regarding risk could be drawn from the population of these accounts. Therefore, one should be able to analyze the number and size of accounts and perform a risk-ranking along with a total dollar value of risk exposure to the organization.

The problem that comes into play is that none of the several hundred accounts could have the same asset mix, and the human element plays heavily on any pending risk. For example, you could have two accounts managed by the same trust officer with identical total asset value. However, one account is composed of U.S. government securities and the other is composed of a chain of gas stations. Obviously the risk exposure in the account with the gas stations is greatly higher due to the potential environmental issues. This can get considerably more complicated when the trusts are made up of varied assets (stocks, bonds, real estate, closely held companies, special assets, etc.) and no two trusts have the same asset composition.

Next, consider the human element. What if you have two identical trust accounts regarding asset mix and value—but one has an experienced trust officer managing it and the other has a first-year officer? Or consider identical accounts with the same experienced trust officer but the beneficiaries or co-trustees on one trust demand and get several and varied disbursements and rotation of assets, and the other trust is rarely touched. Considering the people involved in each example, the actual risk would be very different. A complex quantitative assessment tool to measure this risk would be far too involved and time consuming to use in practice, and a less complex one may never differentiate any difference in risk levels.

To confuse the situation even more, take all of these different variables and mix them up thoroughly in each account. It then becomes very clear that no mathematical formula, matrix, scorecard, or test can honestly assess risk to any useful degree without causing some rather long-winded and impractical exercises. Remember, it must be simple to be effective.

Since a large part of the risk in an organization is not easily quantifiable, and the degree of actual risk is in direct proportion to the number of variables and people involved, the only real answer is to use the people in the organization as the risk measuring tools. Teach them to identify risk and set up the processes and controls to minimize the risk to the desired levels so it all can be managed effectively.

Applying Risk Management

Effective management of risk is critical to ensure an organization's leadership role in the financial services industry. Risk should be minimized to the level where it becomes acceptable for the organization. The key word is "minimized" and not totally avoided. Total risk avoidance is not only impractical but it is often not good business sense. The most profitable and well run organizations are not those that try to avoid or do away with risk completely but those organizations that have learned how to manage risk at its optimal level.

Managing risk effectively requires proper risk training and education, risk definition, and risk identification so risk can then be minimized and managed. In order to ensure that the organization members are properly trained and educated to manage risk, every member must understand the organization's definition of risk and then how to identify it.

Finding an accurate definition of risk has plagued many organizations. If the definition fails to cover a certain event, and that event contains risk, the definition can be incomplete. If the definition involves a certain event and that event does *not* contain risk, then that definition is inaccurate and inefficient as well.

The best way for an organization to define risk is to start with the very broad concept and refine it downward, akin to an inverted pyramid or funnel. Begin with "the big picture" approach, where *any function or event, no matter how small, that can achieve a result different from the desired one, contains risk*. The risk may simply be the necessity to redo a task, or it may have broad financial ramifications. It doesn't matter; both events contain risk. Once risk is defined this way, the next step is for each organization member to identify the risk in their respective areas. It will then be up to the experts (presumably one or more of the following: the risk managers, compliance people, appropriate senior and line management, the legal people, and auditors) in the organization to determine what level of risk should warrant action. Specifically, it must be determined at what point is it cost-effective to revise the function, install monitoring controls to warn of risk, raise the revenue requirements, or stop the action due to legal or civil liability, public relations issues, or unacceptable business risk. How to do this is the next challenge, but one that can be accomplished in three basic steps— define the risk, identify the risk, manage the risk.

I. Definition of Risk

The actual definition of risk will vary from one organization to another depending on its size, market, client base, personnel, and so on. What is considered as "actionable risk," in other words, risk that must be actively managed versus "normal risk," which is monitored through passive controls, will also vary by organization. This may be due in part to the organization's appetite for risk but more so due to their ability and resources to manage it. As a result, there is no firm recipe or complete checklist for risk that will cover every organization; each organization must develop its plan. There are, however, some general areas that will fit into almost every organization's definition of risk. Below is a listing of those general areas, but keep in mind that this listing will not be all inclusive for every organization:

- *Public image.* Although a certain error, fraud, or inappropriate act in an organization may not have a direct financial impact on the organization, it can have much broader public ramifications that could lead to large future liability. In our previous example of the organization that mismanaged their employee 401(k) plan, if this got strong public exposure it could have serious consequences on their public image and ultimately their bottom line. Since this particular organization manages several hundred pension plans, the connection can easily be made that—how well managed could these other plans be if their own employee plan was improperly managed? Other more subtle areas may be organizations that are perceived to be insensitive to the environment or those that appear to be unconcerned with their community needs and only motivated by profits. It at times is a fine line but an important point nonetheless, and the organization must be aware of its public image.

- *Loss of clients.* Losing clients is at times unavoidable; it's an expected risk of doing business. It should not, however, become too expected where ties are not made to the actual and recurring reasons for client loss. Probably the greatest reason for client loss is poor quality service in one or several of the areas in the organization. Poor service can take many forms: both direct, meaning a poor client interaction or relationship, and indirect through poor or faulty processes and systems that cause error. Once a client is lost due to either or these reasons she may be extremely difficult if not impossible to get back. The problems caused by client loss are obvious but the reasons for it are not always. Any issue in the organization must be viewed as a potential risk to the client base.

- *Weak profitability.* Weak profitability can cause major risk to an organization for reasons that are apparent as well as those that are not. It seems almost too often when a particular product or even an entire part of the organization is unprofitable, compliance and risk management takes a back seat. Sometimes the first things to go are the controls and staff that operate them. Cutting expenses is the key word with almost complete focus on the short term while the future is met with crossed fingers. Risk in this scenario takes many forms from lost income and capital to poor perception in the marketplace to legal and civil liability due to errors caused by weak processes and controls. Whenever a product or area shows weak profitability, an immediate red flag must go up to ensure proper coverage and management of all risk.

- *Loss of revenue or funds through errors.* This risk ties into poor profitability; however, this risk can also occur in a profitable setting. Many banks found this out during the 1980s where the beginning of the decade saw high profits from real estate loans, LBOs and junk bonds. Profits were high but so were the many errors made in executing these decisions. During the high profit period no one seemed to notice the errors of bad credit judgment, poor review and controls, and in some instances, just bad business decisions. These errors were a serious risk during the high profit period and it has shown terribly during the downswing of the last decade. Many organizations are no longer around and several are still feeling the pain. One should never simply look at the bottom line and decide revenues are good so everything must be operating well. Lost income through errors must always be unacceptable, regardless of the returns. In some cases it may just be lost opportunity through lower revenues and in others it can be clearly more serious.

- *Loss of revenue or funds through fraud.* Although fraud is always a concern it seems to come up in the places we least expect it. How many times have we heard "he was a dedicated employee" or " she has been with the organization for 15 years?" The best way to prevent fraud is to remove the opportunity and temptation. Since this is not always possible, the existence of risk must be acknowledged. This risk must be recognized and the appropriate controls, education, and monitoring systems established so it can be identified and properly managed. Fraud will hurt the bottom line not only through direct loss but also through damaged public image and employee morale. There will always be dishonest and desperate people; the best defense is to look ahead and be prepared.

- *Inappropriate business fit with current or future plans.* Decide on your future goals and strategic direction and make decisions that fit these plans. If the strategy of an organization is to service the commercial market, they should not buy a retail bank. This may seem obvious but many organizations have made this mistake. Anytime a new business acquisition, market entry, venture, or product is considered there is risk of it not matching the strategic direction or goals of the organization. This must be recognized and carefully thought about in the final analysis. The key phrase today is "core business." Many organizations are shedding businesses and products that don't fit or complement their core business, future goals, and strategic direction and finding they are more profitable in the end. An organization's efforts must be focused on its strengths. If it is spread thin in too many directions, the organization will find that it is largely unsuccessful and exposed to many of the risk categories we are discussing in this section.

- *Poor new product review.* New product review is an important aspect of sound risk management for every growing organization. Perhaps surprisingly, many organizations believe that the only real risk is financial loss through product failure. Although this is obviously a major risk that must be considered, it is certainly not the only one. In considering the profitability of the product the organization must not isolate the product and consider it solely on its own salable merits. As discussed earlier, and among other things, the business fit must be considered. The product can be very successful financially but can cause havoc with other products and parts of the organization. Take the example of the major Wall Street brokerage firm that set up a "vulture fund." This fund focused on investing in the stocks of companies that were potential takeover targets; sometimes they were the target of an unfriendly takeover attempt. Although this fund was extremely successful and made record profits for the firm, they had to cancel the fund because it created a major public relations issue and threatened to seriously damage or destroy other business channels and products. The problem was that this firm was also an investment bank that helped these same type of organizations either execute an LBO or stave off an unfriendly attempt. Besides the public relations issue it also raised some legal ones through "Chinese wall" and conflict of interest. The best approach to new product development is the one many manufacturing organizations are now taking, one of the total team approach. Bring everyone into the loop early on for a complete product review long before implementation. Do away with the linear product development where it goes progressively from one department to the next. Assess the profitability, legality, business fit, ethics, and employee acceptance at the earliest stages. Learning the hard way that a new product is no good can be very costly and expose the organization to serious risk.

- *Poor new account review.* Many of the same reasons that cause new product review to be important also hold true for new account review. All of the risk areas must be reviewed every time a new account is considered. It can be a formalized review or simply a series of questions. Is this new account a good business fit? Does it meet the legal requirements and parameters established by law? Will it be profitable? What are the major risks to the business for account acceptance (credit, environmental, public relations, ethical, etc.)? Can the organization effectively service the client's needs without adversely affecting the current operations or clients?

- *Weak management expertise in key areas.* It is said that a chain is only as strong as its weakest link. To a degree, the same can be said of an organization's management team. A manager with poor expertise in a critical area can hurt an organization several ways and expose it to undue risk. What is meant by expertise is not knowledge but talent, and the ability to make the right decisions and interpret the available data to draw the correct conclusions. For example, a marketing manager must not spend effort selling to high risk clients or clients that the organization cannot service effectively. Of course and as we shall see, knowledge is essential; however, without the proper expertise its application can have flaws. An organization must always strive to recruit and keep the best available people. Availability is often contingent upon resources of the organization but it is important to use those resources at optimum levels.

- *Poor knowledge level (education) of management and staff.* Education and training are critical if an organization is to become or remain dominant in its market. It has been a long understood fact that the majority of errors and losses that occur in an organization are the result of poor education and training and not, as one might suspect, of carelessness or incompetence. This is true of existing employees as well as new hires. The four areas where training and education are essential and can expose the organization to the greatest amount of risk are:
  - Business knowledge—The level of knowledge and understanding that the organization member has of his or her specific job function and business area in general.

- Conflict of interest—The level of knowledge and understanding that the organization member has in regard to conflicts with his or her job function and organization. The employee must know and understand about insider trading, Chinese walls, accepting gifts, proprietary information, moonlighting, personal interests, and so on.
- Policy and procedures—The level of knowledge and understanding that the organization member has of corporate policies and procedures, strategic and business plans, and overall corporate limitations.
- Regulatory—The level of knowledge and understanding that the organization member has of the local, state, and federal laws and regulations that affect his or her job function and the organization itself.

- *Poor risk monitoring and controls.* There is great risk in areas where monitoring and controls of functions and processes are weak, inconsistent, or ineffective. Because controls and processes can occasionally and even often give the correct end result, many errors and potential problems can go unnoticed, which obviously can lead to liability and loss. What makes one process or control strong and another weak depends on its application and intended end result. They all must be reviewed regularly and independently for consistent and desired results. The internal workings of the process or control itself must be tested and not just the end result transactions.

- *Poor strategic and business planning.* Many a fine and profitable organization has stumbled unexpectedly because decisions made that had long-term impact were not planned and well thought out. Every member of the organization must understand the goals and plans of the business or else decisions and actions become short-term and often contradictory to ultimate goals. The real risk in this area is often much greater than anticipated and it is not readily quantifiable and often not definable until after it is upon the organization. The question often asked is: How do you know that you are where you are supposed to be if you didn't know where you were going?

- *Poor contingency planning.* Although this area has historically been relegated to the category of "just write up something to satisfy the auditors," it is relevant and important now more than ever. In the city of London, emergency contingency planning is not only part of every business plan but it is reconsidered on an annual basis and tested, in some cases quarterly. Because of the terrorist activity and all the bomb damage they have suffered, they live on a daily basis with the thought that they may not have an office to come to in the morning. With proper contingency planning, they may not have an office but they will still have a business. Most organizations do not live with the fear of terrorist activity; however, there are a multitude of other situations that can temporarily close an office such as fire, storm damage, etc. All of this risk must be assessed.

With all contingency plans, having one is only half the equation. Testing it to ensure it will work is the other half. There was this manufacturer who was very difinite about the importance of emergency contingency planning. He took all of the necessary steps including installing a state-of-the-art sprinkler system in his factory. He was determined that a fire would not destroy his factory. Well, almost a year to the day after he installed the $1 million sprinkler system, his factory burned to the ground. It turned out that no one had ever tested the system—it was never hooked up to the water main.

- *Noncompliance and direct violations of law.* Although this risk is very real in every organization, it is easily defined and in most cases easily identified. With the appropriate processes and controls in place along with a strong education and training program, this type of risk is effectively managed.

- *Breach of fiduciary responsibility.* Precisely what breach of fiduciary responsibility is for your organization should be defined by your legal counsel. This can be a very broad and vague area but one that should not be taken lightly or ignored.

II. Identify Risk

Effective and timely risk identification is important to every risk management scheme, especially in light of today's limited resources and ever increasing liability exposure. In general terms, when performing risk identification three points must first be kept in mind.

1. *What is the effective opportunity for an event's result to be different from what is expected or desired?* In other words and in very basic terms, what is the real chance of an actual error or fully unexpected circumstance to develop that can cause a nonbeneficial outcome? For example: your organization routinely makes cash disbursements from client accounts for various reasons. What is the opportunity for a pay-out to be made for the incorrect amount or from the wrong account?

    What must always be considered in making an evaluation such as this is:

    a. Difficulty of task (complexity, number of steps, and people involved).

    b. Frequency of event—How many times it occurs on a regular basis (hourly, daily, weekly, monthly, yearly etc.).

    c. Experience/Knowledge of the individuals performing the task—Long time seasoned veterans or transient young staff.

    d. Effectiveness of process and reliability of equipment—How strong and sound the process that causes the desired event to occur is in terms of accuracy and repetition. How reliable the equipment (computers, software, machines etc.) employed in the process is. Does it always detect errors or can they go unnoticed?

2. *What is the effective incentive for an organization member to intentionally alter the result of an event?* Specifically, how can any member benefit if the event were changed in any way through direct or indirect means. Usually the greatest concern here is fraud for financial gain, but there are others. Some of the general incentives are:

    a. Financial gain.

    b. Corporate power or position—Distort the results so a competing manager looks bad and they in turn look good. Take credit for another individual's work.

    c. Personal bias—The member feels no one's ideas are or should be better than theirs.

3. *What is the effective liability exposure if either of the above occur?* In other words, what can happen or cause the organization to experience a loss? Any of the following could be the result:

    a. Repeat the task—Lost time and resources.

    b. Monetary loss—Actual or potential amount.

    c. Civil liability—Exposure to legal action.

    d. Regulatory liability—Government sanction, fine, or legal action.

    e. Public image damage—Short- or long-term harm.

    f. Loss of key personnel—Valuable employee(s) leaves due to unhealthy or "political" environment.

If none of these conditions exist, risk identification may be an unnecessary exercise.

However, keeping these three points in mind, there are essentially two useful approaches for identifying risk throughout an organization. The first is the formal approach and the second is the informal approach. Both of these approaches employ several methods that involve individual as well as team effort.

Formal approach: This employs organized and preplanned methods created and utilized specifically for risk identification and risk management. They require specific intent, clean execution, and good documentation. Some of these formal methods are (not necessarily in order of importance):

    a. *Hold regularly scheduled compliance and risk management training sessions.* This should be a series of training sessions both regularly scheduled and as needed. The periodic meetings should be on recurring topics that need constant discussion, such as conflict of interest, ethics, insider trading, and so on. The as needed sessions would be for new hires, transfers, or special compliance and risk situations that recently occurred or are relevant to the organization and require discussion.

b. *Create formal information services in the organization.*
  - These can be monthly or quarterly compliance newsletters or electronic mail newsletters. Discussed in the monthly or quarterly letters should be:
    - Areas of special concern
    - Compliance and risk considerations for new and existing products or businesses
    - Upcoming or recent audits or examinations
    - Failings of other organizations that have an important lesson
    - Success stories of other organizations that have an important lesson
    - Actual or expected changes in government regulation that could affect the organization
    - Ideas for open discussion
    - Suggestions, recommendations, observations, and so on.
  - Regular circulation of commercial publications. Choose the most relevant and useful publications and circulate either parts or the whole to the appropriate individuals.
  - Compliance and risk alert documents for special situations. This is used for situations where there is serious risk or actual loss sustained by your organization or another organization. It will alert the appropriate individuals to take the necessary action for prevention of similar future events. This compliance alert can also be used for changes in the regulatory environment.

c. *Hold regularly scheduled key compliance and risk management meetings.* Meetings and discussions should be held regularly at all levels of the organization from the board of directors on down to the clerical level. The content of the meetings will vary depending on the group with "big picture" for the board of directors and specific detailed content for the particular areas. The important thing is to keep compliance and risk management current in all the organization members' minds as well as their daily activities. This can only be done with constant discussion and dialog. It is also very important to repeat recurring themes such as fraud, conflict of interest, ethical behavior, and so on.

Keeping everyone appropriately informed is the life-blood of the compliance and risk management program. A compliance department, a compliance officer, or any single group of individuals cannot possibly see or do everything. A continuous flow of the right amount of information (not too much, not too little) can cause the entire organization to work as one with the recognition that compliance is *everyone's* responsibility.

d. *Hold regularly scheduled group risk assessment discussions.* These discussions can be informal talks between the line manager and his or her staff which concentrate on group needs, growing pains, and areas of general, immediate, or specific concern. They should not be complaisant sessions for group members to criticize each other but rather, a way to continually assess the entire group or individual aspects thereof and how changes may or may not improve things. Always look for the better way because it is ever changing. The better way today might not be so tomorrow due to changing needs, environment, requirements, or even technology. Never accept the statement that "it has worked fine for the past five years so why change now." The more that is understood and the more knowledgeable everyone in the area is, the more effective will be the compliance and risk assessment of the individual departments and ultimately the organization.

e. *Develop a compliance validation program.* As we discussed earlier in Chapter 1, a validation is distinctly different from a conventional audit test. The validation seeks to validate the utility, effectiveness, and purpose of a particular function relevant to a specific area, department, and the total organization. It does this through people who are wholly knowledgeable not only of the function but the context in which that function interacts within its department and with the other parts of the organization.

The individual performing the validation does not necessarily need a background in audit, accounting, or any of the financial disciplines. In fact, this type of training is sometimes not the best choice. When it is really analyzed it becomes apparent that typically and historically, considerably greater emphasis has always been placed on the ability to test (i.e., audit and accounting skills) over the ability or knowledge to understand what is *actually* being tested. This way of thinking has always been and continues to be backwards.

Testing is in and of itself a fairly easily learned skill and if there is not enough time to learn it effectively, a simple instruction outline and list of what type of questions to ask during the test are basically all that's needed. On the other hand, learning about a particular function, process, discipline, or business takes time, along with truly understanding the results of the test. Certainly this takes much longer than sitting down for an hour or two to interview the individual who is performing the function, which is a typical audit approach. It has been argued that it is not this simplistic and the auditor very often knows the area or function and is simply interviewing to "get up-to-date." Even if this were the case, which often it is not as the audit function is usually a transient one (and it should be), it would still take considerably longer than a few hours during an interview to get current.

Why should it take weeks, months, and years to train managers and staff about a certain function or job and then expect someone, in many cases someone who is quite unfamiliar with that function or job, to tell these same trained managers and staff if it is working O.K., or if not, what's wrong?

The most qualified person to determine if a function is working well is the individual who knows it the best. True, this expert may need to be educated on generally what to look for and perhaps what the beginning and end result expectations are for the validation. This is where the compliance and risk management experts come in. They will not, however, need to be told *where* to look or even what to look for in terms specific to that job or function.

Since it is enormously easier to have someone understand what your concerns are and what you are afraid of overtelling them where or how they might look to find those concerns, it makes perfect sense to have the experts do the looking. Those experts are the line managers and staff who perform the daily routines and functions. Thinking of it another way, if a machine breaks down or there is a systems problem or there is an error found in a particular area, the experts in those respective fields are looked to for remedy of the problem. Why not use these same experts to identify any initial problems in the first place? Stay with your strengths, reduce the clip-board compliance specialists, keep the approach simple, and it will be much easier to see what needs to be done. It will also get done quicker and at less cost.

Compliance Validation Program

An effective compliance and risk management validation program must have the following:

1. The experts or line managers and staff who perform the functions do the validation.

2. Consistent and organized proactive approach that regularly validates the risk points on a periodic basis.

3. Review and assessment of the findings to effect appropriate change and improvements.

4. Full and continuous support from senior management.

5. Periodic review of the program by the compliance and risk managers and the auditors to ensure its continued effectiveness.

When developing the validation program as in performing the validation process, it is critical to keep in mind the point that the focus of the validation is not the transaction but rather the process and then the control. The transaction (disbursement, signature, overdraft, etc.) is the historical event that only tells you what happened, whereas the process and control tells you how and why it happened. If you know the how and why, the what becomes very predictable.

As this work progresses we will learn how to create and implement a complete validation program. The program includes the 12-Point Risk-Oriented Compliance Validation which is outlined below and discussed in detail along with the Compliance Validation and Certification Program later on in this work.

The 12-Point Risk Oriented Compliance Validation is a procedure that should be performed by the line managers or designates in their respective departments. It can initially be performed in conjunction with the compliance or risk management people but eventually should be performed solely by the line. Its purpose is to ensure complete compliance of all functions in all areas, regardless of apparent importance, and identify all risk so it can be properly managed. This review should be repeated on a periodic and as needed basis. The results of this 12-point review will also be used for the compliance

---

Twelve Point Risk Oriented Compliance Validation:

1. Map and schedule the compliance universe for risk overview.
2. Gain detailed understanding of the area functions and responsibilities of the identified compliance review areas.
3. Create a risk point outline of the area.
4. Risk-rank the points of the Risk Point Outline and identify desired review areas.
5. Flowchart the functions and operations under review.
6. Evaluate the major risk controls and monitoring systems
7. Use statistical sampling during the validation process
8. Develop an effective validation process
9. Perform testing—documentation and evaluation of results
10. Understand the results to identify required changes
11. Ensure implementation of changes
12. Report and follow-up

certification of the organization which is a powerful risk management tool we will discuss later on in this work.

It is critical that the entire 12 steps of the compliance validation are perceived, conducted, and performed in a positive light. The purpose of the compliance validation is not to point fingers, find who is a *screw-up*, or used as a way to grade managers by the number of issues uncovered in their department. It only takes one time to use the validation as a "way to fine the poor managers and staff" and the whole future of the program is doomed. This cannot be stressed enough because using the validation in negative terms will encourage and even force managers and staff to hide problems and issues instead of uncovering them for resolution. Often organizations will "shoot the messenger" of bad news and concentrate on the fact that there was a problem found instead of focusing the resources on the appropriate fix. The first approach causes individuals to spend time and thought in diverting the blame and covering the issues and the latter approach foregoes the finger pointing and instead concentrates on the fix of the problem.

This is another reason why it is very successful to have the line managers validate their own departments because in doing it themselves they do not feel exposed to the rest of the organization. They can identify necessary changes and improvements and have them implemented without the report card and third party involvement that an internal audit would bring. Managers and staff in an organization should not be afraid to expose issues or suggest improvements but instead they should be encouraged and rewarded for such behavior. Reward organization members for fixing problems and not for being perfect and never having a problem. There is no individual, no matter how good, who has not made a mistake or created an issue, so why create an organizational mentality that such an individual does exist and every member should strive for that goal. If you are in business, errors will occur, so focus on the resolution and not on the problems; you may find that the errors will be shorter lived and fewer in number.

Probably one of the most detrimental and perhaps feared acts a manager is subjected to is an audit report that lists a host of "findings" or "exceptions" that is presented in a "you screwed up and now what are you going to do about it" approach. Virtually every manager can remember an episode such as this at least once and then wanting to go hide some place and instead spending a great deal of time trying to discredit the audit results instead of looking for the merit in the report and attending to the issues. The ultimate goal is not to find the errors and problems but to develop and implement the solutions, fixes, and improvements. Finding the errors and the problems is only a way to get there; it is not the prize so a reward must not be given for finding them. Points are not given in a football game for getting your hands on the football; they are given for scoring touchdowns, field goals and the like, but without the football no points can be scored. Likewise, without identifying the problems, resolutions can never be found, but the resolution is the touchdown, not the act of finding the problem.

f. *Perform strong and thorough audits.* The audit function is a critical part of all compliance and risk management. It is essential that the audit programs are comprehensive, review for actual compliance and risk management, and test the processes and controls in place that ensure these things. All audit programs should be periodically reviewed by the compliance, risk management, and line managers to ensure that they are appropriate and comprehensive with accurate application. You should not audit for apples when the organization only grows oranges. It is easy for an audit department to lose sight when they are always on the outside looking in.

The informal approach: This approach relies on the informal network in the organization to accomplish its goal. Although the approach is informal in that it does not require preplanned methods created and utilized specifically for risk identification and risk management, it can be just as powerful as the formal approach. By employing the current structure and leveraging the organization culture, the way people think and act can be changed and strengthened to foster and ensure strong risk identification and management:

a. *Compliance and risk management is everyone's responsibility.* Make it an organization-wide requirement that it is a part of every member's job. No matter how small the task, it must be viewed from a compliance and risk management perspective. Every organization member is his or her own compliance and risk manager. Create a cultural attitude of compliance and risk management and try to build it into the pride of the organization. Once compliance is accepted as *the right thing to do,* it becomes almost second nature to review for compliance in all daily tasks performed. Compliance should not be looked upon as someone else's responsibility or an extra effort that must be done over and above the performance of the task, but as the performer's responsibility to be accomplished along with the completion of the function. Ownership and responsibility of an individual's actions is the most effective way to insure great results. This notion of experts and specialists for compliance and risk management is fine speech and looks good on paper. The real experts are those performing the job, not some third party judging-from-the-side and out-of-the-real-action compliance officer, risk manager, or auditor.

b. *Create the proper environment and incentives so everyone can think compli-
    ance and risk management.* Give incentives that reward this behavior,
    not the opposite. For example, don't say you want proper and com-
    plete execution and only reward for volume, thus forcing the staff to
    cut corners in order to meet these volume demands. The "just do it"
    mentality is wholly deleterious and fully debilitating to an organiza-
    tion. Short-term it may get the job done and meet all the deadlines.
    Long-term it can doom the project or organization with the damage
    it will cause by way of errors, misunderstanding, lack of foundation,
    and wrecked morale.

Postage Due

There was a senior vice-president, who was in charge of operations
in a good sized organization. He prided himself on meeting unrealistic deadlines that no one else would dare try. He used the expression
"just do it" long before the sneaker company made it popular and
even added to it the statement that "I don't want to hear about problems; all I want to hear is that you will meet the deadline." This was
his much used battle cry. It seemed to work, for a number of years—
well, maybe with a few exceptions. There were actually several situations of note where his approach was a dismal failure; we will look
at one of the better examples:

The mail processing unit that had too much mail and not
enough hands to process it. The realistic approach should have had
either much greater automation or twice the staff. Since this cost
money, the senior vice-president would not hear of it and instead
would continually repeat his cry of "just do it" and occasionally add,
perhaps for variety, "or I'll get someone else who can."

One day the manager of the mail processing unit got tired of
fighting and decided to "just do it." He then made an arrangement
with the local post office to only deliver as much mail as he could
process in a day, which allowed him to meet all of his backlog quotas
and deadlines. Of course this meeting of quotas and deadlines was
only on paper, since no one else was aware of the large backlog in the
post office. Well as these things tend to go, this manager eventually
got sick from the stress (although it took over three years), and
needed time off.

As we would expect, his replacement found the backlog, blew
the whistle, and the mail processing manager got fired. The result
was a several million dollar write-off. Most of the backlog was almost
three years old, along with someone coming up with the brilliant
idea that they need more automation and an immediate staff increase. The senior vice-president, of course, blamed the entire incident on the fired manager's poor character and lack of talent. Of

course the senior vice-president demanded strong ethics and did not tolerate such behavior in his organization.

You can't give a starving man a can of beans without an opener and not expect him to try and steal one. If you tell your members to do it by the book and then follow by putting them in unrealistic situations that can only be done by throwing away the book, which when they do they'll usually get rewarded, how can you expect them to do otherwise? In our example, the senior vice-president should have been fired along with the mail room manager.

c. *Foster risk awareness at all levels with everyday functions and processes.* Keep everyone, manager and staff alike, attuned to risk by continually reinforcing the fact that risk is everywhere, and if managed properly it is not always bad. Risk is not just the direct loss of money through theft or error but also the loss through low productivity, resource waste, inefficiency, unused capacity in people and machines, the redoing of tasks due to simple mistakes, and so on. Anytime a process or control is not working at its optimum there is risk of loss to the organization. We are hearing more and more today how companies are making a higher percentage of profit on the same level of sales. They do this through managing their risk situations more efficiently.

d. *Educate every member, management and staff, to assess all witnessed actions for correctness.* Teach everyone risk identification. Don't just have members "do their job" or perform functions. Teach and encourage them to assess and question virtually everything they do: to "look for the better way." Provide incentives and training for this on an ongoing basis. There are many examples where individuals were looking for the better way outside of their realm of responsibility and made their companies and sometimes others a better place and more profitable.

Little Yellow Stickies

A chemist who worked for the 3M company was frustrated over the small notes that were continually stapled or paper clipped to the documents he regularly received. Either the small notes were falling off in transit or he was constantly scratching his fingers on the staples and clips, and those that were taped and stayed on tore the paper when removed, so he decided to look for a better way. Working on his own, the result was the invention of the 3M Post-it™ brand notes or better known as those little yellow stickies. Most people thought that worrying about something as trivial as how notes are affixed to documents was a tremendous waste of time. Certainly time better spent making real money for the company. Fortunately the 3M chemist did not think so and as a result he and many other managers worldwide are now more efficient and productive, and 3M has made several million dollars on the chemist's trivial pursuit. Even the smallest of tasks that can be improved will sometimes have a dramatic effect on the process, control, or organization.

e. *Create and foster a strong ethical and moral culture throughout the organization.* Set up the right rewards and don't send confusing messages. Reward the good and punish the bad, not the other way around. Don't say you require a job done thoroughly and properly and then not allow the time, the resources, or the training to do it, which can often lead to unethical behavior. Lead by example. Don't take refuge in phrases like "I don't care how, just do it or else." Hard work and talent must receive the rewards, not who you know or what you can take credit for. A strong ethical fiber throughout the organization creates a foundation that allows and fosters teamwork, cooperation, healthy competition, sound risk management, and strong long-term profitability which will be the rule rather than the exception.

Manage the Risk

Some General Risk Areas an Integrated Compliance and Risk Management Program Must Focus On

What is precisely meant by risk areas will vary from one organization to another due to the different needs and demands of the business along with the actual personnel involved. The type and size of the business, the marketplace and competition, and the experience and talent of the personnel are all variables in the risk equation. For this reason there is no one formula or solution for every business or even one for each type of business. Unless you are dealing with exactly the same clients, environment, and people, which is rarely the case, the risk can vary greatly. This is not to say that there is no way to identify, assess, and even predict risk. All of these things can be done, within reason; the approach just has to be custom made to the specific situation.

This customization or risk management becomes possible via the continuous assessing of risk through review, validation, and other methods such as risk awareness. There are some general risk areas that all institutions must focus on and should be included in every compliance and risk management effort. Often the best way to begin is to identify an area and simply ask questions. The answers to those questions will often yield surprising results in terms of risk identification and even the additional questions of "why are we doing it this way?" or "why didn't I see this before?" The listing below is not all-inclusive but is rather a general sample of where some of the risk areas might be and where the focus should turn or begin. You may find that you need to add to the questions and even the list.

Some general risk areas:

- Product review (new and existing).
  - Are the products profitable?
  - Are they in line with the strategic plan and goals of the organization?
  - Does the organization have the resources and personnel to market and manage the product?
  - Are the proper controls and processes in place to effectively manage, monitor, and provide a quality product?
  - Has the product received the appropriate legal review?
  - What is the competition doing?
- Environmental policy.
  - Is the policy comprehensive, up-to-date, properly communicated, implemented, and monitored?
  - Did it receive the appropriate legal review?
  - Does it meet the needs of the organization and the current political and social environment?
- Safe keeping of assets.
  - Are the proper controls in place for safe keeping, e.g., inventory, monitoring, disbursements, etc.?
- Function/process (error and fraud).
  - Are the proper controls in place to monitor accuracy and consistency of processes?
  - Is the staff properly trained?
  - Is there appropriate separation of duties, checks and balances, periodic validation performed, documentation, etc.?
- Accuracy of accounting records.
  - Are accounts and records reconciled on a regular basis?
  - Are there proper controls, checks and balances in place?
  - Are audits and compliance validations regularly performed?
- Policy and procedure manuals.
  - Do they exist in all areas?
  - Are they comprehensive, current, and updated regularly?
  - Are they universally acceptable and understood?
  - Does every area have a complete set and are they knowledgeable on the appropriate policies and procedures?
- Education and training of all organization members.
  - Is there a formal and organized program that satisfies the needs of new and current employees?
  - Does it allow for regularly scheduled and as-needed training sessions for:

- Conflicts of interest.
- Corporate policies (key operating procedures).
- Area policies and procedures.
- Applicable regulations (local, state, and federal).
- Corporate mission statement.
- Strategic and business plans.
- Department objectives and goals.
- Cross-training of all vital areas.
- Emergency disaster/contingency plan.
- Emergency disaster/contingency plans.
  - Does a plan exist for each vital area, including the lesser ones?
  - Has it been well communicated to all appropriate organization members?
  - Has it been tested for effectiveness and utility?
- Strategic plans.
  - Does a viable and current plan exist?
  - Has it been well communicated to all appropriate organization members?
  - Is it being followed, utilized, and updated as needed?
- Department business plans.
  - Does each department have a business plan that is not simply a budget? The budget is only part of the department business plan which must encompass the direction, goals, and purpose of the department.
  - Do all members of the department understand and support the business plan?
  - Are there continual updates and comparisons to the plan versus actual results?
- Comprehensive audit programs (consider process, controls, and risk).
  - Do audit programs review the right things?
  - Do they focus on process, controls, and risk instead of transactions?
  - Are they current and up-to-date with the needs and direction of the organization in terms of adequately measuring and assessing performance to identify issues?
- Current and accurate organization chart and description of responsibilities by individuals.
  - Is the organizational human resource structure current with the needs of the organization and demands of the marketplace?
  - For example, are there too many layers of management or not enough?
  - Does everyone understand the reporting lines and are changes communicated to every member in a timely fashion?
- Disbursements.

- Are disbursements properly controlled and accounted for?
- Do the appropriate sign-off levels exist along with accurate recording and tracking of all transactions?
- Is the appropriate exception reporting in place to determine any unusual or improper disbursements?
- Suspense accounts.
  - Are all suspense accounts properly managed and monitored?
  - Are there specific time-limits for resolution of all items?
  - Are the appropriate sign-offs in place to allow items into and out of the suspense accounts?
- Compliance, processes, and controls.
  - Are appropriate and comprehensive processes and controls in place that are regularly monitored, updated, and assessed for effectiveness?

At first thought you may feel that asking questions is not all that useful, especially since the asking of questions usually generates more additional questions than it does answers to the original questions. In reality though, the asking of questions is the best way and sometimes even the only way to get complete understanding and a complete resolution of the problem.

Part III

Establishing an Integrated Bank Compliance Program—The Eight Components

Basic Requirements of an Integrated Compliance and Total Risk Management Program

Before we talk about the components of an Integrated Compliance and Total Risk Management program we need to discuss some basic requirements that are essential to any acceptable program. Without incorporating these characteristics the program will have great difficulty in not only being effective but in sustaining life into the organization's future. It may simply become another one of those well-intentioned ideas that everyone eventually forgot about. "Remember that compliance program we started for a while; it seemed good at the time but whatever happened to it?"

In order for the program to truly become and remain effective and have permanence, some basic requirements must be met:

1. *The program must utilize very limited personnel and corporate resources.* The least amount of people involved and the least amount of funds used to execute the program, the less incentive the bottom-line budget crunches have to wield their knife. Very often during those cost cutting times the first things to go are what are perceived to be the non-income producing areas. Although we have already discussed how sound compliance and risk management is good for business and it actually improves the bottom line, there are still those who may believe otherwise. To some myopic short-term types, sales is the only income producing endeavor the organization has and the back office is a money sponge that they wish could be done without.

This of course is a gross falsehood, but when there is a $1 million budget for compliance it does make their argument easier.

There are other better reasons for keeping the people and resources low, and most of them are straightforward. The fewer people involved in any endeavor the easier and quicker the execution is with a reduced opportunity for mistakes. The best way to spend a lot of money and take twice as long is to involve twice the number of people. Many companies, especially the big ones such as IBM, Hewlet Packard, and Motorola, have found this to be true. At first, some companies did it for cost cutting reasons until they found it made the situation work better than before. By having the individual performing the task also be responsible for the compliance and risk management, you are cutting out an entire layer of fat.

Using fewer people and resources frees more people and resources to other things such as new product development and sales, without either of which the organization would not be in business.

Reduced personnel and resources by their very nature create a simpler program. The greater the simplicity, the easier and quicker the program can react to change, either internal or external, and the easier and quicker it can adapt. And, the simpler the program the easier it is to test and verify its effectiveness and, best of all, the lower the overall cost to practice sound compliance and risk management.

2. *The program must be easily accepted, understood, and implemented.* In a word, the program must be simple. It cannot be complex and involve weeks of training, with loads of documentation and hordes of clipboard compliance specialists running about. Even the best intentions in the world will not save this program from the pile of "good efforts lost." Many a program was cast off with parties, ribbons, and fanfare only to end after the initial excitement died. The program should not make promises it can't keep or require mass amounts of effort to be redirected because eventually those other things that were ignored must be attended to and then the program is forgotten.

The program must be easily accepted, which means that it cannot make difficult demands on already heavy workloads. Easy acceptance also means that it should not change the current power base. Many people may choose to ignore it but every organization has a power structure that is protected quite vigorously. The power structure is the authority and responsibility that certain people and groups control, which allows them to have influence in the organization. Most people will accept more power but very few would willingly give it up. If the compliance and risk management program is integrated into the organization's operations, no one loses power, except the would-be centralized compliance bureaucracy, and most gain it through greater control. This greatly increases the opportunity of acceptance when it is shown to the areas that they will have greater authority and control over their world. They will now have ownership of compliance and risk management and all the benefits that go along with it.

The program must be easily understood, which will also increases its chances of acceptance. For this to happen the program's benefit, utility, and value must be clearly communicated to all of the organization members. They need to be shown that sound compliance means more than following regulations, and risk management is much more than good insurance coverage. They also must be shown that sound compliance and risk management can actually make their departments more productive while using fewer resources. This must be communicated so the members understand that it is best for them and they will *want* to do it, instead of feeling that they are *forced* to practice the program. In order for this to happen the program must have a good education structure in place. The program will require education for the initial start-up, and continuous education for the ongoing success of the program. Senior management can't just write a memo stating that "this is the program." It must be supported with the proper tools, mostly in the form of education.

If the first two parts, easy acceptance and understanding, are accomplished, the implementation can be smooth and swift. Get the program in place as soon as possible so everyone can once again focus on their daily tasks. No one should have to take time out to perform compliance. By having the right education structure in place, implementation can be quick and without many bumps.

3. *The program must have permanence and remain intact and effective long after the initial start-up.* Once the party is over and everyone goes home, will they remember a week later what the party was about? It is great to kick off a new program with a strong show of support and a lot of attention from the top. But if the program is to have permanence and remain effective, besides being a good program, it must continue to receive strong support and constant attention from upper management. It must remain an important and permanent part of the organization. This can be done without great difficulty through various communications, meetings, and dialog that continues on a regular and periodic basis.

Permanence is also accomplished through a strong and continuous education program. Keeping all of the organization members well informed and educated is one of the best ways to ensure an effective and long lived program. As the compliance and risk management program gets integrated into all of the tasks, functions, processes, and operations, so it will also get integrated into the organization's culture. No one should ever have to question, "Why do we need compliance anyway?" They should already have learned through the constant dialog and education programs why it is critical for quality, competitiveness, and profitability.

4. *The program must be flexible and capable of change with the growing demands of the organization, industry, and society (regulations).* Built into the fabric of the program must be the ability to constantly adjust and change. Flexibility is key to the survival of almost everything; a compliance and risk management program is no exception. Flexibility can be achieved through periodic validation and reassessment of the existing program—we must always look for the better way. A process or particular control may have been exceptionally effective when it was first created; however, due to new advances in technology it is now inefficient. Because the process or control still gives the correct answer, someone may assume that it is fine. A periodic validation of the process or control will expose inefficiency along with other issues. This will also hold true for changes in competition, regulation, personnel, and so on.

   If the organization is used to this constant validation and adjustment, changes become no big deal and do not upset daily operations in any material way. Also the best time to find problems or make improvements is when you have the time to make the correction, not when you are forced due to some serious issue. When the change is forced it is usually inefficient and almost always more costly.

5. *The program must be virtually "invisible" to the daily functions of the staff.* The processes or controls cannot be cumbersome and time consuming to execute. If they are either of these they will be cut short or not done at all, which will hinder the work flow, compromise the effectiveness of the process or control, and hurt the overall productivity of the organization. The compliance and risk management function must be integrated into the process and become "invisible" to the organization members so no extra effort is required in its execution. The best way to ensure constant execution of a control is to design it so more effort is required to go around the control than to perform it.

   Many people really don't give much thought to the fact that driving on the right-hand side of the road is a control and a strict aspect of traffic compliance. It is not thought about because it has been integrated into the entire process of learning to drive. The roads and the cars are built to accommodate this, as is the placement of the road and traffic signs. The control, driving on the right-hand side of the road to ensure smooth functioning of the process, the traffic flow, has been built into the entire system. Likewise, by integrating the control into the current design of the process, any new changes are automatically created to smoothly work with the control. When technology allowed for improvements in the road construction, signs, and traffic control devices (lights, signs, message boards etc.), all of theses new changes were devised to accommodate the control of right side traffic flow. That's why when you drive, all of the appropriate signs are on the right-hand side of the road and facing you as you approach them instead of on the left side and backwards. Just think if road or traffic signs were posted facing all different directions, you'd have to stop and turn around to find what road you are on and risk an accident.

The right-hand side driving control is so nicely integrated into the process that the great majority of people, although they execute the control daily, never consider it a control or any extra effort on their part; they do it automatically. The control is virtually "invisible" to the driver since it takes no special effort to perform.

When the control is simple, does not require additional effort or attention to execute, and is not time consuming, it will be performed when required and it will be effective. The best control in the world is only effective if it is performed. Designing the control and the process together with the smooth execution of both in mind will allow for continuous and effective performance for a long-lasting, consistent, efficient, and productive system. Creating after-the-fact controls that try to keep up with a process will cause loss of productivity if they work and ineffectiveness if they are not performed properly or regularly.

Once these characteristics are understood and accepted the components that make up an integrated program can be established. These components do not require any special order and do not demand total adherence to every item and line. They are mostly concepts that can be tailored to each individual organization. The organization type, size, and the people that make it up will dictate the exact mixture and detail of each component. The people in the organization probably will be the most important factor that decides the makeup and degree of each component. This is true because personalities, knowledge, and experience require different levels and degrees of attention.

The real crucial aspect for the program is that at least some form of each component or module is considered in the overall program, and every component is individually and regularly assessed for effectiveness. Each one of these modules addresses an important need for sound compliance and risk management, and therefore must be a part of the overall program. The degree and makeup of the module will vary by organization and will also change over time. But, for example, every program should have a compliance validation effort to substantiate the soundness and effectiveness of the compliance and risk management effort. So the importance of a complete program is high for effectiveness to be achieved.

Once the components or modules are established and in place, they must be periodically reviewed for desired results and effectiveness. It is not enough to establish the components and the entire program and then assume that it will remain viable forever. The education module, for instance, may initially be extremely effective but as the organization grows or the marketplace changes, it is no longer comprehensive and must be revised. Also, technological advances may bring additional productivity or allow for greater effectiveness of a module. The key point is that everything must be continually reviewed so it can always be the best possible program for that organization. This does not mean that every new item to come along must be employed or every new gadget purchased. Five-year-old technology may be fine for a particular organization when economics, personnel strength, or competition are considered. The best possible process for the organization does not necessarily mean the newest or most expensive; it simply means the best possible process to fill the needs of the organization, which always must consider cost versus benefit.

As we have stressed throughout this book, simplicity, flexibility, and ownership must be integrated into the design and implementation of a successful compliance and risk management program. These points hold especially true for the individual modules we will discuss next. The good thing about these modules is that they are in themselves flexible in that they do not have to be followed verbatim. They can and really should be customized to fit and meet the demands of the specific organization. This allows for greater fit into the organization, greater acceptance from the individual members, and ease in implementation.

Module I—
Total Organizational
Management Commitment,
Top Down

Complete accountability and awareness from all levels of management must be achieved through a total organizational commitment to sound compliance and risk management. All management, including and especially senior management, must understand the importance of compliance and risk management. These are daily functions that management must be responsible for. Compliance and risk management is not the responsibility of the compliance department, the risk management department, or the auditors; sole ownership lies with management at all levels. These other groups can monitor, educate, and assist, but ownership belongs to the owner of the task, also known as the manager. The owner of the task is the only one who can ensure constant and daily compliance; anyone else can only ensure occasional compliance through spot checks, periodic audits, and transactional monitoring.

Can you imagine what a police officer would tell you if he stopped you for going through a red light and you said, "you're responsible for traffic compliance and you should have reminded me to stop for red lights"? It's obviously ludicrous to suggest that he should be held accountable for your traffic compliance, especially since he is not with you every day, making it impossible for him to take full responsibility even if he desired. Why should the approach be any different in an organization? The compliance officer is not everywhere all the time, so it is impossible for him or her to see everything. Isn't it equally ludicrous to make that same compliance officer responsible for a staff member's or manager's actions—actions that only the staff member or manager have total and complete control over, just as the driver of a car has total and complete control over stopping for red lights. Some people might say that the manager *is* held accountable for his or her actions, but he or she needs compliance and risk management experts because he or she does not have the knowledge or the time to do these things. As we explained earlier in Chapter 3, why can't managers have the expertise to do their job completely and why shouldn't they have the time? Of course, competent managers have both the knowledge and the time, so these as well as the other arguments are without merit.

Compliance and risk management are not things to be done quarterly or a week before an audit starts; they must be practiced simultaneously with the process if they are to be continuously effective. To suggest that you can hire a team of experts, i.e., compliance and risk management people, who can ensure sound compliance and risk management is equally ludicrous. A third party will never have the knowledge, understanding, perspective, or time to anticipate every future move of an individual performing a task, so why call the third party the expert and make believe they can? There is no compliance crystal ball; instead management at all levels must accept and acknowledge ownership organization-wide and then demonstrate through their actions and performance measurements and incentives that they are truly responsible for compliance and risk management. Although a lot of managers may not agree, self-compliance and risk management is for their personal benefit along with the organization's. The compliance and risk management people can monitor, assist, and educate but they cannot perform compliance or risk management.

Not My Job

A manager in a large organization had a good title, a good salary, and what many considered a good job. He was responsible for a department of 12 portfolio managers and several billion dollars in assets under management. The department was successful for the organization pulling in several million dollars in revenue yearly (and it also enjoyed respectable performance in the fund management community). Everything seemed to be going well, including the manager's annual bonus which grew yearly.

This manager had a philosophy of "spend your time where it counts and don't waste it on nonsense." In other words, his attention was devoted to making money for the clients, the organization, and himself, and all of those unimportant administrative matters like compliance and risk management got attended to only when time allowed. Since he was always so busy, time didn't allow very much attending. But, there were no worries because everything did seem to take care of itself, including his portfolio managers and most of that "administrative nonsense." The proof was all the money they made and the good audit ratings that followed year after year.

The organization did have a compliance department, one of those very impressive kinds with the big budget, centralized staff, annual compliance audits, and plenty of clip-boards. They too gave this manager's department grand reviews and good grades. Everything was wonderful for this manager, but we now know better because this scenario has all the makings of a major failure. As we shall see, and for those who now understand, the failure was very predictable because one portfolio manager did "take care of himself"—a little too well.

To the organization, compliance and risk management was not the department manager's responsibility. The auditors told him, the compliance people told him, the risk managers told him, and even his boss told him; everyone in the organization appeared to know this. They told him directly and through their actions and inactions. Although all of these people openly admitted this before and after the uncovered defalcation, the manager still lost his job. The reason for this is simple: compliance and risk management *is* his and every other manager's responsibility. It has to be because he is the only one who really controls the situation and he is the only one capable of identifying and acting in the necessary ways. Everyone who sat in judgment of our manager concluded this; those same people who said that compliance and risk management belonged to the compliance and risk officers and the auditors. Why did they come to this conclusion? Because they or anyone else for that matter had no choice. You can't give a person a job and then not hold that person responsible for the outcome. You can't do this and be in business very long.

The end of our story was a sad one for everyone. It was found, far later than it should have been, that one of the portfolio managers was performing arbitrage type trades from his home computer with client funds. He would borrow money from client accounts, trade with that money and pocket any increase, and return the original funds to the client account. That was at least the plan, although these things never seem to go that way. The expected happened when the portfolio manager lost money; he kept taking more money to cover his losses in hope of making it back. Like the gambler who eventually sells everything trying to win back his initial losses, our portfolio manager essentially did the same. When he was caught, the red faces were in the dozens and losses were in the millions.

Since all compliance and internal audits in this organization were transactional, third party reviews, essentially outsiders looking in, our portfolio manager had an easy time hiding his little game. The manager could not have stopped the first illicit trade; however, if he would have been doing a routine and very simple compliance validation, he would have found it immediately upon the first trade and could have reversed it, preventing millions in losses while at the same time looking like a hero. Instead he lost his job and severely hurt his career. This manager found out too late that compliance and risk management was not "administrative nonsense" or the responsibility of the compliance, risk management, or audit departments. He had complete ownership all along and he has a pink slip to prove it. It was his job after all.

Discussion Points

- *Total organizational commitment must start at the top with management and work its way down through the organization.* Senior management must publicly acknowledge and then demonstrate their commitment to organization-wide, sound compliance and risk management. Management ownership and accountability must start at the top and be "built in" to and become part of the organization's culture. This can be done two ways:

  1. *Continually talk compliance and risk management.* Management needs to constantly state their strong commitment to compliance and risk management through continuous organization statement. It must begin with discussion at organization meetings, in interoffice memos, in documentation such as policy manuals and corporate literature, and in all discussions regarding job responsibility, performance, and expectations. People should be told to think compliance and risk management and that it is part of every task they perform. Sound compliance and risk management is good for them and it is good for the organization and for business. Incorporate it into all aspects of the organization from the employees' initial orientation through their job descriptions and annual performance evaluations. It is also important to include it in all initial and regular training sessions. Constant reminders will reinforce this understanding and encourage its philosophy.

  2. *Demonstrate through actions, rewards, and consequences that compliance and risk management is everyone's responsibility.* It is not nearly enough to simply talk compliance and risk management; in fact, if all that's done is talk it can be worse than doing nothing, because it can reinforce inaction on the part of the organization members. People get desensitized to words that cause no result or don't carry any rewards or consequences. They even think it a joke after a period of time. "She's always telling us how important it is to put the checks back in the safe when we're done but when I do she never notices and when I don't no one says anything—so why bother?" Management as well as staff must be shown through education and training how and why compliance and risk management is their responsibility and that it is good for business.

They must be rewarded for finding errors, problems, and risk situations and not punished for having them. Serving just one punishment will encourage everyone to hide errors and problems instead of addressing them. It is also important that the reward be in the right place and not reward for the wrong action. The reward should be focused on the resolution of a problem, the correction of an inefficiency, the improvement of a situation, or for increased productivity. The focal point should not be on the *finding* of the error or problem; this should only be recognized as the first step to the final destination of a better situation. Don't necessarily look for what is wrong but concentrate on ensuring that things are done right and how they can be done better. Sometimes it is just a matter of approach and attitude but it can make a world of difference. No one likes to feel that they are being inspected to see if they "screwed-up," but most everyone would like to know how they can do better or make their job easier.

The reward system is critical to the success of the program. If the rewards are in the wrong places, given for the wrong reasons, and not consistent, the whole effort might just as well be scrapped; it will eventually fail anyway. Management must continually demonstrate on a very consistent basis, the behavior and results they want. As we have discussed before, management cannot demand quality and then rank performance only on volume. This is not a demonstration that the organization desires quality; it is, however, a strong statement that the organization just cares about output. The two key elements to success here are first understanding what is actually needed and then providing the tools and rewards to achieve that result. These are simple and obvious steps but ones often neglected in many organizations.

- *Creation of a Risk Management Review Committee.* A Risk Management Review Committee is a group of area managers who are either part of the line or work closely with the line managers and would be responsible for the oversight, on a organization-wide basis, of risk management, assessment, policies, and practices in all areas of the business. Ideally, a manager from each area should be chosen to sit on this committee which would meet periodically to discuss, review, and assess situations, problems, and opportunities.

  The committee will not be in the business of running each department (that's the manager's job), but they will consider major policies, procedures, practices, and issues that affect the entire organization in terms of compliance and risk management. Things considered would be changes in key personnel, new products, expansions, and serious issues that can impact the effectiveness and bottom line of the organization.

Often decisions are made in a "bubble" without full consideration of their entire impact on the organization. Decisions that are made
by a few managers who are not close to the line but affect the managers, along with their areas, who are. The managers who are affected
the most usually learn of these decisions after they have been implemented and when it is usually too late to change them. This approach
not only causes tremendous inefficiency, but many times creates more
problems instead of resolving the current ones.

The committee is designed to ensure better decisions, speed up
the implementation of those decisions, and allow for greater effectiveness. It also creates additional benefits such as better communication,
greater understanding, and stronger teamwork between the areas of
the organization. The details of a Risk Review Committee are discussed and outlined in Chapter 12.

- *Identification of a compliance designate in each area.* A compliance designate is a person who already works in the department but will also be
responsible for the general compliance and risk management concerns
and communication in that department. The compliance designate is a
nonconventional, but very effective, cost-efficient and productive approach to the compliance team. Instead of the organization having a
large compliance staff that must work from the outside in, an actual
staff member in the department is designated with certain compliance
responsibilities. This individual will normally have daily departmental
responsibilities and tasks; however, a portion of their time is dedicated
to compliance responsibilities.

The other individuals in the department are still held accountable for their own compliance and risk management. The designate is
there to help expedite the surfacing and resolution of any problems.
The compliance designate is also an interface and information source
for the department, bringing outside information into the department
in a format that is easily understood and digested. Since this person is
already part of the department, he or she can easily work through the
communication network of the department and assimilate information
without difficulty. It is a very cost-effective, uncomplicated, and easily
accepted and implemented approach to compliance and risk management. The details of a compliance designate are discussed and outlined in Chapter 14.

- *Provide quarterly updates to the Board of Directors, committees and senior
management.* Keeping the top management of the organization well
informed is critical to the compliance and risk management effort.
Without top management support, any compliance and risk management effort is doomed to failure. Simply put, they cannot support
what they do not know. Top management's support is an absolute
necessity if the program is to become and continue to be effective.

In keeping top management informed there is often no need for a great amount of detail; however, enough information must be presented accurately and in a nonbiased fashion. If the top management is good and truly concerned they will require more information in those situations that warrant it. This way a lot of time is not spent by either side on minutia, while still allowing for informed top management.

There are several ways to keep top management informed; whichever way it is done, it must be done in a straightforward manner. The days of the color charts and graphs with the fancy dog-and-pony shows should be gone for the organization. The intent is not to impress or entertain anyone, and top management should not accept or allow this. Fancy shows are costly and usually cause the important information and real message to be lost in the glitter. It is condescending to top management to perform these shows that have little substance, and the organization should take a very close look at any manager, top or otherwise, who insists on such displays. This type of internal communication should never be allowed.

Some of the ways to keep top management informed:

- Hold regularly scheduled meetings with top management to discuss and review general compliance and risk management practices, current and potential issues, issues faced by other similar organizations, impact of any actual or proposed changes in regulation or corporate policy, and internal, external, and regulatory audit findings. The meetings should be structured:
  - Meetings should be formal and preplanned with an agenda for prior review time by attendees.
  - Meetings should be documented and minuted for future reference.
  - Meetings should not be long in duration or complicated in content but structured and organized for important information gathering by attendees. These are not meetings to work out problems but rather information conduits for directors, committee members, and senior management.
- Distribute one- or two-page monthly news briefs written in bullet format where information can be easily scanned. The news briefs should contain compliance and risk management information, updates, regulatory items, and possible concerns. Name, location, and telephone numbers of managers expert in the described information should be listed in the news brief so top management knows where to go if they desire additional information. The top managers should not have to have information requests "filtered" through the organizational layers; instead, they should be able to go directly to the source. This is not only more efficient but it also reduces the

opportunity of misunderstanding and misinformation and greatly increases the communication time frames and effectiveness.

- Distribute compliance and risk management news alerts when special situations arise in compliance or risk management that warrant the attention of top management. They should especially be used in situations where industry or regulatory changes may immediately affect the organization and where issues suffered by another organization surface that could impact them. These again can be written in bullet format where information can be easily scanned. Name, location, and telephone numbers of managers expert in the described information should be listed in the news brief, so top management knows where to go if they desire additional information.

- *Build accountability into all management's objectives.* Everyone in the organization must be held accountable for all of their actions, especially management. No one should be allowed to shirk responsibility or pass the blame on to someone else. If, for example, a department is not performing or there are serious issues in it, the manager should not be allowed to get away with simply pointing his finger at one or two staff members as the cause of the condition. If a manager gets the praise when her department is doing well, she should also be held accountable when it is not. Double standards allow issues to remain, they create inefficiencies and productivity problems, and kill morale.

  A manager is typically given specific objectives that must be reached daily or by week end, month end, year end, and on a recurring basis. These objectives might be to meet a certain sales goal, meet outlined quality benchmarks, complete a special project, achieve a certain knowledge level, reach a specific output, etc. Regardless of the objective, the manager's real purpose is to accomplish the outcome either directly through his or her actions or indirectly through supervision of others. Whenever this is the case, the manager must always be held accountable for the outcome, whether it is good or bad. This seems a common sense thing, but in many organizations the managers are often allowed to get around accountability and ownership of events they are responsible for, especially where issues result. In these situations, management spends more time covering issues and finding blame than they do identifying problems and finding solutions.

  - Give management direct incentives to do it right, hold them accountable for results, and don't reward for creative finger pointing.
  - Reward good results and management behavior that takes initiative and creativity in problem resolution.

Module II—Current and Accurate Policy and Procedures Manuals

The importance of good policy and procedures manuals in an organization is often overlooked by both management and staff. Usually the individuals most aware of their worth are the new hires, because they rely on them as an introduction to the department. After initial review by a new employee the lament is usually something like, "I really wish these manuals were better written and more current." What follows when a current employee sees the new hire reading the manuals is, "Don't bother reading those; besides the fact that they'll put you to sleep, they are old and out-of-date anyway."

There must be a beginning point of reference for anything that is done, no matter how involved or simple the effort. An artist could never paint a true representation of a dog if he or she has never seen at least a picture of one. Someone could perhaps try to describe one to the artist, but without any definite image the painting will probably not look like a dog. If the artist asked more individuals, he or she may get five people giving six different descriptions. The dog may even end up with two tails. The same holds true in all organizations in regard to their processes and controls. A beginning point of reference that is not open to major interpretation must exist. The best way to accomplish this is by clear and accurate policy and procedures manuals.

Every area, major function, and responsibility must be clearly and accurately documented in a policy and procedures manual and approved by the appropriate management. These manuals must be kept current on an ongoing basis and fully reviewed for validity and accuracy at least once a year. This will allow anyone to have a basic starting point for understanding the department, process, or control.

A strong policy and procedures manual is not merely a document to satisfy the auditors, but a ruler to measure the effectiveness of the process or control, etc., in regard to how it should function according to the initial plan. It is a document to define procedure and policy so it can be easily referenced and understood. It is a training tool for new staff, transfers, and existing staff that require additional knowledge. Finally, the policy and procedures manual is a document that allows you to understand the entire process or control without extensive research, investigation, or interviewing scores of people.

There are several different ways to create and structure a policy and procedures manual and many of them will vary by individual taste and organization requirements. What way is best most certainly depends on the organization, so we will not suggest that there is only one best way to develop a manual. There are even many good "how-to" books available with easy to follow templates. Although a good and strong manual can be created by the organization using internal resources, some basic rules are helpful.

The following are suggestions for compiling a manual:

Discussion Points

- Begin by creating a standard outline format for all policy and procedures manuals throughout the organization. Consistency in design is important for ease in understanding, revision, and utility. This becomes especially true in growing and large organizations that may have similar functions in regionally diverse parts of the organization. The style does not matter as long as it is clear for everyone and consistent throughout the organization.
  - Index, chapter, and section numbering, using bullet or paragraph fashion, etc.
- Inventory all current policy manuals needs by department. Determine the updating, revision, and/or creation of new or existing manuals.
  - Develop timetables and set completion dates.
  - Review every manual regardless of its last update or approval by management and/or audit.
- Outline the major responsibilities, functions, and risk areas.
  - List risk points and areas of concern.
  - Work up flowcharts if helpful.
  - Develop individual outlines by function, area, department, business, then organization.

- Ensure that the individual(s) who actually perform the function/manage the function, area, and department thoroughly review and approve the outline as accurate.

- Make it an organization requirement to have accurate, current, and annually reviewed manuals.

- Create a master listing of all manuals with the last update date and line manager responsible.

- Consider the benefit and feasibility of keeping a master policy manual library.

- If the organization has a computer network, consider the benefits and feasibility of putting the policy and procedures manual on the dababase for on-line access. This has several benefits such as ease of update where one change may affect several areas. It would ensure uniformity and consistency.

- Create a policy and procedure manual from scratch.
  - Identify the general area to be documented and then break it up in its component parts. *This is done most effectively by simply making a list of all the different areas and important functions of the department. (It does not have to be in order initially.)*
  - List all of the component parts in relative order of occurrence or flow.
  - Have the individuals who actually perform the functions write summaries of what they do, how, and why.

- Define for the organization the crucial importance of an effective policy and procedure manual.
  - It is not simply a document to satisfy the auditors but a ruler to measure the effectiveness of the business/area/function in regard to how it should operate as compared to how it currently is operating.
  - A document to give a clear definition of a function and policy
  - A training tool for new staff.
  - A document that allows one to understand the entire business/area/function without extensive research, investigation, or the interviewing of scores of people.

Below is a sample policy and procedure manual outline for a mutual funds operation. The only additional step required for this manual is to expand on the outlined points. This particular style of manual, a style we favor, is a bullet point by item for easy review and reference. This style, as compared to the description paragraph style where each item is explained in flowing paragraphs, allows for quick reference through the manual without having to read parts of several passages. By reviewing the index, going to the section, and identifying information desired, one can be in and out of the manual quickly. This will speed understanding and encourage its use by management and staff alike.

Sample of a Policy and Procedure Manual Outline
Policy and Procedure Manual Outline for Mutual Funds
Risk Management and Control Product Review

1. Fund Business Proposition
2. New Fund Introductions
3. Corporate Documentation
4. Service Agreements
5. Fund Prospectus
6. Advertising
7. Adherence to Investment Guideline
8. Portfolio Valuation Process
9. NAV Calculation
10. Accounting Aspects of Fund
11. Fund Securities Transaction Processing/Control
12. Sales Process
13. Shareholder Record Keeping
14. Custody/Control of Fund Assets
15. Investment Process
16. Performance Measurement
17. Trading Policies/Procedures
18. Fiduciary Oversight
19. Staffing
20. Conflict of Interest
21. Corporate Policy
22. Other

Mutual Funds Business
Policy and Procedures Manual Outline

I. Fund Business Proposition

A. *Business Plan/Strategic Plan*

- Creation of a business plan for fund with proper approval
- Product statements covering:

- Specific Investment Process
- Appropriate Accounting Treatment
- Legal Requirements
- Required Documentation
- Regulatory Reporting Requirements

B. *Description of Legal Vehicle*

- Appointment of Directors
- Tax Considerations
- Domicile of Governing Body
- Description of Business Structure
- Administration and Support
- Identification of Parties Involved
- Independent Accountant
- Distributor/Sponsor
- Investment Advisor
- Transfer Agency
- Shareholder Servicing or Subtransfer Agents
- Fund Accounting
- Custody
- Selling Agents
- Independent Auditors

C. *Product Introduction (refer to New Fund Introduction section)*

II. New Fund Introduction

A. *Fund Approval Form*

- Marketing
  - Name of Fund
  - Target Size Description
  - Marketing of Fund
  - Suitability Requirements
  - Special Investment Programs
- Fund Features
  - Open vs. Closed End
  - Load vs. No-Load
  - Exchange Features
  - Redemption Charge
  - Cumulative or Noncumulative Voting Right
  - Advisory Fee

  - Dividend and Capital Gains Distributions
  - Qualified Plans
  - Minimum Investment
- Sales
  - Channels of Offering
  - Geography (Where Available)
- Legal
  - Legal Form of Fund
  - SEC Registration
  - State Registration and Decision Where Shares Will Be Sold
  - Selection of Printer
- Business Structure
  - Fiscal Year
  - Date of Annual Meeting
  - Investment Program and Investment Objectives
  - Capitalization of Fund and Its Par Value per Share
  - Personnel Selections
  - Operating Procedures
  - Brokerage Allocation Policy
  - Shareholder Reports
  - Method and Frequency of Pricing NAVPS of Fund and Its Portfolio
  - Insurance
  - Code of Ethics
  - Adoption of Statement of Policy on Security Transactions
  - Statement of Policy on Inside Information
  - Fund Operations
  - Fund Accounting
  - Treatment and Payment of Organizational Expenses
- Profitability Model
  - Funds under Management (FUM) Minimum
  - Revenue
  - Cost
  - Means of Raising Initial Capitalization
  - Fee Structure

B. Fund Documents Required (Listing of required documents)

C. Legal Opinions Supporting New Structures

D. New Fund Implementation

- Legal
- Transfer Agent/Shareholder Servicing Operations
- Subtransfer Agent
- Custodian Operations

- Investment Advisor
- Selling Agents Training/Operations
- Fund Accounting
- Method of Distribution
- Administrator
- Offering Document; Promotional Materials
- Account Information Document
- Bank Investment "Seed Money"
- Investment Objectives and Investment Restrictions
- Shareholder Programs

III. Corporate Documentation

A. List of All Documents

- Form N-1A Parts A, B and C
- Articles of Incorporation
- By-Laws
- Investment Advisory Agreement
- N-8A
- Officers' and Directors' Questionnaires
- Administrator
- Fund Directors' Resolutions
- Advisor's Board Resolution
- Form of Stock Certificate
- Powers of Attorney for Fund Officers and Directors
- Section 14(a)(3) Undertaking of Investment Advisor

B. Record Retention

- Location
- Contingency Plan

C. Calendar of Filings

IV. Service Agreements for Fund

A. Listing of All Third Party and In-House Service Agreements

- Investment Advisory Agreement
- Administrator

- Distributor
- Subadministrator
- Custodian Agreement
- Subcustodian
- Transfer Agent Agreement
- Shareholder Servicing Agent

B. *Record Retention*

- Location
- Contingency Plan

V. Fund Prospectus

A. *Listing of Prospectuses*

B. *Filing Requirement*

- Detailing of the prospectus development, approval, and publication process (NASD, SEC, etc.)
- Documentation of a control system that ensures compliance with regulatory and corporate policy

VI. Advertising (Promotional and Marketing)

A. *Advertising and Approval Process*

- Compliance with regulatory and corporate restrictions on advertising

B. *Record Retention*

- Location
- Contingency Plan

VII. Adherence to Prospectus Guidelines

A. *Description of Monitoring Process*

- Review and test all funds to ensure compliance with prospectus

B. *Fiduciary Review*

- Fiduciary review committee structure, process, and funds review
- Investment and performance measurement process
  - Research process
  - Investment process and acceptable assets guidelines (approved lists)

- Rating of bonds and other securities

C. *Handling of Exceptions*

D. *Fund Prospectus Adherence*

- Compliance duties
  - Reviewing and testing all funds to ensure compliance with prospectus, S.E.C., and Blue Sky regulations.
  - Preparation and review of statistical presentations to the fiduciary committee and the Board of Directors.
  - Preparation and coordination for audits and financial statements.
  - Preparation and review of S.E.C. filings.

VIII. Portfolio Valuation Process

A. *Description of Valuation Process*

- Individual responsibilities
- Monitoring and controls

B. *Supporting Statistical Reports, Adherence to Testing, and MIS*

IX. Net Asset Value (NAV)

A. *Methodology and Process for Calculation of Net Asset Value (NAV)*

- Portfolio valuation and expenses

X. Fund and Tax Accounting

A. *Determination for an Internal Fund Accounting Department or Use of a Fund Accounting Agent*

B. *Daily Accounting Responsibilities*

- Daily pricing (NAV calculation, yields, dividends)
- Daily processing of income and expense accruals, cash postings, and general entries
- Daily reconciliations and controls
- Information distribution, including availability (cash management), buying power, and yields, prices, dividends, etc.

C. *Monthly Accounting Responsibilities*

- Reconciliations
  - Assets held with custodians
  - Open item follow-ups (unsettled trades, uncollected income, etc.)

- Review of accruals
- Compliance and statistical reports
- Proper maintenance of accounting journals and records
- Safekeeping of appropriate records
- Proper calculation of fees and expenses
- Proper allocation of fees and expenses

D. Tax Considerations

- Researching, determining, and communicating implication of changes in securities and tax laws.
- Responding to tax-related issues raised by accounting and/or fund managers.
- Preparing and reviewing tax filings.
- Reviewing tax-related disclosures in shareholder reports and prospectuses.

E. Administration and Technical Reporting

- Compiling and reviewing all fund performance and statistical data (daily, weekly, monthly, quarterly, semiannual, and annual data and reporting).
- Reviewing and authorizing fund performance data used in presentations, advertising, and fulfillment data.
- Collecting historical fund information and maintaining statistical database.
- Distributing all fund accounting information to other departments and outside services (including institutional sales, marketing, and financial publications).
- Addressing changes in accounting policy, which includes acceptable disclosure, new types of securities, and new, complicated funds.
- Maintaining accounting procedures, which includes both the update of the departments' procedures and manuals.
- Establishing and monitoring timetables and deadlines for key activities and projects.
- Reviewing and approving nonfund expenses.
- Preparing and administering department budget and financial planning.

XI. Fund Securities Transaction Processing and Control

A. Description of the Front End Trades Process

- Accuracy/Completeness

- Timeliness

B. Description of the Settlement Process

- Accuracy/Completeness
- Timeliness
- Accounted and Valued

C. Description of the Confirmation Process for Securities Transactions

- Reconciliation Process
- Price Verifications
- Exception Controls

XII. Fund Share Sales Process

A. Description of the Sales Process

- Distributor (Sales Agents, Transfer Agents) agreements
- Distributor (Sales Agents, Transfer Agents) experience and knowledge base requirements
- Procedures for the handling of desired volumes, record keeping, and control of the distributors
- Acceptance of orders in accordance with the prospectus
- Shareholder reporting process

XIII. Shareholder Record Keeping

A. Description of the Shareholder Record Keeping Process

- Shareholder Servicing Agreement

B. Record Retention and Security

- Location
- Contingency Plan

XIV. Fund Asset Custody and Control

A. Description of the Custody and Control Process

- Control and safekeeping (physical and accounting) of actual shares
- Custodian and third party depository agreements
- Daily reconcilement procedures and custodian reporting requirements
- Insurance coverage requirements
- Process for independent checks for asset verification
- Legal regulatory laws (federal and local) and corporate policy

XV. Fund Investment Process

A. Description of the Investment Process

- Research
- Approved Equities List
- Brokerage Committee
- Approved Brokers List

XVI. Performance Measurement

XVII. Trading Policy and Procedures

A. Description of Procedures Used to Execute Trades

- Selection of counterparts
- Best execution
- Soft dollars
- Trading blotter
- Bunching and crossing of orders

B. Corporate Restrictions

- In-house transactions and monitoring
- Investing in bank securities and obligations
- Use of securities underwritten by bank units
- Suitability of investments
- U.S. bank or bank holding company stocks
- Material nonpublic information

XVIII. Fiduciary Oversight

A. Description of the Fiduciary Review Committee

- Detailed scope of review

B. Board of Trustees

- By-Laws
- Minutes of Meetings

XIX. Staffing

A. Personnel Qualifications

- Management Biographies

XX. Conflict of Interest

A. *Personal Investment Review Policy*
- Control and Reporting Process

XXI. Corporate Policy

A. *Adherence to Key Bank Corporate Policies*
- Services to Third Party Funds
- Third Party Funds
- Sections 23A and 23B
- 1972 Federal Reserve Board Guidelines
- Prohibition on U.S. Underwriting
- Purchase of Fund Shares by Bank Units
- Purchase for Fiduciary Accounts
- Lending to a Fund
- Fund Shares as Collateral

XXII. Other Key Controls and Processes

A. *Contingency Planning*

B. *Compliance Verification Testing*

C. *Conflict of Interest Controls*

D. *Education and Training Policy and Process for Management and Staff*

E. *Risk Assessments and Evaluations*
- After approval of the outlines, update and/or write the text as desired in the approved format.
- Conduct management reviews in all areas to determine that all revisions are communicated and understood by everyone.
  - Ensure that all appropriate staff and management have read and understood the appropriate sections of the manual under revision.
- Make it an audit requirement to have accurate, current, and annually reviewed manuals.
- Create a master listing of all manuals with last update date and area manager responsibility.
- Consider the benefit and feasibility of keeping a master policy manual library.

Module III— Ongoing and Thorough Education Program

Many organizations talk about the importance of education for their members and some even have a formal education program. In many situations, however, the effort usually falls short in one or several places. A strong education program is critical for any sound compliance and risk management program and few would argue that point, but many organizations do not realize that a poor education program can be worse than none at all. The answer to this is simple; if the organization is to have an education and training program it must be thorough, ongoing, and continuously cover all levels of staff from junior new hires to senior long-time management. Of course the scope and content of the program will vary by organizational groups—new hire, staff, manager, etc.—but the focus and continuous nature should not. Everyone should get ongoing education and training, no matter how long they have been with the organization and no matter at what level.

Sometimes the education session will simply be the annual update on prohibited transactions and ethical behavior, while other times it might be a comprehensive review of a specific process, product, or department. Again it depends on the responsibilities, current level of knowledge, and need-to-know of the organization member(s) being targeted. This is where the establishment of a formal and organized program is essential to any effort, because otherwise it will be impossible to consistently identify these needs.

There are numerous good reasons for having a thorough and ongoing education and training program; we will look at some of the more impor-

tant ones, albeit probably the top of the list is that a well-trained and educated employee is more productive and makes fewer mistakes.

Some of the more critical reasons for having a thorough and ongoing
and organization-wide education and training program are as follows:

- *Better trained and knowledgeable organization members.* Contrary to some
  beliefs, the majority of errors are made through poor training, lack of
  knowledge and understanding and not through laziness, incompetence, or lack of concern. A strong program will rectify this.

- *Clear and consistent understanding throughout the organization.* Proper
  education and training will lead to greater teamwork through more
  consistent behavior and a sense of belonging. When people are moving in the same direction due to shared knowledge and consistent
  approach, there is natural development of similar attitudes and culture. This will always allow for greater efficiencies and productivity,
  which is created by less time spent in understanding various approaches and the requirement to learn new information and solutions
  that already exist.

- *More efficient, effective, productive controls.* When the knowledge level of
  the organization members is higher the controls in general need to be
  less sophisticated. This is possible because the managers and staff are
  more aware of what can go wrong and can be more attuned to potential problems. The members themselves, in effect, become part of the
  control system. Anytime this is accomplished you will always create
  greater efficiencies and productivities through the increased simplicity
  and flexibility of the systems, which in turn causes things to be easily
  accomplished and more effective.

- *Fewer errors and fraud.* With a strong and ongoing education and training program, the organization members are more aware of the consequences of fraud and more conscious of its existence. As a result,
  knowing the serious consequences and the high probability of getting
  caught they may be less likely to attempt an impropriety; and being
  more knowledgeable there is a greater opportunity of a fraudulent act
  being spotted by another organization member.

- *Reduce liability.* In mid-1991, the United States Sentencing Commission
  released new federal guidelines on the sentencing of organizations and
  individuals. These guidelines established strict penalties that can go as
  high as several $100 million, including jail time, for the organization's
  members and its officers for criminal offenses committed by the organization's representatives and agents. Considering the sentencing
  guidelines along with the other existing laws such as the Financial
  Institutions Reform, Recovery, and Enforcement Act (FIRREA), Truth
  in Lending Act, Fair Credit Reporting Act, as well as others, the or-

ganization is faced with a host of laws to punish illicit behavior by its members.

The government and the corporate sentencing guidelines specifically look for the presence of a strong program that educates its members on the illegality of certain acts. If it is demonstrated that the organization has a comprehensive and continuous program to educate and train the organization members on fraud, the government tends to be less harsh on that organization whose agent has performed a criminal act. For this reason a critical case is made for a strong, thorough, and ongoing education and training program.

There are three important points to be kept in mind for every program:

- *Education.* Every organization member from the mail room clerk to senior management must be properly trained to do their job right along with being given the appropriate education for:
  - Conflicts of interest
  - Corporate policies (corporate manual, etc.)
  - Area policies and procedures
  - Applicable regulations (local, state, and federal)
  - Cross-training of all vital areas
  - Ethical standards

  Keep all the organization members current with their job requirements and skills.

- *Ownership.* Every organization member must be charged with complete responsibility and ownership of their actions. They must be held accountable for their areas of responsibility and control and not allowed to "explain away" ownership of issues. Someone who has ownership will have concern for doing the job right. Someone who has ownership will have concern for correcting problems quickly and effectively.

- *Recognition.* Every organization member must be given the recognition for their knowledge and expertise and for every job well done. No one should be allowed to take credit for another's success. Education and training will be more effective when the individuals know that they will get properly rewarded for possessing strong knowledge and demonstrating effective skills in their job.

The best way to start any program is to establish requirements in the organization to hire competent people. There is no organization that intentionally hires incompetents; however many organizations do not have an effective screening system to identify weak candidates from strong ones. Too often the actual decision is made from a resume and the "chemistry" during the interview. The first part is based on a piece of paper that is usually exaggerated and the second is based on the emotion of the interviewer; both of these methods can be exceptionally inaccurate. It is important to establish a fair and accurate screening process to identify candidates that fit the organization's requirements for the job skills.

Discussion Points

There are essentially two sources of education—internal and external. Both sources must be tapped in order to establish a complete and effective program. The organization must determine how much of each source to utilize. The internal resources and organization requirements will determine the mix along with the actual availability of both.

The External Source

The external source does not necessarily necessitate the sending of employees to seminars, college courses, or having an external trainer or consultant spend time in the organization. These tools can be very useful and effective but also exceptionally costly.

- As an alternative, there is a host of excellent self-study courses, information audio tapes, training video tapes, books, magazines, and other publications that can provide a wealth of information. Using the appropriate and most cost effective approach is not only good business sense but it will allow for a broader and more far reaching program by spreading the finite resources farther.

- The organization should also encourage its managers to be part of a network of their peers. A peer network can spread valuable information ten times faster than a newsletter or other media. If there is a change in the law, a problem, fraud, or violation at a competing organization, change in public opinion, a new product being introduced, or just a better way of doing something, being plugged into the network will get that information to the organization quicker than anything else. It is also an excellent and very efficient way to save on legal and other professional bills. You can get information to a problem or situation from a peer who just experienced the same situation instead of calling the lawyers, accountants, or other professionals who usually charge dearly for any help. Ironically, there are even times when this professional help is not as accurate or useful. Getting into a peer network is not at all difficult; simply choose a well-known trade seminar that has the type of people you wish to network with and then give and get as many business cards as possible. Most everyone is looking for a new source of information and they will be glad to allow you to call them as they will want to call you for informal talks. It's simple, not at all time consuming, very effective, and exceptionally cost efficient.

The Internal Source

Sometimes unknown to many managers is the gold mine of knowledge, information, and help that exists internally. Setting up the right program so this gold mine can be tapped is crucial, but usually not difficult. All organizations possess experts and creative thinkers who can spread their wonderful talents to benefit many in the organization. These people are present in every organization because if they were not, the organization would not be in business. They are present in all levels from clerk up to senior management, and simply need to be sought out and plugged into the program.

- Develop a "shared information" mentality where organization members are not afraid to go to each other for help, advice, and information. There should be no boundaries (with the exception of legal ones) or Chinese walls separating organization member levels or ranks. Everyone should feel they can talk to anyone for help, advice, and information. This means clerk to clerk, manager to manager, clerk to manager, manager to clerk, and so on. There are experts at all levels who can be used as a resource of knowledge. Never go outside for knowledge until it has not been satisfied internally. External sources of information should complement internal sources, not replace them.

- Create an education program that targets and involves all levels of management and staff and keeps them fully informed about all the necessary compliance and risk management concerns. Include regulatory areas and corporate policy as well as culture areas. Customize the programs by area and schedule periodic sessions. *Outline the major required education areas that every organization should cover, then go into the "nice to have" areas. Discuss the alternative of an in-house training staff, hired training consultants, available seminars, and video and written publications. Consider a basic and thorough program and determine what mix best meets the organization's needs.*

- Hold an initial compliance risk seminar in each area, introducing and discussing the importance of compliance and risk management and the risks inherent to the business. *Determine how this should be run including focus and content.*

- Hold quarterly compliance meetings with management directors and line units. *Discuss importance of keeping compliance and risk management awareness high.*

- The compliance people and/or trainers should work individually with the areas and regions where compliance, training, and education weaknesses have been identified. Perform scheduled training sessions in the area. *Discuss how to work this process into the everyday compliance efforts.*

- Require and schedule each area's compliance designate to assist in the internal audit of another area. *Discuss how this can be an exceptional tool for building greater understanding of compliance and audit while increasing the overall awareness of risk.*

When redesigning the current program or developing a new one from scratch, it can be very useful to look at existing programs in other organizations to see how parts or the whole might fit into your plans. There is nothing wrong with copying a good idea; it saves a great deal of time and cost in the long run. Don't "reinvent the wheel." *Customize success* by taking an existing idea and making adjustments to fit your needs.

Perhaps one of the better programs currently out there is the Motorola concept on education and training:

Motorola on Training and Education

- *Top down commitment and involvement.* Support and involvement must originate and continue from senior management.
- *Linkage of programs to corporate initiatives.* All of the individual programs should have a connection with existing initiatives to keep everyone moving in the same direction.
- *Policies that set expectations and are tracked.* Establishing realistic policies that cause benefit to the organization, are measurable, and can be monitored.
- *Curricula that form an integrated system to deliver consistent messages across levels and functions.* Nothing in an organization is fully independent; everything is interdependent in some way, so the education and training must all tie together and relate to the big scheme.
- *Culture and readiness issues considered.* Organization culture is what makes things happen. The strong corporate culture should be supported by the education and training program.
- *Prerequisite skills of the work force are solid.* The best way to have a strong work force is to start with competent people.

Motorola's keys to building a first-class work force:

- *Selection based on testing on job related tasks.* The new hires are chosen by job and related talent, not subjective factors.
- *Assessment of skills of incumbents.* Ongoing reassessment of existing employees. Simple seniority scheme is not acceptable.

- *In-house training and education to develop prerequisite skills/knowledge.* Strengthen and improve the existing work force.
- *Curriculum based, ongoing training and education for every employee to keep pace with the changing job requirements.* Recognition that employee knowledge levels must move forward with the environment.

Motorola's worker of the future, in addition to having basic skills, must also have strong skills in the following areas:

- Knowing how to learn
- Listening and speaking well
- Creative thinking and problem solving
- Interpersonal skills and teaming
- Self-esteem and motivation
- Organization effectiveness and leadership

11

Module IV—Compliance Validation Program

Establish a formal compliance validation program that can be done on a quarterly or semiannual basis (depending on risk ranking of function/area) and that verifies compliance and risk management and the adequacy of controls. This validation will verify specific controls used to ensure compliance in risk areas. It is a "self test" by the organization's line management to determine the overall soundness of the organization's compliance and risk management effort. It is not an audit in the historical sense but a verification that key people, processes, and controls are effective and functioning as desired.

It can be a very powerful tool in many ways by providing much more than the confirmation that the area is in regulatory compliance. Its benefit to management goes well beyond assessing and monitoring regulatory compliance. It can be a training tool for organization members who need to become more knowledgeable on a specific process or in a certain area. It can be a vehicle to constantly reassess the productivity and effectiveness of processes, controls, and people by way of a low cost and easy method for identification of improvement needs. It can greatly reduce liability and risk exposure through early detection of serious issues and errors. An added benefit is that it helps management see and understand the usefulness and importance of sound compliance and risk management because they are the ones who are performing the validation, assessing the results and determining any necessary changes or fixes.

As we discussed in Chapter 1, validation views the process or control that causes a transaction, from start to finish. It follows the process or control's flow looking for inconsistencies, flaws, inefficiencies, improprieties, or poor design. The witnessed process flow is then compared to what the end

135

result should be, including management beliefs and expectations and written documentation detailing how it is supposed to function.

Discussion Points

- Develop a compliance validation for each risk area that will incorporate a standard format to review key policies, process functions, and practices.
- Create a bank-wide compliance certification policy and process whereby each area, according to predetermined schedules, must perform its own compliance validation.
- The validation should be performed by the compliance designate or an appropriately skilled and knowledgeable individual and supervised by line management. When completed it should then be verified and validated by line management. The compliance department will review the results and assist where necessary in the tracking and resolution of all changes and corrective actions. The compliance department *will not* perform the validation; this defeats the purpose and negates almost all of the benefit.

Compliance Validation Program

12-Point Risk Oriented Compliance Validation

What is a 12-Point Risk Oriented Compliance Validation? It is a 12-part progressive process where a validation is systematically performed in stages to determine the status, condition, functionality, and consistency of an area, process, control, or function. It often does not cover the detail of a conventional audit, yet it goes well beyond such an audit in determining the total compliance and risk management of the organization. It does this by not simply revealing *what* happened, as is the case with a conventional audit, but follows through by giving the *how* and *why*.

Below are the 12 stages of the 12-Point Risk Oriented Compliance Validation.

1. Map and Schedule Compliance Universe for Risk Overview

Defining the Compliance Universe

Defining the compliance universe means identifying and mapping every area where compliance should have a concern. This may seem a bit basic; however, it is quite critical, as understanding what there is to review is necessary in order to cover everything that needs to be reviewed. Both are essential for a comprehensive and effective compliance and risk management program. Every department and area must be assessed to determine the breath and scope of their compliance responsibilities.

A. Begin with a general listing of all major businesses/districts/divisions/regions, etc. *Lay this out the way the organization structures itself.* For example:

Bank Division Listing

- Northeast Banking
- Southeast Banking
- North Southwest Custody
- South Northeast Trust Division

B. Next create a listing of all departments. *It is important that this step is started from scratch as you should not rely on any previously created listings. There is a distinct possibility that an area has changed, a new area has been created, or an old one is gone.* For example:

Bank Department Listing

- Investment Management
- Brokerage
- Research
- Operations/Systems
- Trading Desk
- Fixed Equities
- Mutual Funds
- Regulatory Reporting
- Special Assets and Investments
- Trust and Estates
- Custody
- Legal

C. Itemize all the functions within the departments. *This includes minor as well as major functions. If the function is important enough to be performed, it is important enough to be listed. This exercise may also help you identify functions that are still being performed but no longer serve any useful purpose.* For example:

FUND MANAGEMENT

New Clients

Taking on New Clients

a. Once the Marketing Manager has received notification of client acceptance, he or she must:

  - Write a courtesy letter confirming acceptance.

- Notify all relevant parties of the prospective appointment, supplying contact names, address, telephone, and telex numbers.
- Inform systems of the new account.

  To the Client is sent the following:

  i)   Client Agreement

  ii) Investment Guidelines

  iii) Copy of Fee Schedule

  Management may negotiate the Client Agreement and Guidelines with the Client, which may result in a nonstandard agreement. These negotiations must be done in consultation with the Portfolio Manager, Marketing Manager, Systems Manager, and Group Legal Department.

b. On completion of negotiations, the Client Agreement is signed by the Client and the Marketing Manager on behalf of the Organization. The original, signed copy is filed in the document room and copies given to the Portfolio Manager for filing.

c. The Manager of Operations informs all parties of Client details, accounting requirements and initial investment and passes fee details to the Finance Department.

d. The Manager of Finance organizes insurance bonding which must be in place prior to receipt of funding.

   No business should be undertaken in the client account until confirmation of the receipt of cash/stocks has been received and the Client Agreement signed.

Closed Account Checklist

Client Administration Department must establish and document the following:

1. Reason for account closing evidenced in client file.
2. Document evidence of a validated client authorization to terminate relationship.
3. Determine how the account is to be closed, i.e., liquidation or transfer.
4. Prepare final client reconciliation.
5. Supply appropriate information to finance department for the completion of the final management fee invoice.

Finance must perform and document the following:

1. Complete final management fee invoicing.

Marketing must perform and document the following:

1. Draft termination letter informing Client that instructions are complete and the Organization holds no further responsibility for management of client funds.
2. Obtain termination approval by Marketing Manager or this designate and send termination letter along with final management fee invoice to Client.

D. Collect all lists into an organized compliance universe book. Essentially what is created is a written schematic or a business tree of the entire area and eventually the organization. Another explanation might be a detailed organization chart by function instead of individual. *This organization map must be all encompassing and eventually include every business, division, department area, and function of the organization.*

   • A strong beginning for this effort is to use the existing policy and procedure manuals to create the listings. In most cases the finished book may look much like the policy and procedures manual for that area. *It is important not to rely solely on the manuals in creating this book, as there is a tendency in most organizations to not keep manuals current and/or comprehensive.*

E. After the compliance universe book is created indicate, for each function and department, who has direct responsibility (name of line manager) and support responsibility (compliance designate or staff member) for compliance. *This identification is especially important as these people will be directly involved in the assessing, structuring, and monitoring of compliance as well as any necessary fixes.*

2. Gain Detailed Understanding of the Area Functions and Responsibilities of the Identified Compliance Review Areas.

Once the areas to be reviewed are identified and the compliance universe book is complete, the compliance officer and/or compliance designate should schedule with the line manager a timetable for review with start and end dates. The essential point here is to gain a detailed and working knowledge of the area so the risk points are outlined along with the flow of the major functions, processes, and controls. *Knowing where to start is sometimes difficult since you may not be fully familiar with the risk aspects of the department. Sometimes it is helpful to begin by identifying the work inflows and outflows and then simply follow them through and map and document as you go along. The puzzle will then fall together fairly quickly.*

A. The line manager must set a timetable and schedule for review where necessary, for the detailed understanding of the area's functions and responsibilities. *Area/department management and staff participation and cooperation in this review is essential for necessary knowledge level.*

Review Function/Area	Manager	Start Date	End Date
Investment Management	Ms. Candy Profit	May 5th	May 8th
Loan Processing	Mr. Len D. Buck	May 6th	May 8th

B. Along with the specific functions and responsibilities reviewed there are general points that are consistent throughout the organization and must be included in the overall assessment.
For example:

General Areas for Review

- Policy and Procedure Manuals
- Strategic Plans (Business Plans)
  - Mission statement
  - Strategic and short-term goals and objectives
- Contingency Plans
  - Containment measures
- Education and Training
  - Departmental program for training and education
- Business Identified Issues
  - Review all identified, potential regulatory and policy issues that may require business involvement for resolution.
- Audit Results
  - Review previous audit findings.
- Etc.

3. Create a Risk Point Outline of the Area.

During or after the compliance universe review, develop a Risk Point Outline. This is a listing of all the points in the area/department that appear to contain a degree of sufficient risk and therefore must be reviewed. This Risk Point Outline will be used for an overall risk and compliance soundness check, the basis for compliance validation, and ultimately incorporated as the policy and procedures manual outline. *Essentially this is your departmental listing of functions with all the nonrisk functions excluded. If there is an uncertainty whether or not risk exists, include it in the outline. It always can be removed at a later date.*
Example of a partial outline:

TRUST ADMINISTRATION RISK POINT OUTLINE

Authority, Regulatory Environment, and General Policy

- Regulation 9 of the Comptroller of the Currency Compliance
- Summary of By-Laws and Board Resolutions Regarding Administration of Fiduciary Powers
- Audit and Examining Committee
- Confidential Information
- Files and Documentation
- Signing Authorities
- Outside Directorships, Outside Employment, and Conflicts of Interest
- General Counsel and the Referral of Legal Matters
- Service of Papers and Pending Litigation
- Governing Fiduciary Laws

New Business and Account Opening

- New Business Review and Criteria
- Successor Trustee Appointments
- Compensation and Fee Schedules
- Legal Review and Criteria
- Designation of Management Responsibility
- Execution of Trust Instruments
- Documentation
- Account Opening—Administrative Procedures
- Pending Establishment of Trust

Trust Account Management

- Trust Account Management Generally
- Timely Analysis of Key Elements and Events
- Client Contact and Response Time
- Complaint Letter File
- Use of Legal Counsel
- Litigation and Potential Loss Tracking
- Fiduciary Operating Losses
- Security for Files and Assets
- Control of Expense/Revenue

4. Risk-Rank the Points of the Risk Point Outline and Identify Desired Review Areas

Establish a risk ranking scale, perhaps 1 to 5 with 5 being the highest and the lowest or what ever suits your needs such as 1 to 10 or letter ranking, A, A–, B, and so on. The scale used is not that important as long as it is consistent in its application. The object of the ranking is to allow the bulk of the focus and the main resources to be applied in the greatest areas of need. By determining the priorities in this manner the organization defines clearly for its members the areas of greatest importance and does not force, through nonclarification, the organization members to do this individually. When priorities are determined individually and in an isolated fashion by separate members, they are not always chosen in the order of most importance to the entire organization but rather relative to the members' area, department, or limited corporate perspective. Complete and effective communication is critical to every organization's success and this is another significant part. Risk ranking also becomes more meaningful during limited resource and time constraints.

During the initial ranking the actual risk may be unknown, which will cause estimations and assumptions. This should not be a concern. Adjustments can be made as the entire process progresses and even into the future as needs and events change. An important point to keep in mind is not to get too technical with the initial ranking, as this can prove time consuming and unproductive. Finite precision is not essential for excellent results; in some cases it can be a hindrance when complexities result. It is critical that the ranking is kept simple; this will ensure ease of understanding and smooth application, which in turn allows for effectiveness.

A. In creating a schedule for review of the desired functions and areas, outline the *major* points to be considered and rank them according to risk. For example:

Risk Ranking 1 to 5	General Areas for Review—Ranked by Apparent Risk
5	*Policy and Procedure Manuals—Review for the Following:* • Current and accurate as written • Contains all the relevant policy • Describes in the appropriate amount of detail how the policy is implemented • Policy and procedure as outlined in manual matches actual practice • Copies to all appropriate management

Risk Ranking 1 to 5	General Areas for Review—Ranked by Apparent Risk
5	*Strategic Plans (Business Plans)* • Mission statement • Strategic and short-term goals and objectives • Detail of action plans • Implementation • Accountability • Measured results
5	*Contingency Plans* • Meets regulatory compliance • Meets corporate policy • Risk assessment • Containment measures
4	*Business Identified Issues* • Identify all potential regulatory and policy issues that require business involvement for resolution.
5	*Audit Results* • Ensure all audit findings have been resolved. • Be prepared to discuss reason for finding and how resolution will be effective.
5	*Education and Training* • Departmental program for training appropriate management and staff in regulatory and policy issues

B. In creating a schedule for review of the desired functions and areas, outline the *specific* points to be considered and rank them according to risk. For example:

Risk Ranking 1 to 5	Area and Functions
5	**Mutual Fund Structuring Process; New Business and Product Programs**
5	• Product Statements Covering:
	▪ Specific Investment Process
	▪ Appropriate Accounting Treatment
	▪ Legal Requirements
	▪ Required Documentation
	▪ Regulatory Reporting Requirements
2	• Appointment of Directors
3	• Tax Considerations
2	• Identification of Parties Involved
2	• Independent Accountant
4	• Method of Distribution
4	• Target Size; Marketability
3	• Investment Objective and Investment Restrictions
4	• Shareholder Programs
5	• Offering Document; Promotional Materials
4	• Methodology and Decision Making with Respect to:
	▪ Cppointment of Committee to Spearhead Creation of Fund
	▪ Name of Fund
	▪ Legal Form of Fund
	▪ Use of Joint Prospectus
	▪ Fiscal Year
	▪ Date of Annual Meeting
	▪ Etc.

5. Flowchart Functions and Operations under Review

Every area/process/control/function/task should be flowcharted where useful. Flowcharting process flows is a step that is not absolutely necessary in some situations, but can be a powerful way to allow a complex process to be easily understood. It is true that it's more of a tool for expediting understanding than it is a required step in the validation. Sometimes a process will be flowcharted and after it is understood the flowchart will not be referenced again. Sometimes a process or control can be understood, changed and managed fine without a flowchart. Regardless of these facts, we have found that a flowchart can usually enhance and speed up the learning and the problem resolution process.

A flowchart does this by giving a visual picture the individual can study and follow rather than forcing the individual to mentally draw his/her own, which happens when one reads a document or hears an explanation. When people read a document they must mentally sketch a picture of what they perceive; this can sometimes be fuzzy. At best, it is time consuming and usually inefficient. When the process is explained to them verbally it is also difficult and even more time consuming. A properly diagrammed flowchart gets around all of this.

The flowchart also proves very useful when management is considering a change in a process or control. It is much easier to move pieces around on paper, moving or changing boxes, than it is to try to mentally envision these changes and what their impact will be. With a pencil and eraser one can rework an entire process several times over. It is just a very basic way to comprehend the full cycle of a process. There are several additional benefits such as: a useful learning tool for new hires and transfers, an historical document for future comparison, an information source for comparative analysis with different areas, and a time saving tool for explaining the area to auditors and examiners.

The steps to creating a flowchart are simple: using a flowchart template or flowchart software, diagram the process/control/function etc. on a step-by-step basis until it is accurately and clearly represented. Determining what flowchart rules to use, such as box types, directions, and so on, is not as important as ensuring that all charts follow the same rules. Consistency is critical if the flowcharts are to be useful and if they are to be properly understood by everyone.

Following are two examples of processes that have been flow charted—one simple process and another more involved.

Figure 1 Completion of the Client Data Sheet

1. Go to Finance Screen to obtain merchant name, merchant address, and SIC Code.

2. Write up data sheet.

2a. Merchant—22 characters.

2b. City/State—18/2 characters.

2c. SIC Code—4 characters.

3. Obtain proper sign-off at AVP level.

4. Submit to Accounts Processing for keying.

5. Returned from Accounts Processing?

6. No, follow up with Accounts Processing.

7. Yes, file data sheet in binder by merchant name.

Figure 1   Client Data Sheet (continued)

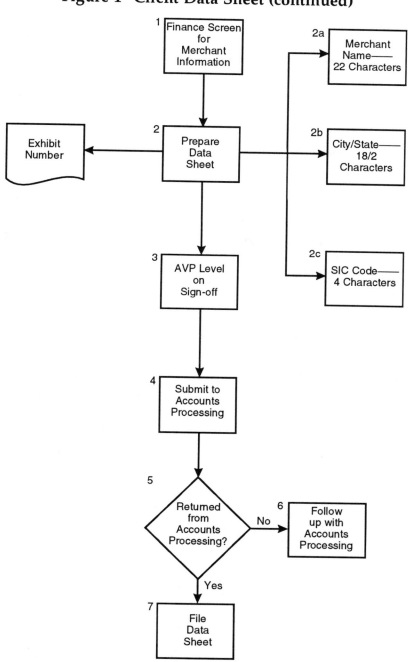

Figure 2   Process for Writeoff of Uncollectable Items

1. Receive media from Operations with printed report.

2. Match each item with report and mark off.

3. Total all items and enter in pending on MIS.

4. Review each item and categorize.
   a. With sales slip
   b. Without sales slip
   c. Credit sales slip
   d. Unrecoverable items (dead)
   e. Merchant chargeback

5. Items with sales slip.

6. Authorized item for full amount.

7. Did you get a valid authorization?

8. Yes, go to Step 10.

9. No, add to unrecoverable items and subtract from pending.

Figure 2 Write-off Items (continued)

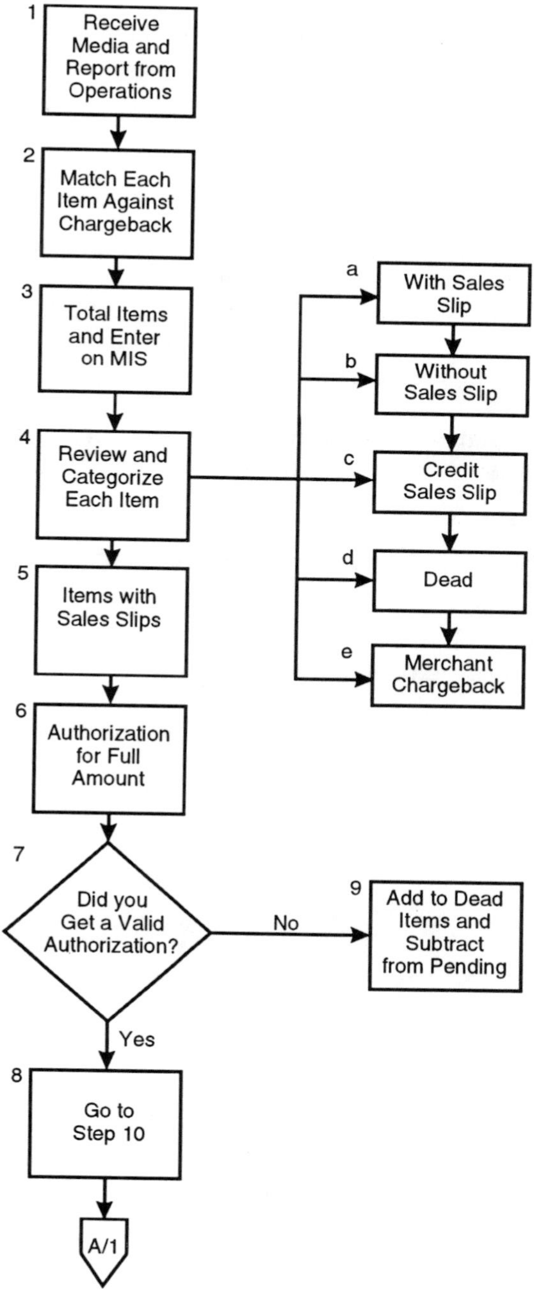

Figure 2   Writeoff Items (continued)

10. Note on item date of authorization, amount, and authorization code.

11. Is Data Sheet available?

12. Yes, go to Step 14.

13. No, see instructions for Data Sheet and go to Step 14.

14. Put in merchant order.

15. Make two copies of each sales slip.

16. Write up batch summary for each merchant and separate copies as follows:
    a.   Tissue copy of summary
    b.   One copy of sales slip behind remaining summary
    c.   One copy of sales slip to file

17. Total up tissue copies.

18. Total up pile of summary with attached sales slip. Should match Step 17.

Figure 2   Write-off Items (continued)

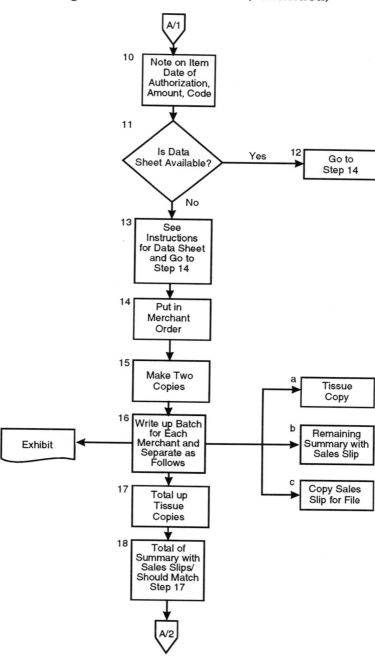

Figure 2 Write-off Items (continued)

19. Enter tissue copy on PC under OP Loss program.

20. Enter total amount in ledger and give a batch number.

21. File tissue.

22. Send summary with sales slip to Operations to process.

23. File sales slip copies separating MasterCard and Visa and put in money order.

24. Enter processed items on Daily MIS and subract from pending.

25. Items without sales slip.

26. Authorization for full amount.

Figure 2 Write-off Items (continued)

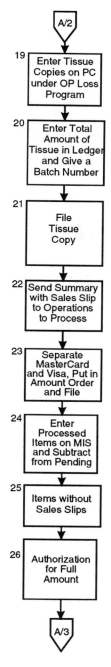

Figure 2   Write-off Items (continued)

27. Repeat Steps 7 through 14.

28. Go to Finance Screen and enter merchant number, city, and state on item.

29. Key on PC under Facsimile program.

30. Run three copies of each facsimile.

    a.   One copy with media

    b.   One copy to file

    c.   One copy with summary to process

31. Repeat Steps 16 through 24.

32. Items where credit was issued.

33. Note on item credits and original sale date.

34. Repeat Steps 26 through 31.

Figure 2   Write-off Items (continued)

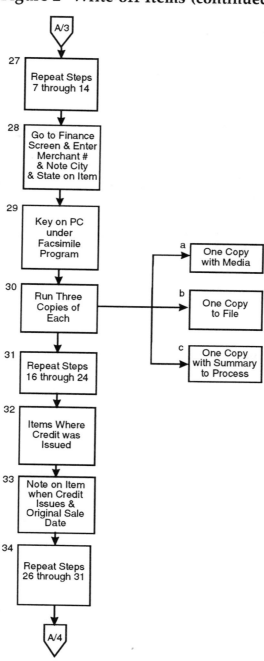

Figure 2 Writeoff Items (continued)

35. Unrecoverable items

    a.   Items without media

    b.   Items missing partial media

    c.   Cannot pass authorization

36. Enter on MIS as unrecoverable and subtract from pending.

37. Merchant chargeback..

Figure 2 Writeoff Items (continued)

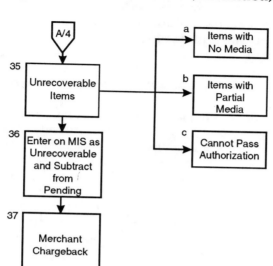

6. Evaluate Major Risk Controls and Monitoring Systems

A highly critical part of any compliance and risk management program is the effectiveness of its risk controls and monitoring systems. It is essential that these systems are in place, effective, and periodically tested to ensure proper functioning. *It is sort of a two-part check system as the controls ensure that the high risk business processes are functioning with an acceptable level of risk and the monitoring system ensures that the controls are consistently performed and remain effective.*

These controls and monitor systems must be continually assessed for accuracy and effectiveness to ensure the proper results. The best control in the world is worthless if it is not used or is looking at the wrong things. As we have discussed, all controls and monitoring systems must be simple, flexible, completely understood, and fully communicated in order to be effective. It is quite common for something to become complicated over time due to continuous changes and "improvements" by well-intentioned members. For this as well as other reasons it is critical to continually reassess all controls and monitoring systems. In assessing controls and monitoring systems one aspect that must be constantly kept in mind is the overall value of the control or monitoring system. It might be a working and effective control, but is it necessary or is it overkill? Ultimately, it is important to have controls that work but it is equally important not to have unnecessary or overly burdensome controls and monitoring systems.

The following is not an all-inclusive listing but rather an example of some of the major risk controls and monitoring systems:

- General Compliance
  - Compliance designate
  - Compliance validation
  - MIS and reporting
- Risk Assessment and Ranking Program (at All Levels)
  - Account (new, existing, closed)
  - Product (new and existing)
  - Environmental
  - Safe keeping
  - Function (error and fraud)
  - Disbursements
  - Accounting records
  - Etc.
- Environmental Risk Management Program
  - Compliance with regulation
  - Effectiveness of monitoring and reporting
- Business Risk Management Review Committee
  - Compliance and risk management meeting schedule
  - Completeness of minutes

- Follow-up and implementation
- Current Policy and Procedure Manuals
  - All departments are included in appropriate sections
  - Every area has complete set and is knowledgeable on policies and procedures
- Preclearance and Insider Trading Controls
  - Employee Investment Policy
  - Reporting and monitoring
- Education and Training
  - Conflicts of interest
  - Corporate policies (corporate manual, etc.)
  - Area policies and procedures
  - Applicable regulations (local, state, and federal)
  - Cross training of all vital areas
  - Ethical standards
- Contingency Plans
  - Tested and current
- Strategic Plans
  - Current and fully communicated
- Department Business Plans
  - Current and fully communicated
  - Ties with a realistic budget
- Area Audit Programs
  - Comprehensive, well communicated and satisfies corporate needs
- Current and Accurate Organization Chart
  - Description of responsibilities by individual
- Disbursements Policy and Process

A good way to assess these controls and monitor systems is to begin by developing a list of questions that cover the major concerns and that must be addressed in order to satisfy the soundness of the controls for a specific area. One must ask—have these important questions been answered satisfactorily or do they raise more questions and perhaps issues? This is what must be looked at and considered in the assessment process.

An example:

Concerns in the Brokerage Trading Area

Procedures—Best Execution

Q—Is there or should there be anything written down on Best Execution?

Q—What are actual procedures followed by us for Best Execution?

Q—How strong are processes for managing and monitoring in-house crosses, self-dealing, TBC-19, etc.? Are they well documented?

Equity Side

Q—What is evidence that committee has reviewed the flow of commissions?

Q—How do we document and defend commissions to firms not on approved list?

Q—How do we document and defend commissions to firms we do not have soft dollar obligations to?

Brokers Approved List

Q—How do brokers get on list (process, policy, and criteria)?

Q—How do we document and define use of brokers not on list?

Q—What is the policy and procedure for third party arrangements—is it documented?

Q—Do our third party arrangements fall under the safe harbor provision (28E)?

Q—Does our price arrangement make sense?

Q—Does the Brokerage Committee review and approve all arrangements?

Q—Is the distribution of soft dollars appropriate? Committing a major percentage of funds to a small number of brokers can be a problem, as it limits flexibility.

Q—How well is our commission flow monitored? It must be reviewed closely for possible fraud, favoritism, kickbacks, etc.

Third Party Services—Soft Dollars

Q—What are policy and procedures for soft dollar distribution? Is there anything documented?

Q—How do brokers, who are not approved by the Committee, get onto the system with business transacted? The Brokerage Committee may not be aware of these arrangements.

Q—Does the possibility exist that commitments were made to brokers not on the approved list that are not showing on the system because no business has yet been transacted?

Q—How do we identify all brokers being used (entire population) or pledged soft dollars? The nonapproved brokers are the risk.

Q—Do we have a policy and procedure manual for the Brokerage Committee? Is it current and complete?

7. Use of Statistical Sampling during the Validation Process

In some cases it is necessary to sample a population of files, documents, account entries and so on. Since the entire population usually cannot be tested due to size, time, and resource limitations, it becomes necessary to seek an alternative approach. When this occurs an appropriate sample can be just as effective in identifying the condition as actual testing of the entire population. There are many different techniques in choosing samples that at times can get fairly complex. The intent here is not to be scientific but rather to get a sample representative of the population in a cost effective and time efficient manner. Since the initial premise of validation is to understand the process, the sampling does not have to be as pure as it would be with a conventional audit where the process is not reviewed or fully understood.

The objective of compliance validation is to verify or certify sound compliance and risk management; therefore, it is not always necessary to spend the extra effort required in performing a sample test in strict accordance with regulatory guidelines. The annual internal audit should accomplish this goal. It is important to remember that compliance validation and an internal audit have different purposes and they should not in any way duplicate each other. There is no point in performing a validation that is identical to an audit test or vice versa. This would not only be a waste of resources but time as well, because the validation would yield the same results as the audit if they were performed identically and both done correctly.

- *When planning the sample, consider the relationship of the sample to be taken to the specific purpose of the validation in regard to what is being validated.* In other words, determine what is actually being looked for and what the intended outcome of the validation is before the sample is taken. If you are verifying the loan review process for all loans over $1 million, don't sample from the loan officer's entire portfolio, which might include loans under $1 million. Only review the process that approves the loans in that category. This will allow your sample and scope to be limited and therefore save much time and effort along with allowing the results to be clearer, because there is less superfluous information that may cloud the facts.

- *The sample should be selected so that it is representative of the full population.* The sample does not necessarily have to be random but it must be typical of the process that is being reviewed. If the goal is to validate the month-end journal entry process into the general ledger, don't have the sample include a large number of adjusting entries when they only happen occasionally due to errors. It may happen that the particular month you are doing your review a disproportionate amount of adjusting entries occurred. If this were to happen, choosing a truly random sample will give you a population that is not characteristic of the normal process. In this event you can intentionally choose your sample to show a normal mix, which will give you a representative sample population and an accurate validation. Since management is performing the sampling, inappropriate bias in the sample selection can be discounted. It should be assumed that management will not try to cheat themselves.

- *Use the common sense rule.* Ensure that the sample is not biased by poor selection, preconceived conclusions, or contamination by other factors. Don't choose the sample haphazardly or strictly through convenience. Ensure that it is planned and well thought out. Don't allow any pre-conceived notions to guide the sample selection by assuming what the conclusion will be before the sample is complete. "I just know I'm going to find that this process works well so why go down the hall for part of my sample; I'll just take it all here." Don't let outside events such as witnessed results from another validation, a recent audit, or an opinion from another manager influence the sample. Unless these events are directly related to the specific validation, they should not be taken into account.

8. Development of an Effective Validation Process

There is no set technique for validation, although depending on the organization structure some clearly work better than others. Essentially, the main purpose of validation is to determine if the area/process/control/function/task is operating as intended and serving a useful purpose to the business in a cost effective manner. It is strongly recommended that the typical audit approach is not used; this does not mean to imply that there is anything wrong with this approach, but rather that validation is really looking to determine a different result. *Validation should never duplicate an audit as this not only defeats the purpose but it is also a tremendous waste of effort and resources.*

The validation approach is simple; have an individual who is experienced and knowledgeable with the process, usually assisted by the compliance designate, perform a review to determine the overall effectiveness in regard to accuracy, consistency, risk management, productivity, efficiency, and cost effectiveness. The individual does not have to be an expert in any of these categories, just in the process itself. If the individual truly knows the process and how it interfaces with others, then to understand if it is accurate, consistent, productive, efficient, etc. is basic common sense. By asking simple questions such as—Is this the only way to do it? Is this the simplest way to do it? Can it be done as good or better using less people, steps, and time? Often a process can be improved in terms of accuracy, time, and cost by just involving fewer people and reducing the steps. Remember, the simpler a process is, the easier it is to perform and learn, the less time it takes, the lower the cost, the easier it is to identify any problems, the easier it is to modify or change, and the easier it is to perform a validation.

What is an effective validation process? We can begin by looking at what a validation is not:

A Validation is Not:

- *A checklist compliance test.* A validation is unlike a conventional audit or compliance test in that it does not test a predetermined series of items listed on a document that is used each time a review is performed. Conventional compliance testing, which is basically the same as a typical audit test, is more like a traditional dance that is passed down from year to year with the same steps performed and little changed. A validation is more like a free-style dance that changes with the music and although it may be similar between dancers, is still unique in performance with each individual dancer. The benefits of this approach are several, due in large part to the varied knowledge levels and understanding of each organization member performing the validation along with the particular situation. Validation does not and should not treat every similar situation the same. In other words, all loan officer files are not necessarily reviewed in the same fashion. The general structure is in place for the review, but the specifics in the application may vary. This approach creates efficiencies in completion time, resource use, and problem resolution.

  This free-style approach also is necessary because the process, instead of the transaction, is verified. An individual can look at a transaction and determine if it is right or wrong without needing to or being able to understand why. The transaction is fixed; it will not change. You can go back to it ten times and it will still be there unchanged; it has become history, whereas the process is always moving, mostly in the same direction. The free-style approach allows the individual to move with the process and study it in progression at the rate and detail commensurate with the individual's knowledge and goals. Since they only have to prove to themselves that the process is working fine, they do not need to waste time performing unnecessary steps and completing documentation to support their findings. This only needs to be done when a problem or risk is found and others must be involved. Instead of a checklist that itemizes all the steps and points to review, a validation replaces it with a structured approach that involves only as much detail as necessary.

- *Concerned with wholesale sampling.* Sampling should not be done simply to meet a regulatory requirement or to satisfy the need to show a test was performed. In some cases with an internal audit, a sample must be taken even when the results are already known. This is necessary to show a third party that a review did take place; with a validation this is unnecessary. With a validation, sampling is only done when specific data are required.

- *Transaction testing.* A transaction is a historical event that has occurred some time in the past. A transaction can be any number of things such as a cash disbursement from a client account, a loan to an individual or corporation, an executed trade, a signed contract, a document in a file, a memo sent, or letter written. All of these things are the end result of an action or process. A transaction can never be changed and by its very nature is old news. Therefore, looking at or concentrating on a transaction is largely unproductive as it will never tell a current and complete story. A transaction can only tell what happened—the disbursement occurred, the letter was mailed, the loan was made—it cannot tell you why or how it happened. In order to understand the why or how you must look at the process. Understand the process that created the transaction and you can understand what the transaction is and what caused it, but it cannot be the other way around. Validation focuses on the current processes and controls, not on what happened in the past or in this case, the transaction. What happened cannot be changed; what is yet to happen can be changed.

- *Testing every aspect of the department or organization.* There is neither time nor purpose to test everything. The validation should concentrate on the risk points of the department with regularly scheduled reviews established for risk sensitive areas. If something is deemed low risk, or it has recently been audited, or the line manager is highly confident it is fine, then a review should be a low priority. The intent is not to have a great deal of time spent "making sure" everything is working well, which would leave less time to actually work the functions and run the department. The goal is to apply scarce resources where they will provide the greatest amount of good for sound compliance, risk management, and profit.

A Validation is:

- *Concerned with tactical sampling.* Using the smallest possible sample size while still getting accurate results. A validation samples only where necessary.

- *Verifying the effectiveness of processes and controls.* Focus on processes and controls and their overall effectiveness, not on individual transactions. It takes someone knowledgeable to understand the process and control along with requiring someone knowledgeable to understand the real issues.

- *Uncovering excessive and/or duplicative processes and controls that eventually hamper productivity and profitability.* A process or control may actually work fine; however it may be superfluous, duplicate another process or control, or give information that is unnecessary. It is sometimes a strong temptation to "double check" or redo a function to ensure that it is correct. This may be mistakenly thought of as a control when in fact it is nothing more than a redundant and costly action. A control should never redo something already done; it should verify its accuracy through some predetermined test or action that takes a different route from the process.

- *Identifying training and education needs.* Most errors committed by individuals are not due to incompetence but are usually the result of poor training or understanding. Through validation, these needs can be easily identified and corrected.

- *Identifying need for risk awareness.* Risk is not something that should be totally avoided or diminished. There is a degree of business risk that is necessary in order to maintain an acceptable level of profitability. Risk awareness is where management is aware of the risk, has taken the appropriate precautions, and has determined an acceptable level that can be monitored. A process can be functioning as desired but it may contain a degree of risk that is not fully appreciated by the staff. The proper level of sensitivity can go a long way in mitigating overall risk. Part of a validation is to determine the appropriate level of risk awareness and identify any need for raising awareness.

- *Validation of the overall soundness of compliance and risk management of the area.* Identify all of the risk points in the area and conduct a validation to see if they are being managed appropriately in terms of compliance and risk. Below is one way to lay out a validation module for the development of a compliance validation:

Validation Module (sample)

Area

Portfolio management of client investment management accounts

Specific Objectives

1. Determine whether the organization has adequate procedures for:
   a. Review of overall investment policy and potential investment problems. These must be reviewed at least annually.
   b. Communicate portfolio management policy to appropriate personnel and include it in committee minutes, directives, and memoranda.
   c. Review investment decisions for the purchase or sale of assets to ensure they meet account objectives.
   d. Review the frequency of investment changes to avoid excessive trading practices.

Approach

Consider the processes and functions that relate to these points:

- The Fiduciary Review Committee process
- Individual portfolio manager process
- Client account administration process
- Corporate investment objectives and client investment objectives
- Brokerage placement practices

Review

- Fiduciary Review Committee actual meetings, minutes, and interview members.
- Portfolio managers' consistency, accuracy, knowledge, workload, and investment performance.
- Client account administrators' consistency, accuracy, knowledge, workload, and account administration timeliness.
- Investment objectives to ensure they meet corporate standards and client account requirements.

Sampling

Dimension and list the sample areas, items, and size.

- *Area:* Fiduciary Review Committees (which includes all pre-preparation, i.e.: checklists, logs, etc.)
- *Items:* Account files, logs, computer MIS, checklists, and minutes
- *Size:* Randomly choose and list 20 accounts for review of account files, logs, computer MIS, checklists, and committee and meeting minutes.

Expectations

Verify that area functions are in accordance with sound compliance and risk management practices.

9. Completed Validation—Documentation and Evaluation of Results

Once the validation is complete the next steps are to catalog and consider the facts collected and the conclusions reached. Just as it is important to collect clear and accurate results, it is equally important to ensure that those same results are clearly and accurately documented. This is necessary so the correct action can be taken and when future comparisons are made, they begin with accurate data.

The results of the validation can be broken down into four basic conclusions:

1. The results show proper and efficient functioning with all risk identi-
    fied and acceptable. The process or control that was validated is op-
    erating precisely as desired in a productive and efficient manner. The
    associated risk is identified, defined, and properly managed.

2. The results show proper and efficient functioning. It has been deter-
    mined that the process or control is operating as initially intended
    with the acceptable results. It has also been determined that changes
    can be made to mitigate some of the current risk, and/or increase the
    accuracy and efficiency of the outcome without additional cost or
    complexity.

3. The results show proper functioning in accordance with current ex-
    pectations; however, the process or control is unnecessary/duplica-
    tive/inefficient/not cost effective and constitutes some degree of
    unacceptable risk. It has been determined that changes can be made
    to mitigate some of the risk, and/or increase the accuracy and effi-
    ciency of the outcome without additional cost or complexity.

4. The results show a degree of improper functioning with previously
    undefined risk. The process or control that was validated is not oper-
    ating as originally expected. The process or control is flawed or no
    longer meets its intended need. There are previously unknown areas
    of risk that need to be fully defined with the appropriate changes
    determined.

It is clear that the first result requires no action and the other three
appear to require some degree of further investigation and possible change.
At this point the manager of the area will consider the full impact of the
current findings and what any changes might mean to the department and
organization. If change that may affect any number of people in and outside
of the department is required, then the manager may consider discussion
with other management. If help is needed to interpret the findings, devise a
resolution, and/or implement change, the manager may request assistance
from the appropriate experts such as other management, compliance, or
audit.

Below are the partial results of a sample compliance validation:

Compliance Validation of the Investment Management Area

Determine whether the area has adequate policies, procedures, and controls
for:

A. Review of overall investment policy and potential investment prob-
    lems. These must be reviewed at least annually.

VALIDATE:

Fiduciary Review Committee meets each month to review every portfolio's holdings to ensure that all investments meet the investment objectives of the account and all securities purchased meet the criteria set out by the organization with regard to issuer and/or rating, as applicable.

Investigate accounts on log and MIS to determine last Fiduciary Review Committee review date and verify that it falls within parameters.

SAMPLE:

Monthly Fiduciary Review Committee review with supporting schedules

EXPECTATIONS:

Walk through the review process for an account to ensure that all requirements are met. If an exception is noted, document the follow-up procedure with the Portfolio Manager and Fiduciary Review Committee.

FINDINGS:

All investment policy issues noted were minor in nature and have been or are being addressed by the full committee.

Fiduciary Review Committee meets as scheduled and performs all required duties appropriately.

RESULTS:

See Monthly Fiduciary Review Committee Files

Validation has concluded that there are no special or unusual risk areas. The results show proper and efficient functioning with identified and acceptable risk.

B. Communicate portfolio management policy to appropriate personnel, and verify its inclusion in committee minutes, directives, and memoranda.

VALIDATE:

Monthly Fiduciary Review Committee review.
Weekly portfolio team meetings
Weekly portfolio administrators' meetings
Identify sources of documentation to support communication of policy (minutes, memos, etc.).

SAMPLE:

Fiduciary Committee and meeting minutes

Portfolio team meeting notes
Portfolio administrator meeting notes

EXPECTATIONS:

Confirm that investment policy is monitored and communicated to all the portfolio managers and portfolio administrators and reviewed monthly by the Fiduciary Review Committee.

FINDINGS:

Corporate investment policy is not communicated on a consistent and comprehensive basis. Word-of-mouth is relied upon too heavily for individual portfolio managers and administrators. When the department was small this was effective and acceptable; however with department now triple in size over the last three years, a more comprehensive and effective process is necessary.

RESULTS:

Validation has concluded that there are risks in the current process where an individual portfolio manager can work contrary to corporate investment policy. Weekly team meetings must include discussion on corporate investment policy with supporting memorandum outlining any policy changes or considerations.
Details to be outlined by senior portfolio manager and approved by Fiduciary Review Committee.

C. Review investment decisions for the purchase or sale of assets to ensure they meet account objectives.

VALIDATE:

Portfolio management team meetings
Corporate investment policy guidelines.
Client portfolio holdings

- Determine what procedures the portfolio managers follow to ensure that all accounts are actively managed in regard to research, documentation, and support.
- Review client portfolio investment process and determine whether assets held conform to provisions of the investment objectives of the account and corporate investment guidelines.

SAMPLE:

Client account portfolios
Review committee
Portfolio team meetings

EXPECTATIONS:

Confirm that investment guidelines and objectives are met and that the client portfolios are monitored prior to a security being purchased by the portfolio manager and reviewed weekly by portfolio management team

FINDINGS:

Portfolio management team meetings are held weekly with active discussions on individual investment and research strategies. Group discussions are interactive and produce good results for portfolio management. High investment composites agree with this observation.

With a few exceptions, security purchase and sales are properly monitored to investment guidelines and client objectives.

General corporate investment guidelines are not strictly followed due in large part to poor communication in the group.

RESULTS:

Validation has concluded that there are no risk areas other than communication of corporate investment guidelines. This is to be dealt with as suggested in Validation B.

Summary of Findings

With the exception of communication gaps in the corporate investment policy which is to be addressed immediately, the area validation has found no major risk issues.

10. Understanding the Results to Identify Required Changes

Before any changes are made due to the validation findings, all results must be thoroughly reviewed by the appropriate management (line management) and the respective compliance and risk management experts, where necessary. *It is essential that all of the ramifications are understood, which includes the risk if left unchanged and the risk and benefit of change.* Contrary to popular belief, it may be appropriate to leave a previously unknown risk situation alone, providing the necessary steps are taken to manage it effectively. Risk is at times fully acceptable as long as it is identified, completely defined, and properly managed. As we have discussed previously, situations that contain a high degree of risk, if properly managed, can be very profitable. For this and other reasons change must be thoroughly considered to ensure that it makes sense:

- Does the change make the situation less complex?
- Does it use the same or fewer resources?

- Will it have a positive impact on the other areas, processes, or controls it affects?
- Is the change cost effective in the long term?
- Will the change reduce risk in this or other situations?
- Will the implementation of the change be smooth and without major disruption of the work flow?

The answer to all of these questions does not have to be yes in order for a change to be effective and positive. Depending on the group needs and other alternatives, a yes response to one or two of these items may be enough to make a change favorable. However, the more affirmative responses to these points achieved by the change the greater the benefit to the organization. On the other hand, if the answer to all of these points is no, then a change, unless required by strong corporate policy, legal regulation, or an unavoidable need, should not be made. An organization should not allow any major changes strictly on the basis of a manager's personal preference or for the sake of change itself. This can be quite disruptive and hurt productivity, efficiency, accuracy, control, and morale.

An example of a partial compliance validation that outlines some of the issues found and the discussed changes is outlined below.

A compliance validation was performed in the following areas:

Compliance Validation Areas

- Trust and Estates
- Investment Management Services
- Brokerage Placement
- Proxy Services
- Investment Research Services
- Mutual Funds

Summary of Validation Findings

AREA: Trust and Estates
MANAGER: Mr. Will E. Trust
PERFORMED BY: Ms. Ida Checkit, Portfolio Administrator

1. *Disbursement Process.* Current process is manual with requests being made both verbally and on various notes and documents. There is no official request form and no consistent and appropriate secondary review. There is also no exception reporting for large or unusual transactions. Under the current disbursement process, unauthorized and fraudulent transactions could be processed, possibly exposing the organization to significant financial loss.

2. *Documented Procedures.* The validation has found that several processes are not documented properly in the respective area's policy and procedure manual. The manuals were found to be out of date and not comprehensive in respect to current processes. Certain departmental members, especially new and junior ones, rely on these documents for reference. This can lead to inefficiencies and errors and must be corrected with a schedule for continuous review and updated enacted.

3. *Management Review.* The validation has found that management review in the areas of documentation storage and closed account processing is not adequate. The lack of management attention in these areas unduly exposes the organization to financial risk and customer dissatisfaction. Current, accurate, and easily accessible records are essential to this department. Regularly scheduled management review and assessment must be performed.

4. *Weak Controls and Management MIS.* The validation has found that in some areas risk review controls are weak and lacking and need stronger development and attention by management. These areas include: brokerage (commissions, nonapproved brokers, soft dollars), uninvested cash, contingency planning, P.C. risk assessments, and internal administration requirements (vacation scheduling, absence records, etc.). In some cases it appears to be a matter of better documentation and in others, better MIS reporting in terms of clarity, consistency, and accuracy. Since these reports are only used for control purposes they have not received the attention they deserve. Management must review these areas closely and make the necessary changes and adjustments to improve reporting.

Results

After line management reviewed the findings it was determined that assistance outside the department would help interpret the findings and determine the necessary actions and resolutions. The compliance officer and the line manager from the Investment Management department were consulted for a thorough review of the facts. The followings actions were concluded:

1. *Disbursement Process.* Automation of the current process will be investigated along with the development of exception reporting for large or unusual transactions. There will be an official request form developed with the proper level of sign-offs required for consistent and appropriate secondary review. The policy and procedures manual will be updated and regularly scheduled semiannual validations performed for continuous assessment.

2. *Documented Procedures.* All department policy and procedure manuals will be reviewed and updated for accuracy and comprehensiveness.

3. *Management Review.* Consideration will be given to a supervisor in charge of documents management to ensure accurate and current files and documentation along with proper security of sensitive and original documentation. This will not initially be a full-time position as this individual will have other duties. This individual will be responsible for all aspects of document management and quarterly validations, and will report directly to the Senior Investment Manager.

4. *Weak Controls and Management MIS.* The supervisors in the areas of Brokerage, Cash management, P.C. systems, and administration which includes contingency planning, will be required to review in detail their MIS reporting and control needs for discussion on possible modifications. The systems area will be appraised of their needs and give feedback on realistic alternatives. Management will then consider the options for strengthening the risk controls in these areas. Semiannual validations will be scheduled going forward.

Schedules and action plans to develop and implement these changes are required in one week.

The following, final two points are perhaps the most important because all of the beginning work becomes meaningless if the conclusions reached are not acted upon and are not monitored for completion. It can actually be more harmful to uncover errors and acknowledge their existence and then do nothing about them than it would be to never have made the effort in the first place.

11. Ensuring Implementation of Changes

The best way and perhaps the only way to ensure implementation of the necessary fixes or changes is for the line manager and compliance officer, if necessary, to be involved in the planning and scheduling stage, and provide assistance where needed and monitor the progress closely while requiring explanation for delays and missed completion dates.

The process to do this is a simple one by setting realistic action plans with milestones and completion dates. The actual approach can vary by organization and even department depending on resource availability, size of the department, the actual tasks involved, and individual preference. Some members may prefer progress charts while others checklists and still others daily reports. The tools used, although they must be clear, uncomplicated, and effective, are not as important as the requirement of monitoring and tracking the progress of the implementation. This must not only be done by the department line manager but also the staff members involved in the effort.

Two very effective and useful ways to do this are:

- *Hold formal departmental compliance reviews and progress reports where necessary.* Depending on the issues and the line manager, these can be informal meetings. It is not important to create a bureaucratic process as this may intimidate the line into pushing through or trying to lessen some problems. Even a simple bureaucracy has a way of growing and becoming self-justified where more time is spent telling people what was and will be done and less time spent in getting it done. Don't forget the goal is to resolve the problems and not to broadcast or publish the departmental failings to the world or make a federal case over the fact that the department has problems. Once the line understands that the mission of the compliance effort is compliance soundness and not "gottcha," they will not only cooperate fully but look to the compliance effort for guidance on future concerns.

- *Require the issue and resolution process to be documented from start to finish. Establishing weekly or monthly progress reports is helpful.* When we speak of documentation we do not mean a detailed diary of all past, present, and future events. It is simply good business sense to record what has happened so you have something to look back on and be sure the same mistakes are not repeated. It is important to let the line understand that this documentation requirement is not to create a record of their problems. Rather, it is essential to record the progress steps in the event a change of direction is needed. It is also helpful in the event the same or similar issue can or does exist elsewhere so the fix can be swift. Also the historical record created can help prevent a recurrence of the same problem in the future.

The following is an example of an implementation schedule:

Example I
Banking Group—Investment Division
Status of Compliance Validation Identified Issues

Banking Trust & Investments	Total Assets	Report Number	Report Date	Comp Rating	Risk Rank
	500B	12345	2/15/9?	1	5

Significant Findings	Corrective Action	Target Completion Date			
		Orig.	Revised	Actual	Rev#
I. New Account Openings—Poor account opening process; weaknesses in adequacy and completeness of documentation; lack of proper legal review.	I. Account opening process must be reorganized with new procedures under development. Management team must be put in place to implement proper documentation and reviews	4/15			
II. Asset Reviews—Asset reviews not done in accordance with corporate policy.	II. New asset review process to be developed.	4/15			
III. SEC Disclosure Rule—Not uniformly followed.	III. Formal process and controls will be established to ensure conformity. Staff will be educated on the important of this policy.	3/15			

Example I (continued)
Banking Group—Investment Division
Status of Compliance Validation Identified Issues

Banking Trust & Investments	Total Assets	Report Number	Report Date	Comp Rating	Risk Rank
	500B	12345	2/15/9?	1	5

Significant Findings	Corrective Action	Target Completion Date			Rev#
		Orig.	Revised	Actual	
IV. Brokers—Brokers dealt with are not on Approved Brokers list; evidence of investment authority being exercised that was not empowered by the governing instrument.	IV. Brokerage committee will be reorganized. Brokerage placement policy and procedure will be developed. Key operating procedures to include controls to ensure only use of approved brokers.	3/15			
V. Customer Fees—Fee tables in system (which dictate fees charged) do not match negotiated fees in contract.	V. Fee table database not updated. To update automated system and implement verification control.	3/15			
VI. Record Keeping Requirements—Trade tickets were not time stamped or order dated.	VI. To purchase time stamper and create log.	4/15			
VII. Policy and Procedures—A current and comprehensive policy and procedure manual does not exist.	VII. To develop comprehensive policy and procedures manual for entire operation.	6/15			

12. Reporting and Follow-up

Reporting and follow-up by both management and where necessary, the compliance officer, are essential to the effectiveness of the process, not only from an execution standpoint but also from a cooperation standpoint. If it is shown that there is no earnest or consistent follow-through the staff will not take the initial efforts seriously and react accordingly, resulting in overall ineffectiveness of the undertaking. Without a complete and accurate follow-through all of the beginning and middle work may become a waste of time.

The reporting is necessary to keep the appropriate people informed. It is also useful from a historical records standpoint so future comparisons and records can be maintained. This becomes especially important as the organization grows and management changes over time. With a good historical record there is a much better opportunity for prevention of repeating past mistakes.

The reporting and follow-up can be accomplished several ways depending on the situation, the people involved, and the organizational requirements. Probably the most common ways are through formal and informal meetings and by written status report. How it is done does not matter, as long as it is done consistently and effectively.

It is important to note that a good deal of time should not be spent in documenting and reporting in great detail. Reports and documents are tools for understanding and assistance in accomplishing a goal. They do not physically accomplish anything themselves, so too much time spent on making them perfect is largely unproductive. The reports and documents should be just detailed enough so they are understood while being brief as possible. It is much more efficient in the long run to document evidence in one page rather than three. People have a tendency to read short documents whereas long ones are scanned or ignored; it is easier to find the desired information on a short report versus a long one; short documents are easier to remember and therefore reference in the future. Short documents also live longer because they do not need as much storage space and can provide longer historical value.

When Do I Get to Do My Job?

Six managers in a large organization got selected for a task force that was created to help their organization review and prepare for an upcoming major regulatory exam. The organization extended a large effort for review of every department to ensure compliance and identify any possible problems. This new team of six managers reported directly to a senior manager who in turn reported to a manager more senior than him, who basically controlled the task force effort but was overseen and directed by the director of compliance. Although the compliance director, who was newly hired for the effort, reported to the regional director of the organization, he was also required to give updates to the divisional director who demanded a good exam.

With all this fire power it appeared that the organization was sure to have an easy pass on their exam. What actually turned out to be the most difficult thing of all was for the six task force managers to find the time to actually do any work. In truth, the entire effort could have been performed by two or three people in four to six weeks while being just as or more successful. Instead it took nine people whose combined annual salary was over $1 million about four months to prepare for the upcoming exam. One may wonder how this is possible; well, the culprit was mostly the reporting and follow-up.

In some organizations a manager's job is to manage, not do anything, just manage. This was one of those organizations. In this kind of environment when you have managers only managing managers it can get pretty interesting because then—who does the work? In our situation the top three managers improvised; they delegated all the work down and since the six task force managers had no one to delegate to, they were stuck "doing the work." What was also interesting is that while our top three managers were very good at delegating all the work down, they were equally talented at taking credit for all of the work on the way up, but that is another story.

With all of this delegating and taking credit, our top three managers had much going on so they felt they needed thorough and comprehensive reporting and follow-up to keep on top of things. The compliance director started by requesting written updates from the top senior manager on a daily basis. So she could prepare for these updates, the top senior manager requested from the senior manager comprehensive reports tracking every action that was accomplished, was in the process of being performed, and was going to be performed. There were action dates requested with revision dates, reasons for missed dates, revisions for the revised dates, and a schedule of new items to be added along with those deleted. All of this was requested daily for the night before her meeting with the compliance director.

Our senior manager, who had the six task force managers directly reporting to him, also needed his reporting and follow-up so he could apprise his senior manager for her daily report to the compliance director. He in turn requested of the six task force managers a daily morning schedule or a "to-do" list of what was done the end of the previous day and what was to be done the current day in addition to those tracking reports his senior manager wanted.

After the six managers completed their morning list they were called into a "team meeting" by the senior manager for an overview, status, and a keep-everyone-informed meeting. After this meeting was over the six managers had to go back and update their tracking reports which kept a detailed log of the all the separate departments and areas they were working in

along with what has been accomplished. After a period of time these combined tracking reports totaled several hundred pages.

By the time their morning lists, meetings, and tracking report work
was done it was time for lunch. After lunch they were able to get down to
the serious business of reviewing and working with the departments and
areas to assess the compliance soundness. They got to do this for the entire
balance of the day—except, that is, when they had to sit in a departmental
meeting to brief those managers of their progress of the review effort. Since
each task force manager worked with more than one department and area,
these meetings usually took up between one to two hours of their day. After
these meetings they could then get back to the business of review. Except
when they had to prepare for the weekly review with the compliance director. This usually took about two to three hours to prepare for and another
two to three hours for the meeting. Now they could get back to the business
of review—except when they had to prepare for and have the monthly
meeting with the divisional manager, which took one whole day to prepare
for and another half day for the meeting. After that they could get back to
the business of reviewing the departments and areas for compliance soundness, until they had to stop for the end of the day update. At the end of
every day before they went home, they had to give a brief update to the
senior manager they reported to so that he felt comfortable at day's end that
they were accomplishing their goals. Needless to say he was usually very
satisfied because "these important task force assignments are always time
consuming."

Although this may seem exaggerated, it is a true depiction of events at
a large institution. But this can and does happen in many organizations,
albeit in lesser degrees. The important point is that we can't get carried
away with reporting and follow-up where it becomes counterproductive.
Reporting and follow-up are excellent and necessary tools but they should
not be allowed to become major efforts in themselves.

Below are two different examples of a status report:

Example I
Ucan Trust US—Status Update

Date: April 15, 199?
Re: Compliance Validation of Trust Business
Compliance Validation Process: Performed March 5, 199?
Manager: Mr. Lyne Manager

To: Managers file

1. **Completion of the Closed Account Transition Process** (closed accounts)—Determine disposition of closed accounts that may still have balances and account files that have not been properly reviewed (audit finding).

2. **Policy and Procedure Manual**—Development of the manual is in progress with the first section completed.

3. **Fiduciary Review Committee Process**—An official Fiduciary Review Committee has been established and Board approved. The next steps are to create an entire system of process and controls (logs, database, MIS, etc.) to monitor and manage the process.

4. **Segregation of Authority and Duties**—There are two major issues here: the first is disbursements, which is a systemic issue and is being addressed from an overall business standpoint; and the second is access by temporary personnel to the account system, and whether or not the temporary help is properly bonded in relation to their responsibilities to the business.

5. **Account Administration/Transaction Process**—Work still needs to be done to develop and implement a documented, overall process that allows for the proper management (MIS and systems), control (sign-offs and checklists), and review (fiduciary and administrator) of the accounts.

6. **Original Documentation Storage and Security**—This issue has been looked at and the appropriate resolution is near. We will probably purchase a fireproof file cabinet.

7. **Department Compliance Validation Program**—There currently is no program; however, before this can be firmly established more work must be done addressing the other major issues.

8. **Risk Evaluation**—A preliminary risk evaluation has been performed on identified accounts and approximately 26 have potential litigation liability. Thirty-two accounts have been placed with outside attorneys for assistance and 14 are on a watch list. There is also some possible risk with some remaining employee benefit accounts.

Example II
Banking Group—Investment Division
Status of Compliance Validation Identified Issues

Banking Trust & Investments	Total Assets	Report Number	Report Date	Comp Rating	Risk Rank
	500B	12345	5/10/9?	1	5

Significant Findings		Corrective Action	Target Completion Date			Rev#
			Orig.	Revised	Actual	
I.	New Account Openings—Poor account opening process; weaknesses in adequacy and completeness of documentation; lack of proper legal review.	I. Account opening process must be reorganized with new procedures under development. Management team must be put in place to implement proper documentation and reviews	4/15	5/15		1
II.	Asset Reviews—Asset reviews not done in accordance with corporate policy.	II. New asset review process to be developed.	4/15	5/15		1
III.	SEC Disclosure Rule—Not uniformly followed.	III. Formal process and controls will be established to ensure conformity. Staff will be educated on the important of this policy.	3/15		3/30	

Example II (continued)
Banking Group—Investment Division
Status of Compliance Validation Identified Issues

Banking Trust & Investments	Total Assets	Report Number	Report Date	Comp Rating	Risk Rank
	500B	12345	5/10/9?	1	5

Significant Findings	Corrective Action	Target Completion Date			Rev#
		Orig.	Revised	Actual	
IV. Brokers—Brokers dealt with are not on Approved Brokers list; evidence of investment authority being exercised that was not empowered by the governing instrument.	IV. Brokerage committee will be reorganized. Brokerage placement policy and procedure will be developed. Key operating procedures to include controls to ensure only use of approved brokers.	3/15	4/15	4/30	1
V. Customer Fees—Fee tables in system (which dictate fees charged) do not match negotiated fees in contract.	V. Fee table database not updated. To update automated system and implement verification control.	3/15	3/30		1
VI. Record Keeping Requirements—Trade tickets were not time stamped or order dated.	VI. To purchase time stamper and create log.	4/15	5/15		1
VII. Policy and Procedures—A current and comprehensive policy and procedure manual does not exist.	VII. To develop comprehensive policy and procedures manual for entire operation.	6/15			

12

Module V—Strong Compliance and Risk Management Controls

Strong and effective controls are essential in order to ensure sound compliance and strong risk management. There are several beginning steps for implementing strong controls: understanding the definition of a control, identifying where the controls should be, installing controls that are not there, removing controls that don't belong, and modifying the remaining desired controls.

Keep in mind that simplicity, flexibility, and necessity are three vital characteristics of controls which will produce a strong and efficient process.

Defining a control. There are essentially two types of controls; the first is a control that requires an event to be executed in a specific way, such as a stop sign, red light, and so on. We call this type of control "rules." The second type of control is any system or function that regularly assesses the effectiveness and accuracy of a process and identifies any inconsistency, inaccuracy, or exception in that same process. The control does this by verifying the accuracy of the results of the process either by periodic testing, sampling, or performing a procedure that mimics but not duplicates the original process. The control can look at every transaction processed or just a selected number. The identified risk of the process usually dictates the extent of the control and the verification of the process. An example of this would be the traffic cop with his radar gun.

Another example of this would be the authorization requirements of cash disbursements. An organization could establish a control that requires only a manager's signature for all disbursements under $5,000, a vice-president's signature for anything over $5,000 and up to $1 million, and the president's signature for anything over $1 million. This control would then cause the president to review only specific transactions, not every one. Another example is a control such as a compliance validation that only assesses the accuracy and effectiveness of a process on a periodic basis, perhaps two or four times a year, and not at every occurrence.

A control is not a procedure that duplicates the original process. It must verify it from a different approach. This is important because if there is a flaw or inefficiency in the process, simply redoing the process will repeat the entire event and make it difficult to identify any problems. In other words problems may not be as apparent when the same route is taken; if they were then a control would not be needed. The problem would be seen as the process is being performed. Besides all this, repeating a process is a gross waste of resources. It also defeats the purpose of a control, which is to identify problems in a cost effective fashion. If confidence about a process is so low that the process must be repeated to ensure that it is giving correct results, then that process should be changed. It obviously is error prone and inefficient.

Identifying where the controls should be. Putting the controls in the right place is critical for effective processes. For long-lasting effectiveness, the controls must be integrated and become part of the process. As in our driving example, the traffic compliance controls have become part of the process of driving your car. The driver essentially executes the controls (following signals, speed limits, etc.) as part of the overall scheme of transportation. The additional controls—policemen, radar and so on—oversee and monitor the entire system, processes and controls alike. This is done for the most part without disruption of the system except where violations occur, such as speeding etc. Having the process completed and then executing the controls is cumbersome, time consuming, and inefficient. What eventually happens over time to a control that takes extra effort is short-cutting and sometimes even total avoidance so the control does not have to be executed.

Perhaps one of the best ways to identify the need for controls is through a 12-Point Risk Oriented Compliance Validation, where a step-by-step evaluation is performed on the identified process. Employing this process will allow you to identify the necessary review areas and assign a risk ranking to determine the need and extent of any necessary controls. It is also a good starting point for understanding the process and ensuring that it is fully effective.

Installing those controls that are not there, removing those that don't belong, and assessing and modifying the remaining desired controls. After the compliance validation is complete you will be in a position to evaluate the need for additional controls and assess the existing controls to determine whether they need to be revised or eliminated.

- Through employment of the validation, identify key policies, processes, and practices and assess their associated controls, if any, for effectiveness and utility. Determine any need for creation, revision, or removal of those controls. All three areas, creation, revision, and removal are equally important. Not having a control where one belongs, having a control where it is unnecessary, and having poorly designed and functioning controls can all cause increased risk, reduced effectiveness, and poor productivity. *It is critical to understand the importance of management's involvement in this entire process. Management has the best expertise and knowledge of their area of responsibility. The compliance or risk management people can assist and train management on how to identify and assess their processes and controls, but management ultimately knows what does and does not work. Any final evaluation of controls must include management involvement; no implementation or changes should be made without the understanding and input of the area management.*

- Develop a priority listing of concerns, an action plan, and timetable to address any issues. *This can be accomplished either individually by the manager, if the issues are isolated, or by utilizing a management team for development of the resolution where it is appropriate.*

- Using the priority listing, systematically execute each action plan and revise each identified weak process and control. Be sure to update the policy and procedure manuals where necessary. *It is important to keep senior and other appropriate management informed of any major issues and/or planned changes.*

Besides the specific controls, there are also some general organization-wide controls that are very effective, such as a Compliance Certification Program and a Risk Management Review Committee, both of which we will discuss next.

The Total Business Compliance Certification Program

The Total Business Compliance Certification Program is an essential part of the Integrated Compliance and Total Risk Management Program as it effectively guarantees proper compliance and risk assessment at the source of occurrence, thereby allowing for a pro-active management approach instead of a reactive management response. This will always result in lower risk, liability, and reduced losses.

What the certification program means to the organization is a highly cost effective way to enjoin management in the detail of ensuring the compliance soundness, strong risk management, and productivity and effectiveness of their areas of responsibility. In doing this it allows management to get a current and valuable assessment of their area without major disruption of the department, which often occurs when utilizing a third party auditor or compliance person. Using third party reviewers as compared to having management do it also consumes a considerable amount of time and resources on both sides without giving a greater benefit.

The key components and basic steps of this program are:

1. Line management has the actual responsibility and complete ownership for compliance and risk management in their respective areas. It is the line manager's and not anyone else's job to assure compliance and risk management in the department. The line managers have sole ownership for the success or failure of the effort, and part of their assessment as effective managers must be their management of compliance and risk in their departments. When a difficult or complex situation arises, the line manager must seek help to resolve the issue, which may include involvement of the compliance or audit staff. However, it is not the compliance or audit staff's responsibility to identify and inform the manager of any problems.

2. Line management has the actual responsibility for performing a compliance validation which will then allow a compliance certification by the line manager. In order for a compliance certification to be complete, a compliance validation must first be performed. The validation must be performed by the line manager or someone on his or her immediate staff. It is important that the validation is performed by staff internal to the department as this is critical to the effectiveness of the effort. After the validation is complete and the results are fully understood and documented with any identified problems being addressed, the compliance certification can be completed and verified by the line manager.

3. The compliance department has the responsibility for ensuring that the compliance certification has taken place and is accurate. The compliance department must also assist in the monitoring and resolution of any identified problems. The compliance department is to only assist and not manage or perform the fixes themselves, as it is management's complete responsibility.

4. The compliance department has the responsibility for reporting on the overall soundness of compliance and risk management businesswide. They must collect the completed compliance certification forms from all responsible areas, check them for completeness, but not the complete accuracy of the validation as this is the manager's job, and then make one statement to senior management and the Board of Directors that the organization is compliance sound with any noted exceptions.

    It is important to note that the compliance department should check, from time to time, the accuracy of the validations performed that the certifications are based on. However, it is not the compliance department's responsibility to promise complete accuracy and validity of every validation. If a manager is intentionally misstating the results of a validation or intentionally not performing the validation fully and completely, this is a management problem and not a compliance problem. Every manager must be held fully accountable for all aspects of his or her job and held to the highest standards for all areas, including the compliance validation and certification.

5. The basis of the program is for line management to perform scheduled compliance validation reviews on a regularly scheduled basis. These validations can be done quarterly, semiannually, or annually, depending on the risk sensitivity of the department. Most departments should do them at minimum, twice a year, and all departments should do them at least once a year.

6. The results of the validation reviews are then collected and assessed by line management to determine weaknesses and/or compliance and risk situations. Only after the validation is performed is the compliance certification completed.

7. If a weakness and/or compliance and risk situation is identified by line management, it must be noted in the certification. It is not necessary to detail the problems in the certification unless they are of a very serious nature. Any identified situations must be scheduled to perform the fixes (sometimes assistance from other areas such as compliance is required). These fixes must be documented and tracked through completion.

8. When the validation is complete and the test results finalized, the line manager will complete a certification form attesting to total compliance soundness (listing any exceptions) in his/her area. The compliance certification form must be completed, signed, and sent to the compliance department.

9. The compliance certification form is an official document that is collected and recorded by the compliance department. The certification form should carry the weight of an affidavit signed by the line manager with strong disciplinary action taken against any manager who has not completed the certification in a timely or accurate fashion. If a manager is found to have falsified or intentionally misrepresented or omitted any facts on the certification, then it should be grounds for immediate termination. It is critical to the success of the certification process that it is taken seriously and executed properly. Any half-baked effort is a waste of time and organization resources.

The compliance department collects all of the certifications from each area, notes the exceptions, and tickles them for monitoring and follow-up. After this is complete, the compliance department then makes one general certification to senior management and the directors that the entire bank is compliance sound (with the noted exceptions).

Some of the specific benefits of a compliance certification are:

- *Line management that is very knowledgeable and kept current of area systems and processes.* By employing the compliance certification, it causes the line manager to pay continuous close attention to his or her area's processes and controls because he or she is required to do the assessments, and then attest to their soundness. Quite often line managers, because they are so busy, tend to not review those processes and controls that appear to be working and only concentrate on immediate areas of concern. The certification, in effect, forces the line manager to look at everything, even those processes and controls that appear to be working. Managers who do this get to know their areas of responsibility in an intimate way, become more knowledgeable, and in turn, pass those benefits on to the organization through improved systems in their departments.

- *Strong awareness of compliance and risk management at the grass roots level.* Compliance and risk management no longer becomes something to think about only when there is an audit or an exposed risk in their area. The certification causes the line manager to learn the importance of daily compliance and risk management and all the benefits that grow from this awareness. This is then passed on to the entire staff which follows the lead of their manager.

- *Accountability is placed where it belongs and with the people who can affect the change.* The big "O" or ownership is placed right where it must be, in the lap of the people who do the job. As we discussed before, no one else can be responsible for traffic compliance but the individual driving the car. The driver makes all the decisions of when to stop, go, turn, and what speed to drive. It then follows that no one else but the driver can be held accountable for any traffic law violations. When accountability is placed in the hands of the individual responsible for the action, it gives very strong assurance that the action will be performed properly and thoroughly. Every organization member has a number of responsibilities they must accomplish; they will naturally worry about the most and do the jobs first whose results will reflect upon their performance.

- *Effective use of existing resources.* Instead of calling up a special effort that must be planned, organized, and executed using both third party and departmental resources, to accomplish a review, a compliance certification uses existing departmental resources. Using a certification, the review can be done in stages that are planned around the busiest times of the day and week. It does not force everything to slow, stop, or turn upside down because the third party reviewers have a small time frame and deadlines to meet. Additionally with a certification, since the reviewers are internal to the department and understand it much better than any third party reviewer ever can, the review can be done more completely and in less time. And best of all, when the review is done everyone goes back to their normal routine and the organization does not have to support an entire department of third party compliance reviewers, which can turn into a major bureaucracy very quickly.

- *Lower staff costs by not utilizing whole groups or departments of third party reviewers (checkers and auditors).* Overall organization staff costs are lower since there is no "compliance army" to support. A compliance department is still a good idea, but as in the Barnett Bank example, it need only be a handful of people versus an entire staff of six or ten. Effectively, what is accomplished with a certification is that the review portion of the compliance effort is integrated into the departments instead of having it stand alone with dedicated resources.

- *Ultimate and very beneficial by-products of this approach are increased efficiency, productivity, and overall quality.* This is achieved by having the people who are most expert with the process do the assessment, changes, and implementation rather than being forced to waste time or cause errors through third party miscommunication. Too often it seems that a third party reviewer asks or requires line managers to make changes in their department for the sake of "better control," when that decision is really made out of poor understanding by the third party reviewer. If the line manager abides by this type of request or requirement, it causes inefficiency, possible errors, and greater risk.

Outside Looking in or the Closer You Are the Better the View

Organization XYZ has a central compliance department staffed by dedicated compliance enforcers and reviewers where "better control" requests are routinely made to the line managers. During one particular review the third party compliance enforcers felt that under the current circumstances there was too great of an opportunity for someone internally to forge a client's signature for their own advantage. As a result of their belief, they requested that the line manager update all of the client signatures on an annual basis. This meant that every client had to be sent a document to sign annually so their signature could be kept current on file.

Obviously, the third party compliance people clearly did not understand the organization's clients or the client market, the department, or the real risk of performing this new procedure. If the line manager had agreed to implement this procedure, which fortunately he steadfastly refused, it would have in fact increased the organization's risk in several ways. First there would have been greatly increased loss of client risk due to the suspicion, aggravation, and inconvenience created by these annual requests. Some clients would go elsewhere due to what they would have felt was unprofessional and unnecessary behavior on the part of the organization. Increased organizational risk would also have occurred if additional resources were not secured to accomplish this mammoth task. This would be caused by the other tasks that would have to be ignored in order to perform the annual mailing. Additionally, if more resources were added to do this process it would impact the organization's profitability. And finally, increased risk of forgery, exactly what the compliance people were trying to prevent by this requirement, could actually have occurred. This could easily happen because of all the paper flying back and forth between the client and the department. Surely some people would eventually get confused over which is the current signature, and which client did not respond. This would present an opportunity for someone to just "make up" a new signature.

This entire process in reality would have made it easier for someone to perpetrate a fraud by simply slipping in their handwritten signature in an account that did not respond. They would then have had no trouble at all matching the file signature since it would have actually been theirs. With all of the paper going back and forth, this would have been fairly easy to accomplish.

In this case, the manager, who understood his clients, the market, and his department and the related risk of the suggested procedure, refused to perform the request of the third party compliance people. The manager knew what the consequences would have been and it was very good for the organization he did refuse. Line management, if properly educated for compliance and risk management, will always be in a better position to understand what is best for their department and ultimately the organization. The by-product of this will be increased efficiency, productivity, and overall quality.

The following is an example of a Compliance Certification Form:

Compliance Certification Form

April 15, 199?

Bank Compliance Officer
32nd Floor

Attention: Mr. John Compliance

Re: Quarterly Compliance Certification

Dear John:

This is to confirm that our study and evaluation of the compliance controls that existed during the three months ended March 31, 199?, for the Personal

Trust Administration Department of the Anytown Banking and Trust Company, was made for the purpose of evaluating the compliance controls and overall compliance soundness of the area. Viewed in total they provide reasonable assurance that all functions are performed and transactions executed in accordance with management's authorization and in conformity with the governing policies, procedures, and regulatory laws, and that all records which maintain accountability for the functions and transactions are reliable and represent fairly the intent and correctness in accordance with the above outlined requirements. As a result of our comprehensive review and in accordance with management's authorization, we confirm to the best of our belief, the following representations:

1. We are responsible for a system of internal compliance and risk management controls that provide management reasonable assurance that the functions and transactions which we have responsibility for are safeguarded, and transactions are executed in accordance with management's authorization and in conformity with the governing instruments. It should be understood that in designing compliance and risk management control procedures, estimates and judgments are required by management to assess and balance the relative risk, cost, and expected benefit of such compliance control procedures. Further, because of the inherent limitations of any system of internal compliance controls, errors and/or risk situations may nevertheless occur; however, every effort is made to remedy these errors and/or risk situations immediately upon their detection and all such errors and/or risk situations of a material nature are immediately brought to the attention of senior management and the compliance department.

2. The description of the internal compliance control procedures followed by the Personal Trust Administration Department are detailed in the appropriate sections of the following manuals which are updated regularly:

    Anytown Banking and Trust Company
    Personal Trust Administration
    Fiduciary Key Policy and Procedure Manual
    Computer Systems Key Policy Procedural Manual
    Record Safe Keeping Key Policy and Procedure Manuals

3. We have not knowingly withheld from senior management or the compliance department any information, material or otherwise, that in our judgment would be relevant to the accuracy of our comprehensive review and the understanding and clear definition of the compliance soundness of our department.

4. There have been no irregularities involving any member of management and/or staff that could materially impact, in even a minor way,

the system of internal compliance controls or the compliance soundness of the department.

5. There are no significant adjustments to the bank and trust company's
    books and records (including unrecorded adjustments) that have not
    been disclosed now or in previous reviews.

6. To the best of our knowledge there are no, nor have there been, any
    representations made by us or exist as a result of other events not in
    our control, that may present the facts or condition of our depart-
    ment or its internal functions as being of compliance soundness
    when in fact this is not the case.

7. We understand and fully acknowledge that if any information, mate-
    rial fact, or condition stated or represented in this document is inten-
    tionally or knowingly false it can lead to disciplinary action up to and
    including termination.

I, Mr. Lyne Manager, attest that to the best of my knowledge the Personal
Trust Administration Department is generally compliance sound and that
the above is true and without any intentional misstatements or omissions.

Signed this Day of April 15th, 199?

_____

Lyne Manager

The Risk Management Review Committee

The Risk Management Review Committee is a group of organization managers who have direct responsibility for an area or department and have
control over and responsibility for organization members who perform
tasks that have some degree of risk. The committee is typically made up of
one manager from each area or department; this way each department and
area is represented.

The Risk Management Review Committee can be a very effective tool
for the organization, but care must be taken or it can become another bureaucratic drag on the system. For this reason, the committee must be structured and maintained with very defined rules for operation that focus on a
specific agenda and limited involvement. The last thing any organization
needs is another committee that sticks its nose where it doesn't belong and
tells people how to do things improperly. The committee should meet, discuss, and adjourn with concise and well-defined instructions to issue
throughout the organization. If this cannot be done at any time, the committee should withhold comment until such time that it can provide useful
information.

Below is the definition of the structure, intent, and tasks of the committee as well as the string of benefits from an efficiency and regulatory standpoint.

The Risk Management Review Committee would be responsible for the oversight, on a organization-wide basis, of compliance, risk management, assessment, and policies and practices in all areas of the business.

Risk areas defined here include but are not limited to the following:

- Public image
- Loss of client
- Profitability
- Loss of revenue or funds through errors
- Loss of revenue or funds through fraud
- Business fit with current and future plans
- New product review
- Management knowledge about direct competition
- Management expertise in key areas
- Knowledge level (education) of management and staff
  - Conflict of interest
  - Policy and procedure
  - Regulatory
  - Business knowledge
- Risk monitoring and controls
- Strategic and business plans
- Contingency plans
- Regulatory issues

The General Committee Structure

- Appointed and empowered by the Board of Directors with the appropriate authority to perform its responsibilities. The committee must be empowered and given the proper authority, responsibility, and forum to accomplish its goals.
- Meet, at minimum, quarterly or more often when appropriate. The committee must meet often enough to be kept current on important matters and to be able to respond timely to the needs of the organization.
- Meetings must be official and documented by minutes. The meetings should be formally structured so the discussions and results can be documented for effective follow-up and results. The meetings must

not be rigid as to inhibit lively and creative discussion, but they should be organized so the most is accomplished while taking the least amount of time.

- Every business area (including auditing, accounting, credit, and so on) must be represented. This is critical if the committee is to be successful and accepted organization-wide. The committee cannot become an elitist group of managers who dictate to the rest of the organization how things should be done. By including every area, recommendations have a much greater opportunity of being comprehensive along with being accepted and implemented.

General Outline of the Committee's Review Oversight Tasks and Responsibilities

The committee's overall responsibility is to ensure, by oversight, that compliance and risk are being properly managed in the organization. This includes the responsibility of efficient use of compliance and risk management resources and the appropriate level of risk tolerance for the organization.

The following are some general areas but the list isn't all inclusive:

- *Oversight of risk assessment and ranking program (at all levels).* Ensure on a periodic basis that there is a program and it is effectively employed in all areas of the organization. These areas include but are not limited to:
  - Account review procedures (new, existing, closed)
  - Product review (new and existing)
  - Environmental concerns
  - Safe keeping of assets, records, and valuables
  - Major function review procedures (error and fraud)
  - Disbursements procedures
  - Accounting records (controls and documentation)
- *Bank Environmental Risk Management Program.* Ensure on a periodic basis that it is effective, current, and covers all concerns.
- *Policy and procedure manuals.* Periodically check that they are current, comprehensive, and properly utilized by all areas of the organization.
  - Be certain all are universally acceptable.
  - Every area has a complete set and is knowledgeable on policies and procedures
- *Insider trading and employee securities pre-clearance policy.* Ensure on a periodic basis that it is current and accurately executed.
  - Business-wide policy and tracking
- *Education and training.* Ensure on a periodic basis that the program is working and covers all the necessary lines of the organization.
  - Conflicts of interest

- Corporate policies (corporate manual, etc.)
- *General area policies and procedures.* Ensure on a periodic basis that all policies and procedures general to the organization are adhered to and added to and/or updated and necessary.
  - Applicable regulations (local, state, and federal)
  - Cross-training of all vital areas
  - Employee personnel policies and procedures
  - Organization's ethical standards and practices
  - Compliance validation program
  - Compliance certification program
- *Contingency plans.* Ensure on a periodic basis that the emergency contingency plans for all of the appropriate areas have been tested and are current and clearly defined.
  - Standards and review
- *Strategic plans.* Ensure on a periodic basis that the strategic plan is understood and appropriately followed by the organization.
- *Departmental business plans.* Ensure on a periodic basis that all of the departments have a business plan that is appropriate, current, and adhered to on a timely basis.
- *Audit programs are comprehensive and look at the right things.* Ensure on a periodic basis that all of the audit programs cover the current risk areas and test for organization-wide compliance and risk management.
- *New product review.* Examine and review all new product considerations for the appropriate business fit and all risk considerations. The committee must consider the overall impact and benefit to each and every area of the organization. The committee must also ensure that all new products have been given the necessary legal and cost/benefit considerations.
  - No new product can be introduced or even tested without the approval of the committee.
- *New policy and procedures review (objective setting for all accounts etc.).* Examine and review all new organization policies and procedures to ensure they are compliance sound, and consider proper risk management.
  - All corporate policy and procedures must be reviewed by the committee for sound compliance and risk management.
- *New systems review including enhancements, changes, and deletion of existing programs.* Review all proposed and new systems for sound compliance and risk management.
  - All new systems must be reviewed and approved by the committee before installation.

- The introduction of new and review of existing software and service vendors.
- *Adequate insurance coverage at all levels.* The committee must consider and review on a periodic basis that adequate insurance coverage in all appropriate areas is in place and kept current. The committee also must review and periodically assess the credit worthiness of the insurance underwriters.
  - Develop standards for coverage.
  - Develop standards and qualifications of underwriters (credit rating, asset size etc.).
- *Regulatory exam preparation (OCC, SEC, FDIC, etc.).* Review and keep informed about all regulatory examinations to ensure proper preparation and follow-up for resolution of all identified issues.
  - The intent here is not to duplicate the audit and examining committee but to verify that the preparation process in general is sound.
- *Ensure that the Board of Directors and audit committees have the right level of knowledge and understanding.* Keep the communication lines open with the right level of information given to senior management. Current and continuous flow of information to the directors, audit committee, and senior management will secure their involvement and support on all important matters.
  - Ensure that they are properly informed and have the appropriate level of information and resources available.
- *Standardization of like policies and procedures.* Review all of the major policies and procedures to confirm that there is no duplication and that there is consistency throughout the organization. It is especially important for the policies and procedures to be the same throughout the organization. It causes confusion, inefficiency, and lost productivity when the same process or function is done differently in separate parts of the organization.

Some major benefits of a program are:
- The Board of Directors, concerned committee members, and senior management will find it an exceptionally useful resource for important information as well as a security blanket for their individual compliance responsibilities. With all of the increasing responsibilities and liabilities that directors, committee members, and senior management are being exposed to, it is more important than ever for them to be well informed.
- The regulators (OCC, SEC, FDIC, state, etc.) will look upon this type of effort with extremely good favor as it is precisely what they suggest— a central body of appropriate and informed business managers re-

viewing all relevant facets of the business from a compliance and risk perspective.

- It will allow the business to become more efficient, as important implementations and changes will be reviewed by all areas and not isolated to certain groups. This will negate the situation of a change being made in one area without another affected area not being part of the decision. It greatly increases communication across all levels of the organization and also increases the individual understanding and appreciation of each department.

- There will be a healthy exchange of knowledge and learning from each area's successes and failures. Cross-pollination of ideas and experiences can only help strengthen the organization from a compliance and risk management perspective. It also helps on the individual level in building a stronger organizational culture and a greater sense of teamwork.

- It is a central forum to surface potentially serious problems quickly for resolution before they are critical (pro-active instead of reactive). When serious or potential problems arise, the committee can meet immediately to discuss and determine the best course of action. Instead of serious problems floundering around the organization until they grab enough people's attention, there is a formal body that can act quickly before the risk or loss gets too great.

Module VI—Well and Consistently Informed Management and Staff

Senior management, middle management, and staff must be kept fully informed in order to provide adequate support for compliance and risk management. Communication is key to the effectiveness of every compliance and risk management program; the more people who know, the better their overall judgment and the quicker they can come to the correct decision. When senior management all the way down to the staff is kept fully informed to the degree necessary to perform their jobs effectively, they will be happier, more productive, and generally more dedicated along with making fewer mistakes.

Don't rely on the need-to-know principle where an organization member is giving only that information that it is felt they "need-to-know." Along with individuals' ability to perform their jobs it causes several other problems. Individuals may think they are being given limited information because they cannot be trusted, they are not important enough, there is a secret or something going on that must be hidden from them, or it is a way to keep them in the dark so they can be taken advantage of. All of these reasons may not be true, but every one of them has the potential to seriously hurt morale, productivity, and overall effectiveness.

It is obvious that everyone cannot or should not be told everything, but some organizations seem to spend more effort and resources keeping information from individuals that can or should have it than they do in keeping everyone properly informed. Enough cannot be said about the importance of strong communication throughout an organization. It has been consistently shown that the best run and strongest organizations are those that make a special effort to keep everyone informed at all levels. It is usually not that difficult and does not take any special talent or resource expense; the resulting benefits are tremendous.

On the individual level, when people are properly informed they feel they are: important, trusted by the organization, and better prepared to do their job. They feel that the organization is more honest with them, which usually creates a better sense of loyalty and a stronger sense of teamwork; everyone is part of the same team. From an organizational level, when the communication lines are stronger, information is passed quicker, more efficiently, and more accurately. All of this spells greater efficiency, productivity, lower cost, and reduced risk. Reduced reliance on the "rumor mill" is always a good thing no matter how one looks at it. It also helps tremendously when organization members move to different departments or areas as their assimilation, learning curve, and discomfort are greatly reduced.

Some helpful ways to increase organizational communication:

- Establish formal compliance and risk management briefings with the company Board of Directors, audit and examining committees, and senior management. Depending on the level of risk and the problems involved the meetings can be done on a quarterly basis or semiannually with interim sessions if a special situation warrants. The appropriate structure and level of detail mostly depends on the information being discussed, but also is dependent on the desire of the directors, committee members, and senior management. In general, an overly detailed briefing is not necessary or productive as the audience at this level does not often have the time. The right mix seems to be the most beneficial at this level.

- Hold quarterly compliance and risk management meetings with business heads. As with the most senior level of management, the right mix of information is important. It is critical that the level, detail, and amount of information be determined by the business heads and not by lower management. One cannot act upon something they are not aware of; the business heads must be exposed to everything so they can control the detail flow of the briefing. Typically, the detail is greater than that given to the directors, committees, and senior management but is usually not transactionally detailed unless a special situation warrants.

- As discussed earlier, developing the right training vehicles and creating strong information conduits, be they group meetings, information services both written and verbal, or formal documents, can build strong, effective, and long-lasting communication channels that satisfy virtually all information needs. As can be seen, none of these methods are terribly time consuming or very costly.

For the sake of efficiency we have duplicated here a small portion of Chapter 6.

a. *Hold regularly scheduled compliance and risk management training sessions.* This should be a series of training sessions both regularly scheduled and as needed. The periodic meetings should be on recurring topics, such as conflict of interest, ethics, insider trading, and so on, that need constant discussion. The as needed sessions would be for new hires, transfers, or special compliance and risk situations that recently occurred or are relevant to the organization and require discussion.

b. *Create formal information services in the organization.*
   - These can be monthly or quarterly compliance newsletters or electronic mail newsletters. Discussed in the monthly or quarterly letters should be:
     - Areas of special concern
     - Compliance and risk considerations for new and existing products or businesses
     - Upcoming or recent audits or examinations
     - Failings of other organizations that have an important lesson
     - Success stories of other organizations that have an important lesson
     - Actual or expected changes in government regulation that could affect the organization
     - Ideas for open discussion
     - Suggestions, recommendations, observations, and so on.
   - Regular circulation of commercial publications. Choose the most relevant and useful publications and circulate either parts or the whole to the appropriate individuals.
   - Compliance and risk alert document for special situations. This is used for situations where there is serious risk or actual loss sustained by your organization or another organization. It will alert the appropriate individuals to take the necessary action for prevention of similar future events. This compliance alert can also be used for changes in the regulatory environment.

c. *Hold regularly scheduled key compliance and risk management meetings.* Meetings and discussions should be held regularly at all levels of the organization from the Board of Directors on down to the clerical level. The content of the meetings will vary depending on the group with a big picture perspective for the Board of Directors and specific detailed content for the particular areas. The important thing is to keep compliance and risk management current in all the organization members' minds as well as their daily activities. This can only be done with constant discussion and dialog. It is also very important to emphasize recurring themes such as fraud, conflict of interest, ethical behavior, and so on.

Keeping everyone appropriately informed is the life-blood of the compliance and risk management program. A compliance department, a compliance officer, or any single group of individuals cannot possibly see or do everything. A continuous flow of the right amount of information (not too much, not too little) can cause the entire organization to work as one with the recognition that compliance is *everyone's* responsibility.

d. *Hold regularly scheduled group risk assessment discussions.* These discussions can be informal talks between the line manager and his or her staff which concentrate on group needs, growing pains, and areas of general, immediate or specific concern. They should not be complaint sessions for group members to criticize each other but rather a way to continually assess the entire group or individual aspects thereof and how changes may or may not improve things. Always look for the better way because it is ever changing. The better way today might not be so tomorrow due to changing needs, environment, requirements, or even technology. Never accept the statement that "it has worked fine for the past five years so why change now." The more that is understood and the more knowledgeable everyone in the area is, the more effective will be the compliance and risk assessment of the individual departments and ultimately the organization.

An example of some key compliance meetings:

Key Compliance Meetings

How the right structure can build a strong communication network

Below is a sample listing of regularly scheduled compliance meetings held in some organizations. All of these meetings and with the noted frequency may not be necessary in your organization; however, it is a good model to work from. Keeping the right people informed will always benefit the organization, often in previously unforeseen ways.

Key Compliance Meetings

Meeting	Frequency	Attendance
Business Head Compliance Review	Quarterly	Business Head Management Directors Compliance Director (and other required

Meeting	Frequency	Attendance
Board of Directors Compliance Review	Quarterly	Board of Directors Compliance Director
Audit and Examining Committee Compliance Review	Semiannually	Audit and Examining Committee members Compliance Director (and other required
Management Directors Compliance Review	Quarterly	Management Directors Compliance Director (and other required
Department Managers Compliance Review	Quarterly and as needed	Department Managers Supervisors Staff Compliance Director (and other required
Compliance Seminars	Annually	All management and staff as required Compliance Director and staff

Module VII—
Adequate Staffing in the
Business Units

In order for the compliance function to be successful it must have dedicated resources in the unit areas and departments. There must be consistent and thorough application of the compliance and risk management effort. This is best accomplished by having identified and dedicated resources allocated to the effort. This does not mean, however, that the resources identified must be solely dedicated to the compliance and risk management effort, as this is not always the most efficient use of resources. Shared resources are not only more efficient and cost effective but they can also work better. This is often true because a shared resource usually has a broader knowledge base and a greater perspective on things due to its involvement in more than one task.

This is simply another way to integrate compliance and risk management into the fabric of the organization and its everyday operations. One of the best ways to accomplish this integrated compliance and risk management effort, or shared resource, is through the use of the compliance designate concept. We have talked about it briefly throughout this work; we will now go into greater detail.

The Compliance Designate

The compliance designate is a nonconventional, but very useful, and productive approach to the compliance team. Instead of the organization having a large compliance staff that must work from the outside in, an actual staff member in the department is designated with certain compliance responsibilities. This individual will normally have daily departmental responsibilities; however, a portion of his or her time is dedicated to compliance and risk management responsibilities. In most cases only a fraction of the individual's time (15%–25%) may be directly compliance and risk management related; the other portion is spent performing normal department tasks along with a constant attention to compliance and risk management needs. The person becomes a helpful tool without the burden of extra employees.

Basic Responsibilities

The compliance designates are typically not senior members of the department. They are usually individuals who cross or can cross all areas and levels of the department. They must report directly to the department or line manager and not to the compliance department. It is very critical that this individual is not regarded as a "snoop" for the compliance department or for senior management. The compliance designate must be viewed by all members in the department as an information conduit, an expediter, as a central depository for compliance and risk management concerns, and as an additional resource available when a department member needs special assistance with a compliance or risk management concern. The designate is not responsible for the individual compliance and risk management matters of each department member. Everyone has ownership of their own compliance and risk management; the designate is there to assist them in fulfilling their responsibility.

The compliance designate must:

- Acquire basic knowledge and understanding of the laws, regulations, and corporate policy that directly affects his or her area. *A simple study of the laws, regulations, and corporate policy that directly affect the department is basically required. The designate is not required to become any sort of expert.*

- Review and be thoroughly familiar with the area and department policy and procedure manual. *He or she should essentially know this document inside out as it is the reference tool for the department and an information source.*

- Keep the department fully informed on all relevant compliance requirements, matters, and problems. *Simple informal discussions or a memo with brief comments is all that is usually needed. At times, the designate may actually hold group discussions depending on the importance of the issue.*

- Act as focal point for the department compliance and risk management issues. *It is essential that the compliance designate be very visible and accessible to all members of the department and have an open dialog with the department manager.*

- Keep fully informed and understand the audit programs, approach, technique, and requirements. *A very helpful beginning here is to have designates actually spend time or conduct an audit of another area. This gives them a strong understanding of the audit process that will prove extremely helpful for the preparation of upcoming audits in their department.*

- Assist in the area preparation of all audits. *The auditors typically send an introduction letter announcing the upcoming audit and requesting information and documentation beforehand. The designate should be the one who coordinates and collects this information for the auditors.*

- Act as major information source during all audits. *The designate can expedite audits by gathering information before the auditors arrive and act as a focal point for new information requests by the auditors. This could be very beneficial to the department as it will lessen the disruption auditors may cause during their information requests and also help the auditors to be more efficient by getting information more accurately and quickly.*

- Coordinate and/or perform the department compliance validation. *The designate is a good candidate for performing the validation because he or she is probably the one individual most familiar with the department and will greatly increase their understanding and knowledge of the department.*

- Be responsible for the coordination of all area compliance and risk management education needs. *They should help identify along with the line manager and note individual educational needs, coordinate with the compliance department for education seminars and meetings, and keep the department compliance library current and complete.*

Effectiveness

Once this approach is used many advantages become clear:

- It is cost effective from a resource standpoint as a large compliance staff is not needed and resources are not solely dedicated to the compliance effort. The shared resource scheme is more cost effective and efficient.

- It is effective from a compliance standpoint as firsthand information is easier to obtain because the designate is already a member of the department and therefore knows his or her way around. Since the designate is also part of the department he or she is not looked upon as an "outsider" and will normally have access to more accurate and thorough information.

- It is a more productive use of resources as the designate knows the department well and therefore does not have to "learn it first" before performing a compliance monitoring or testing function. *No matter how well a compliance officer may know an area, he/she will never know it as well as an informed department member. Normal changes do occur (if only in personnel) that would require the compliance officer to investigate whereas the designate would learn these things as they occur, negating the need to thoroughly study the department.*

- It is a more efficient use of resources from a time standpoint, as in most cases it is not necessary to have a third party, full-time compliance monitoring and testing function. Since the designate uses only a portion of his or her time performing this function, a full-time compliance officer for the department is not required.

- It raises departmental awareness of compliance and risk management, as having a daily compliance presence in the department causes the management and staff to focus on compliance regularly. It also reinforces the fact that they have ownership of compliance and not a non-departmental or third party individual.

- The designate is flexible, depending on the needs of the department. If it is a low risk department, less time is spent by the designate on compliance and risk management, and vice versa if it is a high risk situation. Also, if a crisis arises the designate can shift efforts temporarily towards that crisis; be it a compliance or departmental crisis. *Since time is shared between tasks, temporary suspension on either side will not prove overly deleterious to the department.*

Module VIII—Internal Audit as a Team Member

The internal audit department of most organizations is not typically looked upon as a team member in any sense of the word. Independence is the favorite and major declaration of the audit staff. No one will argue that independence is critical for the overall effectiveness of any audit department, but it must not be confused with isolation. Isolation occurs when the concept of independence is exaggerated. What then happens is that the auditors end up continually looking from outside in and losing perspective of their job and the organization.

For fear of compromising independence the auditors do not: share their audit programs and even the results; they do not have constant and open discussions with management; they are located in a different building with locked doors with a controlled entrance; they rarely attend management or organization meetings; they practice and specialize in the surprise appearances; they do not consider line management input on what or how they should conduct their audits; they look upon the adversarial us-against-them relationship as proof of their independence; and they feel that their expertise on control and risk management is considerably better than that of line management. All of this really has nothing to do with independence and everything to do with ineffectiveness, since in reality it isolates the audit effort from the rest of the organization, which inhibits them from having a good understanding and perspective on what is important.

Can We Talk?

A banking organization was going to be examined by the Office of the Comptroller of the Currency (OCC) for regulatory compliance. The exam was to take place in approximately three months, so the organization had some time to prepare. Management was concerned that their compliance and risk management effort was sufficiently comprehensive and that it covered the points most important to the OCC. The OCC had recently made some major changes in their exam approach and their concept of what should be important to the organization from a compliance and risk management perspective. The changes the OCC made were sweeping as they moved away from individual and isolated compliance violations and instead concentrated on management structure, knowledge, and expertise along with a strong focus on process and control. Understandably, management was concerned that they were going to be properly prepared and that their current approach would satisfy the OCC. They decided to turn to the auditors for help in understanding the OCC's new approach and in the assessment of their current compliance situation.

The auditors of this particular organization placed the utmost emphasis on their independence. They showed this both symbolically by placing their offices in a city separate from the areas they audited and organizationally by keeping auditor-management communication at a minimum. Any auditor contact with the line outside of an audit had to be conducted through the proper channels and through formal discussions. Nothing was to happen that might appear to compromise the independence of the audit department.

Management, on the other hand, mistakenly looked upon the audit department as a resource for guidance, information, and assessment. With this in mind they approached the audit department to ask for their input and help in understanding the new OCC guidelines. They thought to ask the auditors to jointly review the OCC approach and make an assessment on where they stood in regard to overall compliance. To the great shock of management, the auditors refused under the claim of compromising their independence. The audit department felt that if they assisted the line with assessment and preparation on the OCC approach, they would have become a tool of management and no longer capable of being fully objective. This entire line of thinking was of course totally ludicrous, but since the auditors were isolated from the rest of the organization for so long they not only felt that they were not a part of the organization, they also lost touch with the organization's needs and their true and actual role.

Management saw this refusal as just another example of the audit department's adversarial behavior and another attempt at sabotage to make them look bad. It was also more proof of why they must hide everything possible from the auditors and cooperate with them as little as possible.

Our story ends with an ironic twist as management took it upon themselves to perform the review and assessment and ended up being in very good shape. They passed their OCC examination with flying colors and saw the OCC cancel a review of the bank for the following year. Since the OCC deemed the bank in good condition, they were placed on a two-year cycle until further notice. The only negative comments the OCC had on the review were not directed toward management but toward the audit department. The OCC found that the audit programs were not comprehensive or current and did not focus on the right risk areas. The auditors and the Audit Committee both received a strong reprimand by the OCC to revise their entire audit focus and update and/or change all of the audit programs. The audit department had been told by the OCC that they were too isolated from the organization. Management, which was trying for years to do exactly that, got two things out of the OCC's comments: more cooperation from the audit department going forward and a small chuckle.

The internal audit department can work very closely with management while sharing almost everything and still keep their independence. As long as the audit department keeps its objectivity and does not allow itself to be unduly influenced by management, they can move back into the organization and become part of the "team" for the benefit of everyone. This includes sharing the audit programs and understanding with management. Auditors can talk to and work closely with management and still keep their independence.

Keeping in touch with management is an important part of the auditor's success, but the other critical aspect is having audit programs that are comprehensive and look at the right things. Audit is a key link in the sound compliance and risk management chain, so it must be strong and cover all the necessary aspects of the organization. To do this the auditors must employ comprehensive and competent audit programs. Below are some of the major points that must be considered in the evaluation of the audit programs:

- Review all of the audit programs to determine if they have the most effective focus for ensuring that the bank meets compliance, risk management, and regulatory requirements. *Does the audit program consider things such as: organizational structure, management knowledge, and expertise in key areas; effective training programs, proper insurance, and legal guidance; emergency contingency planning, new and existing product review, and so on. Ensure that the approach considers all risk aspects and does not only concentrate on transactional testing.*

- Review all of the audit programs to determine if they are consistent in their application and execution. *Ensure that the programs can identify like functions in different areas and businesses and that the audit approach is consistent in its application throughout the organization. Verify that management has a good understanding of the audit programs and their application and that they know what to expect. Nothing the auditors do should surprise management. There should be full understanding from management on audit's approach, purpose, and function in the organization network. This must not be confused with surprise audits; there are times when it is necessary for the audit department to perform a surprise audit in an area or depart-*

ment. Management should be aware that a surprise audit can occur which is different from audit doing something that surprises management. The purpose of the audit department is to monitor, test, and validate that the organization is functioning as expected; it is not to see how many times they can find a management screw-up.

- Review all of the audit programs to determine if they have a process and control orientation and not a transactional focus. *Audit should discuss the difference between a transactional audit and a process and control review. They should review with management how a transactional approach is ineffective and a control and process review is a stronger risk assessment tool. Although every audit must have transactional testing to verify condition, the audit approach must focus on process and control.*

- Review the audit scope to determine if it covers all of the appropriate areas and functions. *Each area should be broken down into its critical components and mapped to the current audit scope to determine if everything is appropriately covered by the audit. It may be determined that certain areas, departments, or functions are not reviewed annually. This should be a conscious decision and not one made by default. Every year the audit scope should be reviewed or revised where necessary. No organization stays unchanged from one year to the next; things get added, deleted, or modified, and so must the audit program. Working off of last year's program and simply filling in the blanks is a sure way to miss something important that has happened.*

In summary, the effective audit program must have a strong organizational focus. It must be consistently applied throughout the organization with a process and control orientation and have a complete scope to cover all required areas.

Part IV

Compliance Ownership and Accountability

16

Developing a Risk-Based Compliance Team

Compliance and risk management is not any one individual's or any specific group of individuals' responsibility; it is a daily activity that is everyone's responsibility. Every member who has a job to do in the organization has the complete ownership of the compliance and risk management of their actions. This concept must be part of the organization's culture so it becomes an accepted way of doing things. Everyone must be held accountable for his or her own actions; compliance and risk management is no exception. The trick is to build it into the processes and controls, so it becomes invisible to the individual performing the function. This is not only possible, it should be an organizational goal.

There are numerous benefits to compliance as a team approach, not the least of which is the decommissioning of the compliance army. The need for a whole army of compliance people or auditors who perform ineffectual, after-the-fact checking and testing on historical events becomes unnecessary. Besides the point that this approach does not work (and causes considerable expense through increased liability and errors), it is very costly in terms of personnel. Though already discussed earlier, a list of compliance teamwork benefits is presented again as a powerful reminder:

- More efficient operations
- Reduced personnel
- More responsive and flexible system
- Better educated management and staff
- Increased productivity
- Reduced overall risk
- Reduced overall cost

Developing an Integrated Compliance and Risk Management Team

In developing an integrated team, the first place to start is to compile a team of competent individuals and define their general responsibilities for the integrated compliance and risk management effort. Clear understanding of every member's role, along with top down management support of each member's responsibilities, is critical for success.

Team members

- *The Board of Directors.* A strong integrated compliance and risk management program must start at the top. Every member of the board must be fully committed to the effort. It must be understood that sound compliance and risk management is good business practice and not something that is forced upon the organization. *The board must be kept informed of concerns, problems and benefits if they are to continually support the program.*

- *The Committees (Fiduciary, Audit, Examining, etc.).* The committees must support the program through their general oversight enforcement of compliance. *Their review must focus on compliance and demand that management supports the evidence of compliance effectiveness and not simply give verbal defense.*

- *Senior management.* They must preach compliance and foster its understanding throughout the organization. *Compliance effectiveness is a downward flow in the organization. It must start at the top or it is doomed to failure. Senior management must make it understood that compliance is everyone's responsibility and it is good business by talking, showing, and demonstrating compliance.*

- *Line management.* Must practice compliance and risk management every minute of every day. No process or task must be developed or performed without integrating compliance into it. No matter how small the task, if it is important enough to perform, it is important enough to practice sound compliance and risk management. *Line management must understand that they have ownership of compliance in their area. Others may help to assess and monitor it but complete ownership is theirs.*

- *Staff.* Must also practice compliance and risk management every minute of every day. If they spot a compliance issue they must report it immediately to their management and encourage their management to keep them well informed. *It is management's responsibility to train and educate staff on compliance awareness and specific policies and regulations.*

- *The Compliance Department.* Must ensure compliance soundness throughout the entire organization. They do this through monitoring, training, assisting, and reporting on compliance and risk management.

They must ensure that the board, committees, and senior management are kept well informed and that line management is practicing effective compliance. They must be responsible for "auditing the auditors" by verifying that all internal audit programs are comprehensive and effective. They must monitor, train, and where necessary, be a part of the fix.

- *Internal audit.* The auditors are effectively the policemen of compliance and risk management. They are there to spot the violations and identify the weaknesses. Compliance and risk management testing must always be a part of their audit programs. *The internal auditors are an essential part of the compliance program and overall compliance soundness of the organization. They are the real litmus test.*

- *Legal counsel.* The lawyers are a strong resource that should be used efficiently. Because of their expense, they should not be consulted for every action. They should be utilized to help define and identify a potential liability situation, regulatory violations, and civil concerns. *Don't wait until after the organization has been sued to bring the attorneys into the picture.*

Compliance Oversight and Responsibility

Responsibility of oversight for compliance and risk management rests in the three upper levels of management. It is their job to guarantee that the right programs are in place and are supported by adequate processes and controls along with the availability of appropriate resources. These three upper levels must provide strong and continuous support for the entire program through review, guidance, verbal discussion, reward, and recognition. The three upper levels are:

- Board of Directors
- Fiduciary, Examining, and Audit committees.
- Senior Management

Actual compliance takes place in the line areas and is the complete responsibility of line management. This is where the ownership and actual execution occurs.

Board of Directors and Audit Committee Responsibilities

The involvement of the Board of Directors must go beyond what has been in some cases traditional support of senior management until something serious has occurred. It is not suggested that the directors should get involved in the daily management of the organization; they should be very knowledgeable about the organization's strengths, weaknesses, direction, challenges, and opportunities. The board should also be very familiar and have met personally the organization's key management to help support their role in the organization.

The Board of Directors is presumably made up of senior and very successful managers and business people from other organizations. This being the case, they should have a great deal of top level support and guidance to offer the organization in its effort to be successful. If the directors are to simply show up once a quarter to be given a slide show of how great the organization is doing and this becomes their only source of information, they will have little of value to contribute. Some have made the strong argument that the board members do not have the time to get more involved. If this is the case, then perhaps they should resign and make room for members who do.

In many boards there are several hundred years of business experience along with a tremendous amount of brain power and business networking capability. It is up to the organization's managers to tap this fantastic resource. To spoon feed or censor the information to the board does not serve management in the long run; all serious problems and weaknesses that are not dealt with eventually come out. Why not use the Board of Directors as an additional resource? They are a high powered resource that is essentially free.

Board of Director Responsibilities

- Review the organization's strategic and business plan for appropriate direction, business fit, and overall soundness. Ensure that it meets the current and future organization goals. *It is important that the board and senior management see eye to eye on where the organization is going.*

- Each board member must be given a copy of the Key Operating Policy and Procedure Manual for review. Each member should have a general understanding of the document and comment when appropriate. *This is not to suggest that they should read it in detail from cover to cover. Each director should be aware of the document's content and use it as a guide and reference source for future need. The directors should also be made aware of any major policy or procedure changes, deletions, or additions.*

- Review quarterly, the actual financial and business results of the organization in comparison to expectations and plan. *The directors should require from management an explanation for all major variances and exceptions. These explanations should be support with fact and detail and not simply comment that "it is under control." Understand and comment on direction and next steps.*

- Affirm and require on a quarterly basis, evidence of the organization's compliance with the laws, regulations, and corporate policies. *This can be easily accomplished through the organization's compliance certification program. The directors should use this as their main source for compliance information and verification. They should also understand and review:*

1. General fiduciary policy and officially approve.
2. Quarterly Audit Committee's review results, including:
   - Audits
   - Integrated compliance and risk management program
   - Risk assessment policies
   - Management controls

- Periodic review and approval of the organization's major risk areas and functions. *The directors should at minimum annually, review and approve the organization's process and controls for the "high risk" areas such as control and management of assets, cash disbursements, new account acceptance, litigation issues, insurance coverage, etc.*
- Act as the Management Operating Review Committee. Review and pass recommendations on all major operations changes and considerations. *This is not to suggest that the directors become involved in the day-to-day operation of the organization, or even the general detail. They should simply be appraised of any major considerations or changes in the operations of the organization, such as the desire to outsource all of the data processing and close the computer department.*

Audit Committee Functions

Audit and examining committees are being looked upon more and more by the regulators to play an active role in the oversight, monitoring, and management of compliance and risk in the organization. They must take an active role as an independent body that objectively ensures the organization's risk and monitoring systems are working properly. Their major concern must be that the auditors are independent and not isolated, current, and successful in their effort to monitor and test the organization for verification of overall compliance. This of course is done largely through strong comprehensive and effective audit programs.

The audit and examining committees also go beyond the approval of the audit programs to look at the other vehicles the organization uses to ensure sound compliance and risk management. This would include review and understanding of all compliance and risk management programs such as the compliance validation, the compliance certification, any risk identification and ranking programs, training and education programs, emergency contingency plans, and all other top level risk and compliance programs that cross the organization levels. These committees have a special responsibility as an outside independent oversight that can be fully objective and supportive on the organization's management of compliance risk. Like the

Board of Directors, this is another powerful resource. To summarize the key points, the following are presented:

- Each committee member must be given a copy of the Key Operating Policy and Procedure Manual for review. Each member should have a general understanding of the document and comment when appropriate. *This is not to suggest that they should read it in detail from cover to cover. Each committee member should be aware of the document's content and use it as a guide and reference source for future need. The committee members should also be made aware of any major policy or procedure changes, deletions, or additions.*

- Perform a quarterly review and assessment of the organization's Integrated Compliance and Risk Management Program to determine if it meets the needs of the organization. Require documented proof of effectiveness and proper functioning. Review quarterly compliance certification program. *This review doesn't have to be overly detailed, but it should be detailed enough to get a good understanding of the organization's program. Since the program is large and the committee does not meet for more than several hours, they can review separate parts at different meetings and only repeat those topics that are of special concern.*

- Review financial statements and reporting results for major variances and exceptions. Require explanation for any strong fluctuations. *Understanding the financial situation is key to oversight of risk. Strong indicators of where risk "hot spots" are can often be found in the financial reports.*

- Review annually the organization's major risk policies. *Ensure that they are functioning properly, are fully comprehensive, and meet all of the risk management needs of the organization. Among other things consider:*
  - Methodology used for risk assessment
  - Key risk areas and policies
  - Management procedures and controls

- Assess and attest to the internal and external audit independence. Require substantive proof, and if necessary, testimony verifying the independence. *Understand the relationship of the auditors to management to not only confirm their independence but also their understanding of the organization and its needs along with their ability to work effectively with management.*

- Review the plan and scope of the internal audits based on assessment of organization's risk. Determine that is complete and comprehensive. *The committee must ensure that the scope covers all of the appropriate areas and give special review to the new growth areas of the organization. The committee should review the scope and plan with management and get their agreement on its comprehensiveness.*

- Review and formally approve annually the internal audit programs and schedule of audits. Ensure that the programs are comprehensive, updated annually, and with the proper focus on compliance and risk management. *The committee must also review and get testimony of the audit department's approach and staffing. The committee must validate that the audit approach meets the needs of the organization and the regulatory requirements. In doing this they should get comment and feedback from management on their view of the utility of the audit programs. The committee should also review the staffing requirements of the audit department to determine that they are properly trained.*

- Review all internal audit results. Ensure that all major risk issues have been identified and are being addressed by management. *In reviewing the results the committee should make comparisons with the prior year to check progress and require explanation for recurring events. Special attention should be given to regulatory violations and serious risk issues.*

- Give a report to the Board of Directors on a quarterly basis, on the committee's evaluations, conclusions, and recommendations on the condition of the organization's compliance and risk management activities and the effectiveness of its policies, procedures, and controls, and whether the organization administers its activities in accordance with regulation, law, corporate policy, and sound compliance and risk management principles. *This report should not be overly detailed but it must contain accurate assessment and dialog that is clear and concise and provides real benefit to the directors in their understanding of the organization's operations and practices.*

- Review all external audits and examinations by outside accounting firms and government regulators. Ensure that all major risk issues have been identified and are being addressed by management. *In reviewing the results the committee should make comparisons with the prior year to check progress and require explanation for recurring events. Special attention should be given to regulatory violations and serious risk issues.*

Role of Line Management

- Line management has primary responsibility and accountability for complete compliance and risk management in the organization. *Line management has the strongest knowledge of processes and controls and their strengths and weaknesses which translates into effective ability to manage risk and compliance.*
  - Compliance is a daily responsibility
  - Line management and ownership of effectiveness and results
- Keep policies and procedures current and accurate. *The manuals must be updated on a continuous basis and at minimum annually. It is the line manager's responsibility to ensure they are comprehensive, current, and easily accessible to staff and audit.*

- The policy and procedure manual is the how-to book of the manager's world.
- Must be kept current for reference, training, and testing needs.

- Develop and maintain internal compliance controls in their area and department. *These controls must be tested and kept current. Line management should enlist the help of the audit department and the compliance people in the development and assessment of the compliance controls.*
  - Compliance controls must be built into processes and functions.
  - Compliance controls must be maintained and verified for accuracy.

- Develop with compliance and maintain a compliance validation and a compliance certification program for their area and department to identify potential compliance and risk management issues. *The effectiveness of these programs must be assessed on an annual basis.*
  - Compliance validation is a vital compliance management tool.
  - Compliance validation aids greatly in increasing efficiency, productivity, and identifying training needs.
  - Compliance validation allows management to be pro-active instead of reactive.
  - Compliance certification gives assurances to the directors, committees, and senior management on the soundness of line management's practices.

- Take immediate corrective action on all identified issues. *It is line management's complete responsibility to monitor and resolve all problems and required changes in their area or department. If assistance outside of their area or department is needed, it is up to the line manager to request and secure the help. Ownership of final resolution rests in the hands of the line manager.*
  - Responsible for implementing and tracking corrective action even if fixes are not performed by management or their staff.
  - Identify and resolve issues before they become serious.

- Keep staff educated and maintain high compliance awareness. *Working with compliance and the training staff, the line manager must identify, schedule, and ensure that his or her staff is properly trained and educated on an ongoing basis. Keeping the staff current in their respective job functions and compliance and risk management awareness is critical to productivity, efficiency, and sound compliance and risk management.*
  - Require that staff achieve and maintain compliance awareness in applicable areas.
  - Require the training of new staff and the ongoing training of existing staff.
  - Reaffirm the importance of compliance at staff meetings and individual staff reviews.

Role of the Compliance Officer and Compliance Function

- Review the organization's Integrated Compliance and Total Risk Management Program for adequacy and effectiveness. This would include compliance validation, the compliance certification, and a 12-Point Risk Oriented Compliance Review. *Work directly with all levels of management and the audit department to understand the organization's needs, scope, and expectations. Ensure that the program addresses all compliance, risk, and regulatory concerns.*
  - Review control programs at least annually or as requested by management.
  - Verify adequacy, effectiveness, and adherence.
  - Review for lack of controls and implement where required.
  - Review for unnecessary controls and have them dismantled.
  - Keep abreast of current trends in new technology and industry techniques.
- Assist in the development and maintenance of policies, procedures, internal controls, validations, and training and education programs. *It is important for the compliance officer to keep current with all new technology and techniques. Not all of the new approaches will or should be utilized; however, keeping current will make them available for the organization to employ when the time is appropriate. One of the best ways to keep current is through a peer network. Through constant communication with other compliance peers in the industry, the compliance officer can give and get a wealth of current and valuable information.*
  - The key word is *assist* management and not *perform* any of the development or maintenance for management.
  - The compliance officer does not know the area nearly as well as management; therefore, he or she should only assist in the structure and development and not in the detailing of the text.
  - Using industry contacts, interface with peers to discuss issues and methods and share information. *Don't reinvent what already exists.*
  - *Customize success.* Take from elsewhere what already works and customize it for your organization. The "only created here" mentality is time consuming, inefficient, and very costly.
  - Insist on the "keep-it-simple" approach. Complex process or controls are ineffective and often totally useless. They are something to be avoided, not completed. The simpler and more flexible, the better.
- Monitor the organization's management of risk and compliance and the effectiveness of its controls. *The important point is the compliance officer is not responsible for the soundness of the organization's compliance*

and risk management; management has complete ownership and account-ability. The compliance officer is responsible for the maintenance and monitoring of the Integrated Compliance and Total Risk Management Program and ensuring that all of the necessary information is made available to management so they can perform their duties.

- Centrally monitor overall management of compliance, risk, and control of the entire operation through attendance at meetings, review of appropriate documents and information, quarterly, semi-annual or annual compliance meetings with management, confirmation of the management compliance validations, collection and reporting on the compliance certifications, and basic use of good compliance judgment. Keep current with the industry, technology, and government regulation.

- Conduct spot testing to confirm overall compliance. *On a periodic and as needed basis, verify the accuracy of the compliance validations and compliance certifications in the various areas and departments. Do not perform a full scale audit as this would require too much time and resources, and is unnecessary. What the spot review is trying to identify is poor execution by the manager or actual misrepresentation. It should not be the responsibility of the compliance officer to double check every validation. If everyone if fully committed and properly trained, spot reviews are sufficient.*
  - Verify the accuracy and effectiveness of the management compliance validations, the vital processes and controls, training needs, and overall compliance awareness.
  - Do not test transactions, test processes, and controls. If processes and controls are effective the transactions will be fine.

- Act as interface between auditors and examiners. *The compliance officer can act as the information conduit between the manager and the auditor. This can save time on both sides with the efficiencies in communication and information transfer it creates. Since the compliance officer has a good understanding of audit and a general understanding of the manager's department, he or she could expedite the information transfer by preplanning with both the manager and the auditor before the audit. The compliance officer can also act as a mediator at times when there is a misunderstanding, disagreement, or poor communication.*
  - Assist management during all audits and examinations and interface directly with auditors and examiners before and during actual audit or examination.
  - Work closely with internal auditors before, during, and after audits to ensure audit effectiveness and access to all appropriate information and facts.
  - Scrutinize all internal audit programs to confirm they are looking at, verifying, and testing for the appropriate risk points. Be sure programs are comprehensive and current with regulatory require-

ments and concerns, sampling is accurate, information gathering is not flawed, and auditors possess the appropriate knowledge of the area, process, or function they are reviewing.

- Require that the auditor *define* the risk of any change or implementation of control or process required by the auditor. It is not enough to say there is an inconsistency or a risk; it must be defined in identifiable business terms.

• Monitor regulatory changes and ensure that compliance requirements and corporate policy are current. *It is important for the compliance officer to keep a close eye on the regulatory environment for any changes that might even marginally affect the organization. Surprises in this area should not happen and if they do can be quite disruptive.*
  - Review appropriate publications, attend compliance seminars, and become part of a compliance network of industry peers.

• Be responsible for the oversight of the training and education program. *This is a critical part of compliance and risk management, so it must be watched closely by the compliance officer. Although actual training and education is the responsibility of management, the compliance officer must ensure that the resources are effectively employed and available to the appropriate individuals.*
  - Keep training schedules for every area and department for the entire organization. Verify that they keep current and are adhered to closely.

Role of Audit

• Ensure compliance and risk management effectiveness by performing strong audits that focus on sound compliance, and risk management processes, controls and practices, and the concerns of regulators. The auditors must also confirm adherence to corporate policy, which especially includes the important areas of business planning, emergency contingency planning, personnel management and training, risk assessment and identification, and the compliance program. Audits must be comprehensive and current with sound risk and compliance management approach. Audit issues must be communicated to management in a format they understand. *The auditors must monitor and enforce the rules. They must also create a healthy and strong atmosphere and dialog with management that does not have them perceived as an adversary. They must work closely with management to help develop and secure a strong organization.*
  - Foster an open dialog with management. Educate them on audit's importance, role, and support to the business. Prevent the "us against them" atmosphere and show how everyone works for the same company.

- Audit the compliance function and ensure its effectiveness with risk management and control.

Role of Legal

- Support the compliance and risk management effort through legal review and opinion of actual and potential issues and management considerations. They must be a constant reminder of what can happen if issues are allowed to grow and the proper attention to detail is not paid to risk situations. *The legal people should be a part of the assessment process of every identified risk situation where it is an issue or a new product or business opportunity. Do not wait until a lawsuit is received before the legal experts are consulted. We are not suggesting that no move be made without a lawyer at your side. In situations that are identified with strong risk or where the risk is unsure, consulting the attorneys can save a great deal of time, money, and resources.*
  - Keep the legal experts in the loop for risk assessment. Ensure that they are properly skilled and kept informed.
  - Require the legal people to have a good regulatory and legal library that allows for quick reference of needed facts. Ensure that the legal people are current with technology and the industry and possess the necessary knowledge.

17

Common Challenges in Developing an Effective Program

There are some major obstacles that may be encountered during the creation and implementation of an Integrated Compliance and Total Risk Management Program. It is important to identify, discuss, and review all of the possible obstacles with management and staff before, during, and after implementation. There are times when the execution of the new program will require a partial or sometimes major change in the culture or mind set of the organization. Individuals who previously assumed that compliance or risk management was the auditor's or compliance department's responsibility would take the position that as long as no one said anything they were fine. If they had a compliance or risk situation, the auditors or compliance people would tell them; if these issues were not pointed out it was because the auditors or compliance people were not doing their job.

With an integrated program, compliance and risk management is the responsibility of those same managers who assumed it was not. This requires a new way of thinking and a new behavior and management style. However, once this new approach is explained to management they will understand that it is not such a radical approach and that, in fact, it has tremendous benefits for them individually, as well as for the organization in general. When Integrated Compliance and Total Risk Management gains acceptance it will become the way to do business and it will have permanence.

The specific issues the organization may face will vary from one organization to the next; however, there are some general issues that can be discussed. The most important point is to recognize that problems in implementation will arise and the beginning may be a bit bumpy. The more effectively these problems can be anticipated and the more quickly they can be discovered, the smoother and faster the implementation can be accomplished. Even if most of the problems are not initially anticipated or identified, just by letting everyone know that there will be problems and to anticipate their possibility will greatly assist in the overall task of execution of the program.

Four of the most common challenges in developing an effective Integrated Compliance and Total Risk Management Program are:

1. *Organizational structure: The importance of the right culture.* In some cases the actual structure of the organization must be changed in order to achieve a successful program. Several things are meant by organizational structure, which includes the physical makeup of the compliance and risk management function as well as the reporting lines and accountability. In some organizations the compliance function is a centrally organized department that usually reports to senior management. This central body typically goes from area to area checking and testing for compliance and often employing a conventional audit style checklist approach. The compliance auditors make their rounds, document their findings, and add them up for a final conclusion on the organization's overall compliance.

   Some organizations attempt this with a small compliance staff while others try it with a large one. In either case, there are dedicated resources specifically assigned to the task of testing for and enforcing compliance. These types of compliance departments are usually held accountable for the overall compliance of the organization. If no violations have been found it is assumed that they are doing their job. They usually do not get much press, except if there is a problem, in which case they get plenty of attention.

   The costliness of this approach is usually recognized but it is tolerated on the assumption that ensuring sound compliance and risk management costs money. It is not until serious problems have arisen (that perhaps had festered for many months or even years but were never found) that failure of this approach is recognized.

   As a result of conventional beliefs and the fact that the organization had not, as yet, had any serious compliance or risk problems, acceptance of the integrated approach may be challenging. The mentality that "we have not had any problems, which is proof our current approach works" is sometimes strongly embedded in the minds of management, along with the belief that the integrated approach will cause them more work and possibly get them in trouble. This makes it not only difficult to perform a change but often even more difficult to have it accepted. Management must be shown that a lack of problems does not mean everything is fine and that an integrated program will require less work in the long run and keep the organization out of trouble.

- By change we mean things such as understanding who is responsible for compliance. In many organizations compliance is the responsibility of the compliance department and not something management typically concerns itself with. *"The compliance officer checks my department to make sure things are correct; I'm too busy to worry about those things."*
- Another change may be structuring the processes whereby compliance is built into the task and not a stand-alone function. *One example of this may be to create a new account opening checklist. The checklist requires completion in order for an account to be opened instead of opening the account and then having someone go back at a later date and check that everything is in order.*
- One more change may be getting everyone in the organization to accept the fact that compliance is everyone's responsibility and that it is a teamwork effort. Everyone in effect is the compliance and risk manager of his or her own jobs. *Integrated Compliance and Total Risk Management is not only good sense; it is good business as it creates efficiencies and fosters quality service, reduces liability, and lowers cost.*

2. *Compliance and risk management areas: They exist everywhere.* Every area, department, process, control, and aspect of the organization must be concerned with sound compliance and risk management. If it is important enough to do in the first place, it must be important enough to do right. Sound compliance and risk management is all about doing things right. Since the entire organization must be focused on doing things right, they must be focused on compliance and risk management as part of the process of doing things right.

   In many organizations it is often assumed that compliance or risk management is not a concern of certain areas, departments, or processes simply because they are not viewed as having a need to comply with regulation or they do not possess any risk. We have already shown in Chapters 1 and 2 that compliance and risk management both have much broader definitions than historically believed. With these definitions in mind we can see that the compliance and risk management focus must be everywhere. Even in those areas such as personnel or the mailroom and those functions such as filing or record keeping, that typically are not viewed as compliance or risk concerns, must be part of the integrated program. This view may be seen as overkill and looked upon as a waste of time. It is important to demonstrate otherwise and anticipate the need to prepare for this argument.

The argument that resources are finite and so must be concentrated in the greatest areas of need is a true and accurate one. Organization resources are limited and must therefore be used in the most efficient manner where they can have the greatest impact. The organizations that do this the best are the ones that are the most profitable. For this very reason, it is critical to recognize that compliance and risk management areas are everywhere in the organization. This recognition allows the utilization and deployment of existing resources in every area to focus on sound compliance and risk management and negates the need for a compliance army along with the ability to employ the very efficient pro-active management approach.

- Ensure that compliance validations and risk reviews are performed in every area and for every process. *If everyone performs their own compliance and risk management there will never be a shortage of resources.*
- Establish an organization culture where everyone is focused on "doing it right." *The smallest of tasks, when improved, can have a great impact on the organization's quality, profitability, and competitiveness.*

3. *Resources: Every organizational member is a team resource.* Since compliance is not a "revenue producer," management always seems to have the strong temptation to either cut back or not supply enough resources. If there are no current problems, compliance is usually not given a great deal of consideration. When there are no problems this is often one of the hardest "sell areas." Compound this with the suggestion that management is responsible for compliance and risk management and it becomes even tougher to sell.

When every organization member is seen as a team resource the entire compliance and risk management scheme not only becomes more effective but it can become a "revenue producer" by better managing risk and improving overall quality and productivity.

It is very important, but sometimes proves difficult, to resist the urge of having your compliance people become policemen and/or auditors. In reality they must do a small amount of each at times; however, neither should become their main purpose or function. A compliance staff should be small, very flexible, and responsible for monitoring, training, and assisting management with any compliance fixes. Employing the available resources effectively and efficiently is key to a successful program.

- When we speak of resources we don't mean hiring a large compliance staff. Resources are compliance designates, monitoring systems, compliance validation, a library, etc. *Any and every tool used in the compliance and risk management effort is a resource.*
- Educate everyone on the value and benefit of the team resource concept and how it is good for the individual and good for busi-

ness. *Utilizing everyone in the most efficient and effective way is employing a very valuable and limited organizational resource in the most productive fashion.*

4. *Motivational requirements: Compliance is the right thing to do.* In the beginning management and staff must be motivated and given a strong incentive to "think compliance." The initial reactions from management are that they do not have the knowledge, and they certainly do not have the time, to perform any compliance function. They may view the program as a low priority, a waste of time, and perhaps a serious infringement upon their ability to perform their job effectively. An integrated program is of course none of these things. This can and must be clearly demonstrated to both management and staff so they are fully convinced. Another important incentive is the strong and continuous support that must come from senior management. When this support is recognized by management and the staff, they will consider it a high priority and treat it accordingly.

   It is critical to the success of the program that everyone is properly motivated and the organization provides the correct incentives to foster this motivation.

   - The organization must provide strong incentives to management and staff alike for the practice of sound compliance and risk management. Part of the appraisal and assessment of a good manager and considered in any promotion reviews should be their attention to and effectiveness in managing compliance and risk. The same rules should hold true for all staff members. *It is very easy for them to rationalize and think that compliance is an unproductive waste of their time.*

   - Educate and perform ongoing training for all management and staff on sound compliance and risk management. Teach the benefits, advantages, and need for integrated compliance. *Once it is recognized that compliance and risk management is their responsibility, there will be a strong motivation to practice it.*

   - Build all new processes and controls and modify the existing ones to integrate risk management and compliance into their operation. *Once compliance is built into the processes and controls its practice will become invisible in most cases, and performing compliance will not be a burden. The incentive to go around or not practice compliance and risk management will have been effectively removed. Just like the driver obeying the traffic laws, compliance is part of the process.*

18

The Need for Ethical Standards for an Effective Compliance Program

There has been much written and perhaps even more said about corporate, ethical behavior. We have heard often about the social responsibility of an organization and how the public wants and even demands socially responsible organizations. Almost all of these discussions have been followed by statements of how it is the right thing to do, organizations should be forced to behave responsibly, business has an obligation to give something back to the community, and even that social responsibility should be a required cost of doing business. These are all arguments with merit; however, many are difficult to fully support and most are difficult to implement with any degree of continued success.

Regardless of what many people might argue, it would strongly appear that business in general is motivated by the bottom line. Some argue that this is the way it should be. There are several examples of organizations that can be cited to contradict the belief that profit is the motivator, but there are probably two to three times that amount to support it. So why is this whole thing so confusing and why do some organizations talk ethics in speeches, meetings, manuals, and constant dialog and not do it in practice while others are sterling examples of socially responsible, highly ethical behavior? Is ethics one of those things that should only be done by the other guy, or is it just nice to talk about and only practice when convenient? Should we all be forced to practice ethics? All of us have met the individual, on more than one occasion, who always demanded fair play and cheated at every possible opportunity. What seemed to be the worst part of it all was that this individual appeared to continually prosper from this behavior.

Why do some of us cheat? When did we first learn to cheat? How do we stop people from cheating? These as well as the earlier questions are all good questions, ones that have been debated for many years and still defy complete and accurate answers.

The author, who gives many presentations at business seminars nationwide, always ends his presentation with a short, five-minute piece on ethics and why ethical practice is good for business. He once commented that he usually gets complaints that no one wants to hear that part. One sponsor even suggested that he take it out because it may "insult" someone in the audience. But there was always that special time when two or three people would thank him for his courage to talk ethics.

It is clear not only from all of the corruption in some business but also from the general disinterest it seems to generate that strong proponents of ethical practice appear to have a tough job ahead of them. This does not mean that they should stop; it only means they must work harder.

We will not attempt to answer the tough questions posed earlier; they generate difficult and often emotional discussions of right and wrong and who is and is not responsible. Any attempt would require rigorous debate, research, studies, and even some postulation. For us to do that here would take another 200 pages to even give the subject justice. If these broader issues of ethical behavior are important, and eventually they should be, we suggest you read a text on corporate ethics. There is an excellent new book called *Straight Talk about Business Ethics* written by Linda Trevino and Katherine Nelson. Both authors know a great deal of business ethics and their book does a fine job of sorting out and clarifying these difficult issues. Ms. Kate Nelson in particular has a considerable amount of experience in business ethics. As the former head of human resources communication at Citibank, she created the much acclaimed "Work Ethic" board game, which was used to communicate corporate ethics to its 85,000 employees worldwide. The game has also been featured in the *Wall Street Journal, Fortune,* and the *Financial Times.* The ethics game is an interesting approach to ethics training for a large organization. The book does an excellent job of dealing with tough and controversial questions and issues.

We will narrow our discussion down to only one point, and that is why ethical practice is good for business. Although it is only one point and it does not directly talk about the social, political, environmental, or even religious aspects of ethics, this one point we will discuss is possibly the most important point and the only one business really needs to focus on initially. If an organization practices ethics solely because it is good for business, the need to debate those other points is not immediately important as they eventually get addressed along the way. Practicing ethics is the right thing to do and every organization must do it. Doing it because it is good for business is an easy way to focus on a tough topic while accomplishing a difficult task.

Forgetting for the time being about the many somewhat intangible reasons to practice ethics, there are several powerful and very beneficial reasons to have a strong ethical framework built into the organization. All of them relate directly to the bottom line by either causing better results or preventing liability and loss. Strong ethics means fair play, which translates into an environment where people are judged on individual and team merit and not on who they are, who they know, or what they have taken credit for or escaped the blame from. Fair play does not care about race, sex, age, where you went to school, who your uncle is; it only looks at what you know, what you've done, and what you can do. It's true this only exists completely in a perfect world, but to the extent that it should be the goal of every organization.

When people know they are being judged on merit and not on some uncontrollable or immeasurable trait, they will concentrate on doing the best job possible and not spend their time on ways to impress the appropriate individuals. Every individual working for the better way will cooperate collectively and become more effective as a group. This will be accomplished without additional resources and expense and often using less time and money. This will all add up to strong morale, long-lasting employee-employer relationships, which turns into lower overall costs and higher quality, all of which should lead to greater market share and higher profits.

On the reverse side, a poorly controlled unethical organization will often be less efficient as a group simply because everyone is jockeying for the best position and their own self-interest at the expense of others and the organization. Morale will be low, turnover high, productivity poor, and quality spotty. All of these things do fall to the bottom line but the worst is the risk and liability from exposure of the unethical behavior. The organization's public image could be severely hurt as with Solomon Brothers's government securities debacle, or totally destroyed as with Drexel's junk bond disaster. The direct bottom line hit, as both of these organizations experienced, comes from the loss through fraud and the fines and legal actions taken against the them. The much publicized Corporate Sentencing Guidelines among several other punitive type laws is an excellent example of the severe monetary fines an organization can suffer due to unethical behavior.

Organizations or individuals in organizations who cheat eventually get caught. In most cases, admittedly not all, the benefit of their dishonesty is lost, putting them in a position much worse than before the inappropriate act. The risks are exceptionally high with the opportunity for escape very slim. In most cases the gain is short lived and short term. Rolling the dice, which unethical behavior is similar to, seems to be a risky and foolish strategy for profit and growth. Most organizations who fall victim to unethical behavior in their ranks do not make a conscious decision to allow or foster illicit acts. They simply do not do enough, if anything, to prevent them.

We could spend the next 50 or so pages recounting the instances and examples of organizations who lost "rolling the dice," but most have been well publicized and are well known. We can also detail how ethical organizations, fair play and judgment by merit all contribute to a stronger bottom line. Most of us already know this having experienced it sometime during our careers. If anything it seems simple and straight forward common sense. Besides, going into the detail of ethics causes us to make value judgments and forces us to start talking in degrees and specifics of what constitutes ethical behavior and where to draw the line. This is not for us to do here; it will be left up to the individuals to draw their own lines and decide what to do and why. We will just point out some ways to approach ethics in general.

No organization or no one for that matter can completely stop unethical behavior. The annual cost to American business has been estimated at well over $25 billion. What an organization can do is to greatly reduce unethical behavior internally by taking away the incentive for such behavior along with creating a healthy environment where ethics can become the rule.

Everyone acts for a benefit, whether it is material, emotional, physical, or perhaps otherwise. Take away the benefit received from that behavior and the rational individual will eventually stop that behavior. Leave the benefit and the behavior, even at the risk of a strong punishment, may be lessened but will still be practiced. We can establish severe punishments if the individual is caught in the act of the undesired behavior and make that punishment well known, but if there is still a possible reward or incentive for that behavior, many may still take the risk.

Removing the incentive and leaving the risk seems to be a way to curtail the behavior. Criminology has studied this for decades and although there are plenty of laws and penalties for criminal behavior it still exists. Everyone knows you will go to jail for robbing a bank, yet bank robberies are still fairly common. So why do people still rob banks? Obviously it is for the possible reward of free money. But what if banks did not have any money to rob, how many people would still try to rob one? Take away the reward and the illicit behavior will end. This of course is easier said than done in most cases, as a bank can't operate without money. There are, however, alternatives and ways to lessen the reward, as many banks have done by making it more difficult, and reducing the possible reward by limiting the cash in the tellers' drawers and the vault at any one time.

Creating a strong environment without the incentive for inappropriate behavior is also easier said than done, especially in a well-established organization. Like everything else that is important it must be seeded from the top and grown from the grass roots of the organization. Senior management must fully demonstrate and strongly support ethics in order for it to become part of the organization's culture. It can be accomplished for the end result of a better and more profitable organization. It must first be desired and then worked hard for.

In order to create such an environment there are three basic principles that should be followed:

1. *Establish an incentive and reward system based on excellence and hard work.* Creating a system that is based on job quality, knowledge, and individual expertise is a strong beginning to establishing an ethical culture in the organization. When organization members know that they will get rewarded for hard work, they will concentrate and focus more on the quality and level of their work while giving less attention to organization politics and the rumor mill. The organization must encourage hard work by providing the incentives for it and not by rewarding people for ways to get around it. This is done when organization members are given promotions, bonuses, and other benefits for making themselves look good instead of actually being good. The measurements must be in the right place and not focus on the wrong things. An example would be the manager who grades her staff on the number of hours they stay past 5:00 p.m. each day instead of the actual quality and quantity of their work. One staff member who leaves at 5:00 p.m. every day can actually do more work with better quality than another staff member who stays until 7:00 p.m.; yet the 5:00 p.m. member is looked upon with less favor. Ability and merit, not subjective and immeasurable traits, should dictate promotions and rewards. Although this is a difficult ideal, the organization still should strive continually to get as close as possible to the ideal of a complete incentive and reward system based on excellence and hard work.

    A critical factor in accomplishing this ideal is ensuring that the measurement system is fair, equitable, and accurate. The right things must be measured, so accurate results can be achieved. Then follow this by placing the incentives to encourage the desired results and the rewards for hard work, and the organization will have created an incentive and reward system based on excellence and hard work

2. *Develop an ethical environment that can foster and sustain responsible decisions.* The "just-do-it" mentality we spoke about in Chapter 6 must be totally unacceptable. No organization member must be put in a position of breaking the rules in order to succeed. The environment must be able to recognize these situations and prevent them from occurring. The organization must ensure that all of the appropriate checks, balances, and controls are in place to identify and take away the temptation and easy opportunity for inappropriate behavior. People cannot easily steal something that they do not have access to. The environment must allow an open and healthy exchange of ideas, clear expectations, and well-defined responsibilities. Organization

members should not be afraid to speak up if a request they were given will cause them to break the rules if completed. No rules should ever be broken. If any rules are too restrictive, prohibitive, or unnecessary, they should be changed or removed immediately. Organization members should not be taught how to "work around the rules" to do a better job. They should be given a flexibile environment and a chance to react quickly in times of need. Breaking or seriously bending the rules should never be an alternative.

3.   *Build a system of ethical practice throughout the compliance program and the organization.* Such a system is begun at the top and built into the "grass roots" of the organization. It is accomplished mostly through education and training of every organization member. It is also done by example. Senior management must show their own actions and rewards for ethical behavior. Incentives for cheating must be removed while keeping everyone well informed so that there is the least number of surprises possible. Let all of the organization members know on a continuous basis what is and is not appropriate behavior. Don't wait until someone steals the cookie jar to "set an example."

Continuing Integrated Compliance and Total Risk Management Long into the Future

It is one thing to get everyone excited and kick off a well-intentioned program with lots of fanfare and press, and quite another thing to keep it going after the initial excitement has died. There are many favorable reasons for integrating compliance and risk management into the fabric of the organization and one of the most favorable is that it has a strong basis for permanence. By integrating compliance and risk management into the process it becomes part of the process; therefore, performing the process is also performing the compliance and risk management. It also becomes part of the organizational culture of ownership, responsibility, and accountability and the accepted way of doing things.

Any system where people have to "take time out" to perform the compliance and risk management will eventually fail. It seems to be human nature to be immediately concerned with something right after the individual or someone close to the individual had just experienced or been told about it. Then after a time, if that experience is not repeated, the concern becomes less and less until it is eventually forgotten. The same is true in taking caution with a situation; at first we may be very careful to do everything correctly but as we get more comfortable we tend to cut corners and take a little more risk.

When performing a task that we need to take extra steps before or after each process, those steps tend to get shortened each time we perform the task until they become an abbreviated version of the original. If no one seems to notice, complete steps may even be cut out altogether. This is precisely what happens when compliance and risk management is performed outside of the process. After a period of time, if nothing has gone wrong, it becomes more of a perfunctory duty rather than an actual control or concern. It eventually gets pushed farther down the priority list of important actions until it gets cursory attention or is ignored altogether. Only after a problem arises does everyone once again pay it any attention. Of course, by this time it is too late and the risk is considerable.

Compliance and risk management, in order to be successful, must be a daily practice that is continuous and repetitive with every job performed. It cannot be something done occasionally or by third party inspectors. That is, it cannot be done this way and also be effective. No job can be successfully overseen by a third party, not unless that third party is with the individual performing the job every minute of the day. The second the third party individual walks away they begin missing the process and the compliance and risk management function has essentially stopped. It may begin again once they have returned, but the in-between time has been left unguarded. In reality this control approach is dependent on timing and luck and can only ensure occasional compliance and risk management; it can never ensure complete compliance and risk management.

Returning one final time to our driving analogy and after understanding all we have discussed, we can see how compliance and risk management *must* be the responsibility of the individual performing the task. We hear of accidents, drunk drivers, and traffic tickets handed out on a daily basis. Imagine the chaos that would result if none of those individuals were held responsible for the accidents or tickets. People would care less, be less attentive, and the police would have to quadruple in size with probably little effect. If all the drivers were not held accountable for their own traffic compliance and they were told that there will be a traffic compliance officer to ensure they are in compliance and the officer will also audit them about once a year to test for compliance, how worried will they be if they miss a stop sign here and there? The typical response would be, "I know I'm in total compliance; I passed my last audit." The fact that the audit could not have possibly looked at everything and that it was almost a year ago, which leaves a great deal of time in between, seems to not matter. In reality it matters a great deal.

Some drivers by their very nature will abide by the rules, but many would find it more expedient to let the compliance officer worry about it. After all, it would be the compliance officer's responsibility to identify and resolve any issues. On the other hand, what if traffic compliance was not built into the system? When people learned to drive they were not taught the "rules of the road." They learned these long after they had become accomplished drivers. In fact, there are "rules" specialists who oversee the entire rules aspect and they must ensure that everyone learns and follows the rules. These rules specialists are different from the driving teachers who focus only on driving.

This then creates a situation where the individual must mentally practice driving separate from compliance. The driver would get in his or her car and then have to think, "which side of the road do I have to drive on" and "I mustn't forget that those octagon shaped red signs with the big word stop mean I must stop and look. I believe it's look both ways." A good example of this is people who learn to drive in America and then go to Britain and attempt to drive. The signs are different, the side of the road everyone drives on is opposite, and the roadways themselves are set up differently. Anyone taught to drive in America must consciously think traffic compliance and be continually aware of the rules lest they risk a serious accident. This person obviously would not be as efficient at driving in Britain as they are in America.

Just think what the roads would be like if everyone had to go through this mental process every time they got in a car to drive. Obviously this seems like a silly scenario, but if traffic compliance was not built into the process of driving from the very beginning where people really don't have to give it much thought, it would not be so silly.

What is also not so silly is that many organizations run their compliance and risk management functions this way. They have removed the function of red lights and stop signs and given it special status apart from the process of driving. They have also elected special traffic compliance officers who are responsible for the compliance of every driver and even given them the authority to audit the drivers to *make sure they are in compliance.* Because we have not *grown up* learning the internal operations of our current organization, it appears much more convoluted than our roadways (some areas in New York may be an exception) but it is really no different. In order for things to get done in any organization they must get from one place to another whether it is through phone lines, computer, verbal meetings, or physical transportation. There are no special secrets that only a select few experts can figure out.

Probably one of the biggest ironies is that the organizations who segregate the compliance and risk management functions from the process do so because they believe they are important and require special attention. As a result of this belief they appoint specialists who are then held responsible and accountable for the compliance and risk management soundness of the organization. What these organizations are doing in effect is taking the control out of the hands of the real specialists and experts, the people doing the job, and placing it in the hands of a third party who cannot even hope to understand any function better that the expert who performs it. These third party compliance and risk management officers are generalists at best in regard to the operations of the organization. They actually lack the very expertise that is critical to ensure sound compliance and risk management.

Instead of trying to teach the compliance and risk management officers to be experts in all areas, it is a far sight easier to teach the experts in the areas to be conscious and aware of compliance and risk management.

Although they should not be large in number, the compliance and risk managers are essential to every organization. It is their role in most cases that must be redefined. Don't try to make them the *doers* of compliance or risk management. Instead, make them the managers of it. They should be the teachers, monitors, and overseers, but the *doers* must be the real experts, the people performing the task. The conductor of an orchestra does not play every instrument and is not expected to. If the conductor was in the orchestra playing even one instrument, who would do the conducting while he or she is trying to be part of the violin section? The compliance and risk management officers are the conductors of the compliance and risk management process; they do not perform the actual compliance or risk management. They only oversee it. Even if they actually tried to perform, who would be doing the teaching, monitoring, and overseeing while they were? An organization must keep its strengths where they have the greatest utility. This is accomplished by keeping compliance and risk management part of the daily process and not giving it special status so it is only practiced occasionally by third party individuals.

By integrating the compliance and risk management disciplines into the everyday processes, the organization has achieved a very productive, efficient, and long-lasting way of accomplishing a function critical to its success. The cost savings are considerable to the organization in terms of smaller compliance and risk management staffs, efficiency and productivity savings, and reduced liability and risk through pro-active management. Continuing Integrated Compliance and Total Risk Management long into the future will ensure these savings.

Index

About the Author

Mark Arthus is the Chief Administrative Officer for Morgan Grenfell Capital Management, Inc., a wholly owned U.S. investment management subsidiary of Morgan Grenfell Asset Management, B. V. whose ultimate parent is the London-based Morgan Grenfell Group PLC. Arthus is responsible for all compliance functions, financial control and various administrative matters; he has played a key role in creating new compliance programs that include some innovative concepts to accommodate the new regulatory demands and financial restraints.

Mr. Arthus has presented his ideas at banking conferences and consulted with banks nationwide. Along with performing and managing audits, he has also held training sessions to educate management and staff in process and procedure changes and compliance requirements.

Prior to joining Morgan Grenfell Capital Management, Inc., Mr. Arthus was employed for more than five years at Citibank and last served at The Citibank Private Bank as the Senior Compliance Officer in the Trust and Estates, Investment Management and Funds areas nationally. Prior to Citibank, Mr. Arthus was the Senior Financial Control Administrator at United Technologies, Hamilton Test Systems; Credit Manager for Westinghouse Electric Company and Controller for two mid-sized manufacturing companies.

Mr. Arthus received his M.B.A. in Accounting at New York Institute of Technology and is currently attending Pace University in NYC for his Doctorate in Finance and Management. He also has a B.A. from Hofstra University and an Associates degree from S.U.N.Y. at Farmingdale.